DICTIONARY
OF
INSURANCE

DICTIONARY

OF

INSURANCE

Lewis E. Davids

Illinois Bankers Professor of Bank Management
College of Business and Administration
Southern Illinois University—Carbondale

Sixth Revised Edition
1983

A HELIX BOOK

Rowman & Allanheld
PUBLISHERS

Copyright © 1983 by Littlefield, Adams & Co.
81 Adams Drive, Totowa, NJ 07512

Sixth edition, revised. Previous editions were originally
published as a Littlefield, Adams Quality Paperback.

Sixth Edition 1984
Fifth Edition 1977
Fourth Edition 1974
Third Edition 1970
Second Edition 1962
First Edition 1959

Reprinted in 1984 as A HELIX BOOK by Rowman & Allanheld
(a division of Littlefield, Adams & Company)
81 Adams Drive, Totowa, NJ 07512

Library of Congress Cataloging in Publication Data

Davids, Lewis E.
  Dictionary of insurance.

  (A Helix book)
  1. Insurance—Dictionaries. I. Title.
HG8025.D3 1983   368′.003′21   83-16091
ISBN 0-8226-0381-0 (pbk.)

84 85 86 / 10 9 8 7 6 5 4 3 2 1
Printed in the United States of America

To. A. R. D.

CONTENTS

PREFACE

Lexicography is of necessity an empirical art, based on the usages that have become established over many years. With the passage of time, subtle changes develop in the connotation of words. In some cases the meanings have become completely reversed. Since English is not a "dead" language and insurance is far from being a "dead" subject, it appears that many of the terms cannot be frozen into an unalterable context. Since insurance covers such a wide area there is some tendency for terms to have somewhat different meaning from one part of the country to the next, as well as from one company to the next company and one section of the insurance industry to other sections.

Court decisions have had a most significant influence in defining the meaning of many of the clauses found in insurance contracts. However, these decisions too have tended to interpret certain clauses in the light of conditions as they existed at that time. The atomic age has caused basic changes in our way of life and also in our evaluation of insurance contracts in so far as certain risks. Many of our problems today can be traced to the difficulty of communication of one nation to another, of one segment of society to another. Studies have been made that indicate many people do not even read their insurance policies; additional research has shown that of those who have read their policies, many are not conversant with the meaning of the various terms, clauses, and phrases found in the policy.

This is an attempt to define, at this time, terms used in insurance. Some of the terms naturally are associated with other fields such as law, statistics, accounting, government, taxation, and real estate as well as with insurance.

Some dictionaries, in the search for accuracy, have devoted literally pages of explanation to the definition of a single word. Such dictionaries may properly be called encyclopedic. This dictionary has not adopted such a technique, but has tried to define the terms briefly and succinctly so that laymen, insurance company employees, and college students of insurance may be able to comprehend the meaning of words and phrases frequently found in texts, publications, and in conversations concerned with insurance.

The traditional alphabetical arrangement is used, but two considered variations have seemed to be desirable to be incorporated so that this study will accomplish its goal. Abbreviations are used in texts, descriptions of policy clauses, and in insurance documents. The more commonly used abbreviations have thus been included with the words that the abbreviations stand for. These abbreviations are found at the front part of each letter. The second variation is based on the thought that the next best thing to knowledge of a fact or condition is to know where one can obtain the correct answer. For this reason the title and location of many of the nonbook sources of information on insurance are given. The executive whose title and address is listed should be in a position to answer questions on those specific questions concerned with his special area. Naturally, book sources should be utilized prior to individual contact with such individuals and institutions.

Proposals have been made both in academic and applied insurance circles that a committee on insurance terminology correct the "terminological inexactitude" that is found in the area of insurance. Until such time as the committee, which at this writing is in the initial stages of formation, has been fully formed and produces its findings, it is hoped that this insurance dictionary will meet the pressing need that is evidenced in several ways.

This study represents the author's findings based upon an interest dating back some twenty years, when, out of necessity in preparing his master's thesis, he collected a number of the terms that are used. Since that time many more terms have been added.

That this edition represents the ideas and works of many individuals almost needs no explanation. Many who helped make predecessor related studies indirectly helped with this study. Especially to be thanked for their kind permission to use some of their definitions are The Rough Notes Company Inc. and Robert W. Osler, Vice President and Editor of the *Insurance Salesman;* The Macmillan Company, publishers of *Modern Life Insurance,* 1st ed. copyright 1939 by Mehr-Osler. Miss Dorothy Hepworth, executive secretary of the National Institute of Real Estate Boards, publishers of *Real Estate Salesman's Handbook.* Dr. John S. Bickley, editor of *The Journal of Insurance.* A. L. Kirkpatrick, Manager, Insurance Department, Chamber of Commerce of the United States; The Institute of Life Insurance, Employer's Mutual Insurance Company of Wausaw, Wisconsin; Hartford Fire Insurance Company of Hartford, Connecticut. The American Association of University Teachers of Insurance and the participating insurance companies in their joint fellowship program should be signaled out for special mention, since through fellowships in both the life and the fire-casualty-marine fields the author was provided with facilities for testing many of his definitions at the Provident Mutual Life Insurance Company of Philadelphia and the Home Insurance Company of New York. William T. Davids of the Metropolitan Life Insurance Company of New York was most helpful in many phases of the study. Any virtues found in this dictionary can be attributed to the above people and their organizations. Shortcomings should be directed exclusively to the author, who welcomes suggestions of terms to be included or modified. In this way continued progress can be made, in an area that will continue to grow and with the growth provide increasingly important social contributions.

Lewis E. Davids, PhD

PREFACE TO NEW EDITION

In preparing this new edition of *Dictionary of Insurance* it was possible for the first time to include the definitions which have been prepared by the Commission of Insurance Terminology of the *American Risk and Insurance Association.*

To indicate and give credit for the permission to reproduce the terms these definitions are followed by the letters CIT. Several terms prepared by CIT had caveats such as "tentative" or included "comments." In addition, the CIT holds "Since all language is dynamic in character, the discussions and recommendations which emanate from the Commission or its Committees should not be regarded as the final solutions to terminology questions."

Appreciation is expressed here to the *Commission on Insurance Terminology* and its over thirty distinguished authorities who are members of the Commission for their permission to reproduce the terms here.

In addition to including terms prepared by CIT this edition has substantially broadened its coverage of major organizations and associations in the field of insurance. This is especially to be noted in the area of Canadian insurance practices and institutions.

The author wishes to acknowledge the cooperation of the Insurance Information Institute (U. S. A.) and the Insurance Institute of Canada. Finally, major court decisions which have a bearing on insurance are identified.

As with the earlier edition of this study, William T. Davids, of the Metropolitan Life Insurance Company of New York, provided advice and counsel.

A NOTE ON INSURANCE TERMINOLOGY

Davis W. Gregg
President
The American College of Life Underwriters

Polonius: "What do you read, my Lord?"
Hamlet: "Words, words, words."
Insurance is plagued by an infernal and exasperating jungle of confusing terminology—words, words, words.

For the sake of public understanding so important to the future of insurance, for the sake of effective communication within the insurance industry, and for the sake of furthering insurance science, something should be done to bring order out of terminological chaos. A specific recommendation will be made in this paper.

THE PROBLEM

It was Humpty Dumpty of Alice in Wonderland fame who said:
"When I use a word, it means just what I choose it to mean —neither more nor less."
Perhaps insurance people have individually and collectively humpty-dumptied the special language of this business to the extent that it is hard even to understand each other. Pity the poor public!

It is not difficult to find examples of current lexicographical confusion. Take the field of health insurance. Is it "health insurance," as one would suppose from the names of the two important trade associations in the field, the Health Insurance Association of America and the Health Insurance Institute? Or is it "accident and health insurance," "health and accident insurance," "accident and sickness insurance," "sickness and accident insurance," "disability insurance"—or what?

Take the word "coinsurance." This term has been widely used in health insurance (or is it "accident and sickness"?) in recent years to mean, in general, a provision under medical expense coverage whereby the insured agrees to share losses in some given proportion with the insurer. But, how does this use of the term jibe with the time-honored use in property insurance? And, what about its still different meaning in the field of reinsurance?

What meaning does such language as "commercial accident and health insurance policies" or "non-cancellable guaranteed renewable disability income" coverage have to the public?

It would seem that at least those in the insurance business could agree as to the meaning of "multiple line underwriting." But even here one is faced with confused usage of the term. If it's a property insurance man expressing himself, the term may mean one thing; but if it is a life insurance man, it may mean something else.

The variety of terms used to describe the life insurance field man who contacts the public approaches the point of absurdity. Is he a life underwriter, a field underwriter, an agent, a career agent, a salesman, a special agent, a field representative, or a special representative? These and probably scores of other titles have been given him over the years. His trade association is known as the National Association of Life Underwriters and his professional designation is known as "Chartered Life Underwriter." In property insurance the designation is "Chartered Property Casualty Underwriter." But can companies, teachers, editors, and the public agree on what to call them? And, what about the confusion with the "underwriter" in the home office who has an entirely different job?

What is the difference between a "general agent" in life insurance and a "general agent" in property-liability insurance? Or, what is the meaning of "agent" in these two fields?

Another example. Is there any language in life insurance less descriptive and less appropriate than "industrial" and "ordinary" life insurance? And, what exactly does "ordinary" life insurance mean—especially to the public?

If any field of insurance be considered—life, health, property, liability, marine, pension, surety, social—the impact of language on the public and those in the business inevitably will be confusion, and disagreement in regard to truly fundamental and basic concepts. Winston Churchill once spoke of "terminological inexactitude." Surely, insurance has more than its share of it.

A PLAN

Could not a Committee on Insurance Terminology go a long way toward solving this problem? Such a committee, soundly organized by insurance educators and people within the insurance industry and determinedly and doggedly devoted to the task of adding clarity and effectiveness to the language of insurance, could inevitably have a substantial and lasting effect.

The philosophy of the Committee might be centered in Alexander Pope's suggestion that

> "In words, as fashions, the same rule will hold,
> Alike fantastic if too new or old:
> Be not the first by whom the new are tried,
> Nor yet the last to lay the old aside."

Inevitably, the Committee would meet distrust and resistance if its recommendations should be revolutionary in form or timing. Yet, through careful study, through the art of gentle persuasion, and, above all through patient devotion to the ultimate good to result, outstanding progress could be made in even a decade.

The American Association of University Teachers of Insurance would seem to be the ideal organization to initiate a continuing study of insurance language for many reasons. In the first place, the Association, by definition, is interested in all lines of insurance. Secondly, as an organization, it can invite all segments of the insurance industry to participate without prejudice to individual interests. Thirdly, the members of the Association are those who are creating insurance literature, especially for education use; and thus it is they who can have the greatest ultimate impact on insurance language. Finally, in a venture of scientific and scholarly nature such as this, it is logical that the Association should take the leadership.

A word of caution should be offered, however. The research will be effective only if the Committee on Insurance Terminology is truly a joint project between the Association and the various segments of the insurance industry. Though the direction and much of the work must be a labor of love of teacher members of the Committee, the full and continuing interest of insurance trade associations, insurance companies, the insurance press, and insurance regulatory authorities will be necessary if the project is to succeed.

Much progress is being made in developing the science of insurance. But, for any science to reach its full fruition, it must have a language of exactness and clarity. Here, then is an area where the Association can devote its resources, human and financial, toward progress. "The difference between the right word and the almost right word is the difference between lightning and lightning bug." (Mark Twain)

DICTIONARY
OF
INSURANCE

DICTIONARY OF INSURANCE

A.A.U.   Associated Aviation Underwriters
A.B.S.   American Bureau of Shipping.
Ac   Accident.
A.C.I.F.   All Canada Insurance Federation
A.C.L.U.   American College of Life Underwriters.
A.C.S.C.   Association of Casualty and Surety Companies.
A.C.V.   Actual cash value.
A.D.B.   Accidental Death Benefit
A.D.T.   American District Telegraph
A.E.C.   Additional extended coverage.
A.F.A.   Associated Fraternities of America.
A.F.I.A.   American Foreign Insurance Association.
A. & H.   Accident and health.
A.G.C.   Associated General Contractors
A.H.I.S.   American Hull Insurance Syndicate.
A. & I.   Accident and indemnity.
A.I.A.   American Insurance Association.
A.I.I.C.   Associate, Insurance Institute of Canada
A.I.M.A.   As interest may appear.
A.I.M.U.   American Institute of Marine Underwriters.
A.I.P.L.U.   American Institute for Property and Liability Under-
writers.
A.I.U.   Aero Insurance Underwriters.
A.L.C.   American Life Convention.
A.L.E.   Additional living expense.
A.L.I.C.   Association of Life Insurance Counsel.
A.L.I.M.D.   Association of Life Insurance Medical Directors.
A.M.I.A.   American Mutual Insurance Alliance.
A.M.U.(B.C.)   Association of Marine Underwriters of
British Columbia
A.O.   At occupation, an underwriting designation for an occu-
pational accident.
A.P.   Additional premium.
A.P.L.   Automatic Premium Loan
A.R.   Accounts Receivable
A.R.I.A.   American Risk and Insurance Association
A. & S.   Accident and sickness insurance.
A.S.   Automatic sprinkler.

1

A.S.A.   American Standards Association

A.S.I.M.   American Society of Insurance Management

Au   Automobile.

AAA tenant   A prime tenant who has the highest credit rating.

Abandonment   The act of relinquishing title to damaged, lost property by the insured to an insurance company for the purpose of claiming a total loss. Some policies provide that there can be no abandonment to the company.

Abatement   The refund of duties on damaged imported goods. The goods may be damaged during importation or in a bonded warehouse. The diminution or the entire doing away of anything: as the abatement of taxes.

Above-Normal Loss (A.N.L.)   A loss made greater than normal by conditions such as weather, delayed alarm, etc.

Absolute   A final and complete order or ruling. It is complete and effective immediately.

Absolute assignment   An assignment of all control and rights in a policy to someone other than the person on whose life the policy is written.

Absolute Liability   Liability that occurs where one has a duty to fill no matter what the circumstances may be. Absolute Liability is often found in cases involving explosives. In many automobile laws an insurance company may be responsible to a third party irrespective of any statutory faults or breaches on the part of the insured.

Absolute ownership   Exists where the interest or explicit right of possession of the insured is so free from limitations, qualifications, or restrictions that it cannot be taken from him without his consent.

Abstract of title   A summary of all conveyances, such as deeds or wills, and legal proceedings, giving the names of the parties, the description of the land, and the agreements, arranged to show the continuity of ownership. A title insurance policy may serve as an alternative.

Abuse of Process   A phrase commonly used in describing an action that is completely without foundation in facts and based upon prejudice or emotion.

Accelerated option   The use by the insured of accumulated policy dividends as well as the cash value of a life insurance policy to pay up the contract or create an endowment.

Acceleration clause   A common provision of a mortgage and note providing that the entire principal shall become immediately due and payable in the event of default.

Accelerative endowment Under this type of policy the dividends instead of being disbursed are applied to the policy and cause it to mature at a prior time.

Acceptance The reception of something by another with the the intention of retainment as indicated by the action of the receiver. In the case of a contract, acceptance indicates and implies agreement to terms and propositions as well as proposals by which a contract is made and the various parties of the contract bound.

Accession The process whereby property which belongs to one person becomes the property of another by reason of its being added to or incorporated with the property of the latter.

Accessory A person who not being present, is concerned in the commission of an offence either before or after the performance of the fact. An *Accessory Before the Fact* is one who procures, counsels, or commands another, to commit the offence. An *Accessory After the Fact* is one who, knowing an offence has been committed, receives, aids, assists or shelters the offender.

Accident An unforeseen, unintended event, something unexpected, something which could not be considered as a forseeable occurrence and consequence of an undertaking.

Accident and health insurance Insurance, benefits under which are payable in case of disease, accidental injury, or accidental death.

Accident and health insurance, group *See* **Group insurance.**

Accident and health premium A premium paid by a borrower for an insurance policy that insures continuance of mortgage payments in the event of a mortgager's disability or illness.

Accident control or prevention *See* **Loss prevention service.**

Accident frequency Rate of occurrence of accidents; e.g., number of accidents per million man-hours worked: A factory employs 1,250 workers who work on a basis of 2,500,000 man-hours a year. If 32 workers suffered disabling injuries in the year the "accident frequency" rate is 12.80.

$$\frac{32 \times 1,000,000}{2,500,000} = 12.80$$

Accident, industrial An unforeseen, unintended event arising out of one's employment.

Accident insurance Replaces a substantial part of earned income lost through disability caused by accidental injury, and also may provide for payment of medical expenses occasioned by accidental injury, and indemnity for death or loss of limbs or sight suffered through accident.

Accident policy Type of business insurance coverage and personal insurance coverage that insures against loss resulting directly and independently of all other causes, from bodily injuries effected during the term of the policy solely through accidental means.

Accident severity A measurement of the seriousness of the results of accidents; e.g., days lost per 1000 man-hours worked. In a plant which operates with 2,500,000 man-hours in a year, one man is killed, another is disabled for 15 days, and 30 others are injured so as to lose 2 days each. As 6,000 days are charged for a death, the total number of days lost in this plant because of disabling injuries would be 6,075.

$$\frac{6,075 \times 1,000}{2,500,000} = 2.43$$

Accidental bodily injury As the term is used in insurance policies, presupposes that the assured could not reasonably foresee that his actions would naturally and probably result in his injury or death. Injury to an insured(s) body as a result of an accident.

Accidental death benefit A feature added to a life insurance policy providing for payment of an additional death benefit in case of death as a result of accidental means. It is often called double indemnity. *See* **Double indemnity.**

Accidental Death & Dismemberment Insurance Accidental death insurance plus dismemberment insurance combined into one policy.

Accidental Death Insurance A form of insurance that provides payment if the death of the insured results from accident. Accidental death insurance is often combined with dismemberment insurance in a form called "Accidental Death and Dismemberment."

Accidental means Unintended, unexpected, and unforseeable cause of an injury. For example, if a man covered by an accident insurance policy should carry a trunk up the steps of his home and a board broke in the step, causing him to fall and injure his back, the injury would be due to accidental means. If he strained his back in carrying the trunk, the injury would be an accidental result and would not be covered under the terms of some accident insurance policies.

Accommodation An obligation assumed gratis.

Accommodation line An insurance company at times will accept from an agent or broker whose entire account is satisfactory, business which would ordinarily be rejected on a strict underwriting basis. Such business is known as an "accommodation line." Insurance that, by itself, would not be acceptable to an insurer, written as an accommodation where the possibility of securing other desirable business seems to justify it.

Accomodation party A party who signs a negotiable instrument (note or bill) as maker, acceptor, or endorser without receiving any consideration to accomodate another party and enhance the credit worthiness of the paper.

Accord and satisfaction Adjustment of a disagreement as to what is due, and the payment of the agreed amount.

Account current A monthly statement to companies by the agent showing premiums written, return premiums, commissions, and net amount due to balance.

Accounts receivable bond Bond guaranteeing that an agent or employee will properly pay incoming accounts to the individual carrying the bond. It affords protection against dishonest acts related to money matters.

Accounts receivable insurance Pays for loss of records showing how much is due the insured. Insurance against loss due to inability to collect outstanding accounts receivable because of damage to or destruction of records by a peril insured against.

Accounts receivable policy Type of business insurance coverage that is "all risk." It may be written in two ways: (1) valuable papers and records form or (2) accounts receivable form, which provides insurance if the policyholder is unable to collect from his debtor because of loss or damage to records or accounts receivable.

Accretion An addition to land through natural causes (opposite of erosion). Generally the mineral deposits left on riparian lands by movement of waters. Accretion must be distinguished from appreciation and increment.

Accrue When a right is vested in a person, that right is said to accrue to the benefit of that person.

Accrued depreciation Depreciation, accrued.

Accrued Future Service Benefit   That portion of a participant's retirement benefit that relates to his period of credit service after the effective date of the plan and before a specified current date.   CIT

Accrued interest   The interest earned for the period of time that has elapsed since interest was last paid.

Accumulation   Percentage addition to policy benefits as a reward to the insured for continuous renewal.

Accurare nemo se debet   Nobody is obligated to accuse himself. The ordinary use of this maxim is that a witness can refuse to answer a question, if the answer is likely to incriminate him.

Acid and chemical damage policy   Type of business insurance coverage against loss caused by acids and chemicals.

Acknowledgement   The act of one who has executed a written instrument in going before a competent court or officer and declaring it to be his voluntary act and deed.

Acquiescence   Where there is an infringement of right either specifically or implied and the victim of such infringement agrees to carry on in spite of it, this is known as an assent. (See also Laches)

Acquisition cost   The cost to the company of securing business, including commissions to agents and brokers, and in some companies field supervision costs.

Acre   A measure of land, 43,560 square feet.

Act of God   An accident or event that is the result of natural causes, without any human intervention or agency, that could not have been prevented by reasonable foresight or care, such as floods, lightning, earthquake, or storms.

Actio in personam   A personal action, in which the plaintiff claims that the defendant ought to give or do something to or for him.

Actions   When used in the policy, refers to legal actions or proceedings in Court. Actions under the policy for claims against the insuring company are ordinarily restricted by the policy, and must be commenced within one year from the date of the occurrence of the loss or damage or, one year after the cause of action arises.

Active life reserve   Also called policy reserve. Type of reserve of company writing accident and sickness policies. Since the claim rate increases with age and a level premium is charged, a policy reserve must be established.

Actual cash value   The present-day value of property measured in cash, arrived at by taking the replacement cost and deducting for depreciation brought about by physical wear and tear, and obsolescence. For example, a burglary policy will insure you against loss as the result of theft of articles from your home. A burglar takes two suits, one three years old, the other a month old. Even though you paid the same price for both, wear and tear and the use you have had of the three-year old suit would make its "actual cash value" less than that of the newer suit. The fact that you may have to pay more to replace these suits with others will be taken into consideration.

Actual cash value policy or policies, mainly automobile physical damage policies, are issued to insure the "actual cash value" of the property, instead of a fixed dollar amount. Premiums based on estimate of value of insured and similar property (autos, same age and model) are also called "No amount" policies because they show no fixed amount of insurance.

Actual damage Damage which really exists in fact, as distinguished from potential or possible damage.

Actual dividends Those dividends paid on a policy during a previous period.

Actual total loss *See* **Total loss.**

Actuarial cost methods Techniques used to determine amount to be made under a defined policy, such as **mortality tables,** assumption of interest rates and expenses, and the like.

Actuary A person concerned with the application of probability and statistical theories to the practical problems of insurance and related fields. He may specialize in life insurance, property and casualty insurance, pension work, government programs, or a combination of these. His responsibilities extend to the calculation of premiums, evaluation of various reserves, forecasting of financial results on both a long-range and a short-range basis, and he often has additional executive duties in connection with the operation of his firm.

Ad damnum That part of a declaration or writ, which sets forth the amount claimed.

Addendum An addition to a written document.

Additional death benefit (a life term) This term is now used in Hartford Life contracts in lieu of "double indemnity." It is a sum of insurance payable in addition to the face amount of the policy but not more than $50,000. (*See* **Double Indemnity**)

Additional extended coverage An endorsement for policies covering dwellings and similar property, extending the coverage to include insurance against direct loss caused by water damage from plumbing and heating systems, rupture or bursting of steam or hot water heating systems, vandalism and malicious mischief, vehicles owned or operated by the insured or by a tenant, glass breakage, ice, snow, and freezing, as well as fall of trees and collapse. A $50 deductible is required in most states.

Additional insurance Additional insurance is insurance which is added to an already existing policy. Unless it is agreed to by the company or its duly authorized agent the insurance is voided.

Additional insured *See* **Insured, additional.** A person, other than the one in whose name an insurance policy is written, who is protected against loss by terms of the policy. For example, if you have an automobile liability policy, anyone who may drive your car with your consent is an additional assured although not mentioned by name in the policy, and is protected against loss by the terms of that policy.

Additional interest The interest of an additional insured. Same as additional insured.

Additional living expense A form of "extra expense insurance" on dwellings. The insurance company provides additional funds to compensate for the extra costs caused by the interruption, e.g., extra cost of living in a hotel.

Additional provisions Provisions in addition to the regular insuring and benefit provisions, and to the standard or uniform proivsions, which define and limit the coverage. Also often called general provisions.

Add-on interest The full amount of interest calculated on the original principal for the term of a loan. It is added to the principal, thereby becoming a part of the face amount of the promissory note.

Adhesion Legal concept which holds that any ambiguities in the working of insurance contracts will be construed against the company writing the insurance.

Ad Hoc For the purpose of the subject matter involved.

Ad infinitum Continuing indefinitely.

Ad initium From the beginning.

Ad interim In the meantime.

Ad libilum At pleasure, as one pleases.

Ad litem For the purpose of the proceedings. A guardian "ad Litem" is a person appointed in particular proceedings, to represent the interests of an infant or other person who is under a disability, and is therefore unable, so long as the disability continues, to act in person or to be directly represented as a party to the proceedings.

Adjacent Lying near to, but not in actual contact with. Nearby. Property near the property insured or discussed. Such adjacent property may increase the hazard of loss.

Adjoining Contiguous; touching, in actual contact with. Property which touches in all or in some part the property which is insured.

Adjustable policy *See* **Reporting policy.**

Adjustable premium The right retained by the insurer in some contracts to change the table of premium rates applying to classes of insureds as a condition of the renewal of the contract.

Adjusted earnings Net earnings from the operation plus the value of insurance in force for growth in written premiums.

Adjusted gross estate The full value of an estate at the time of the death of the owner less such items as funeral expenses and administrative costs.

Adjusted net worth An insurance company's capital, surplus, and reserves plus the value of existing insurance on the books, as well as any unrealized capital gain. From this amount are deducted estimated income taxes and other adjustments.

Adjuster An individual who acts for the company or the insured in the settlement of claims. He leads to agreement about the amount of a loss and the company's liability. Adjusters may be salaried employees of adjusting organizations operated by insurance companies, individuals operating independently and engaged by the companies to adjust a particular loss, and special agents or staff adjusters employed by the company. The term "claim representative" is used interchangeably. Not to be confused with public adjusters who represent claimants only.

Adjuster, average An adjuster who specializes in the adjusting of marine losses.

Adjuster, independent An independent professional man or organization settling claims for insurers on a fee basis.

Adjuster, public One, other than a lawyer, who represents the insured in settling claims with insurers on a fee basis.

Adjustment The process of determining the cause and amount of a loss, the amount of indemnity the insured may recover after all proper allowances and deductions have been made, and the proportion that each company is required to pay under its contract if there is more than one insurance company involved.

Adjustment bureau   Organzation, frequently owned by member insurance companies. It has a staff of adjusters to which the companies refer their losses.

Adjustment expenses   Expenses resulting from the settlement of a claim.

Administration Bond   It is a bond which must be given by a person or Company to guaranty the matters of administration. It is commonly used in wills to guaranty the fidelity of the executor or administrator of the estate.

Administrator   The person appointed by court to manage and settle the estate of a deceased person who has left no will.

Administrator's deed   The legal instrument given by a person who is legally vested with the right of administration of an estate, especially of an estate such as that of a minor, an incompetent such as a lunatic, or of a testator having no competent executor.

Admiralty   Court having jurisdiction on maritime questions and offenses, including suits involving marine insurance contracts and general average adjustments. For example, if you ship goods by a boat and the boat should run aground and make it necessary to throw part of the cargo overboard, an admiralty court (U. S. Federal Court) would give the final decision as to what proportion of these losses would be charged to you under the principle of general average.

Admiralty bond   Bond used to cover maritime matters, to assure release of a vessel or property under libel or security of payment of costs.

Admitted assets   *See* **Assets.** Assets of an insurer permitted by a state to be taken into account in determining its financial condition.

Admitted company   A company is termed "admitted" within a given state when licensed to do business in that state. An insurer of another state or country licensed under the insurance law of a state to do business in that state.

Ad valorem   Designates an assessment of taxes against property. Literally, according to the value.

Advance   In real estate, a partial disbursement of funds under a note. Most often used in connection with construction lending.

Advance commitment (conditional) A written promise to make an investment at some time in the future if specified conditions are met.

Advance discounting for mortality Consideration of the number covered by a plan of insurance such as pension or retirement who will die before reaching the age for the benefits to start.

Advance discounting for severance Consideration of the number of employees who will terminate their employment before retirement. This permits lower contribution by the employer to the plan.

Advanced payments Those payments by the insurance company to cover the insured's expenses due to such things as fire, losses, or medical treatment. These will be deducted from the final settlement of the claim.

Advance premium The payment made at the start or beginning of the period covered by the insurance policy. *See* **Premium advance,** and **Deposit premium.**

Adventure Clause Phrase describing the trip or voyage which is to be undertaken.

Adverse Possession The occupation of land by someone who does not have the true legal right of ownership.

Adverse selection Insurance of risks which are poorer or more prone to claim than the average risk. There is a tendency of poorer risks or less desirable insureds to seek or continue insurance to a greater extent than do better risks. Also there is a tendency of insureds to take advantage of favorable options in insurance contracts. Selection "against the company."

Advisory organizations Function of rating bureaus and similar groups that advise and do not require members to follow recommendations.

Aedificatum solo, solo, cedit "That which is built upon the land goes with the land".
Most commonly found in insurance in the matter of fixtures as becoming part of real property unless there is a specific contract to the contrary.

Aero insurance Coverage against risks of flying.

Affidavit A statement or declaration reduced to writing and sworn to or affirmed before some officer who has authority to administer oaths or affirmations.

Affidavit of claim   A form required when a claim is filed. In general it contains the facts on which the claim is based.

Affiliated companies   Companies between which there are some relationships such as interlocking directorates, common stock ownership, or holding company acquisition.

Affirm   A term usually used when confirming a judgement of an inferior court. To "affirm" the earlier judgement is to agree with it. To "reverse" the earlier judgement is to upset it and rule differently.

Affirmation   A solemn declaration in the nature of an oath, made by persons who have religious scruples against taking oaths.

Affirmative Defence   The defendant's position in a law suit is usually a negative one, that is, his pleadings and proofs in court usually are of a nature denying charges made against him and the offering of evidence to convince the Judge or jury of his freedom from wrong doing.

Sometimes however a defendant may strengthen his defense by pleading and showing affirmatively at trial that the plaintiff was guilty of actionable negligence or contributory negligence. Other such examples of "Affirmative defences" available to a defendant in certain cases are as follows:

(1)   That the plaintiff assumed the risk.

(2)   That the plaintiff had previously released the defendant, prior to suit.

(3)   That the plaintiff's cause of action was outlined by statute 4 etc.

Affreightment   A bill of lading. A contract to transport goods by sea; either a charter party or a bill of lading.

After-acquired property   The property a debtor acquires as security after the execution of a mortgage or other form of indebtedness that additionally secures the indebtedness.

After charge   *See* **Unsafe.**

Age   The last previous birthday in cases of annuities. A period of one year, starting half a year before and ending half a year after the birthday of the individual in the case of insurance application.

Age change   The date halfway between natural birth dates when the age of an individual for the purpose of life insurance rating changes to the next higher age, insurance age being the nearer birthday. Annuity age is commonly the last previous birthday.

Age limits   The limits of age below which and above which the company will not accept applications.

Agency experience A record of the profitability or unprofitability of business an insurance company has written for a particular agent.

Agency plant All of a company's agents or salesmen.

Agency superintendent Officer of company supervising a territorial division's agents.

Agency system Sometimes called the American Agency System. The use of sales and services of insurance agents who are not exclusively associated with one insurance company. This is in contrast to what are called "direct writers" or the use of salaried employees who may operate through the use of mail.

Agent Representative of the insurer in negotiating, servicing, or effecting insurance contracts; he may be an independent contractor or an employee.

Agent, general The general agent is the company representative in a given territory, entrusted with the task of supervising the company's business within that territory. He may appoint local agents whom he services. The general agent is an independent contractor compensated on a commission basis.

Agent, Independent An independent businessman who represents insurance companies under contract in a sales and service capacity and is paid on a commission basis. Sometimes referred to as a "local agent," he is licensed by the state in which he conducts his business.

Agent, local An insurance agent, frequently referred to as a "local agent" or "producer" is an independent contractor. He represents insurance companies in a sales and service capacity and is paid on a commission basis. He is licensed by the state in which he operates. His powers are limited by the terms of his agency contract and by the state laws. An agent to whom a small territory is assigned, and to whom limited authority is usually given.

Agent, policy-writing A local agent who is authorized to write and sign insurance contracts for his company. Although there are a number of technical divisions of producers, as a general rule, in all forms of stock company insurance except Life, an agent has such authority and responsibility, while a broker has not. Agents at times are improperly called brokers. At times a policy-writing agent is correctly called a recording agent.

Agent, recording *See* **Agent, policy-writing.**

Agent, resident A licensed agent who is a resident of the state by which he is licensed.

Agent, special, or Agent, state   The special agent or state agent is an employee of the company. He serves as the personal contact between the company and its agents in a given territory.

Agent, surveying (fire term)   A surveying or survey agent is a local agent who does not write policies for his company, but instead submits business to the company by means of applications. This type of agent has otherwise the same authority as a recording agent.

Agent's authority or power   The agent's authority or power is that which is granted in his agency contract. By case law, the authority which the public may reasonably expect the agent to have. Agency power sometimes includes claim adjustment and settlements. It never includes authority to change or waive the provisions of a policy, to alter an application, or to make an amendment or rider. The last two are valid only when signed by an officer of the company.

Agent's balance   A statement compiled periodically showing amounts due to or receivable from agents.

Agent's Commission   The payment by a company to the agent who places and services insurance, usually expressed as percentage of premium, new commission being that paid in respect of the first policy year and renewal commission that paid in respect of subsequent policy years.

Agent's License   A license stating that authority has been granted by the state or province entitling the agent to solicit and sell insurance.

Agents' qualification laws   State laws that establish minimum qualification requirements for insurance agents.

Aggregate contractual liability   The total amount of money which the company insuring will pay under the terms of a liability policy for claims which arise as a result of the liability assumed by the insured insured under that contract.

Aggregate excess of loss reinsurance   *See* **Stop loss** and **Excess of loss reinsurance.**

Aggregate indemnity   A maximum dollar amount which may be collected for any disability, period of disability, or under the policy.

Aggregate limit   *See* **Limit, aggregate.**

Aggregate operations liability   The total amount of money which the insurance company will pay under the terms of a liability policy for claims for damages caused by the insured or his agents in the operation of a business. It usually applies only to property damage liability.

Aggregate products liability   The total amount of money which the insurance company will pay under the terms of a liability policy for claims which arise out of the distribution or use of the products covered by the contract.

Aggregate protective liability   The total amount which the insurance company will pay under the terms of a liability policy for claims which may arise from acts of independent contractors. This is frequently found in the construction field.

Agrarian   Pertaining to fields or lands, or their tenure.

Agreed amount clause   Policy provision in which the holder agrees to carry a stated or determinable amount of insurance. An amount of insurance specified in the contract as being sufficient to nullify the effect of coinsurance, average, or contribution clause of the contract.

Agreement   Where two or more persons come to a mutual understanding with respect to their rights and duties.

Agreement for deed   *See* **Conditional sales contract**.

Agreement for sale   A written document in which the purchaser agrees to buy certain real estate (or personal property) and the seller agrees to sell under stated terms and conditions.

Agricultural machinery insurance policy   Type of marine insurance coverage. Self-explanatory.

Air passengers policy   Type of business insurance coverage. Self-explanatory.

Air rights   The rights vested by grant (fee simple, lease agreement, or other conveyance) of an estate in real property to build upon, occupy, or use, in the manner and degree permitted, all or any portion of space above the ground or any other stated elevation without vertical planes, the basis of which corresponds with the boundaries of the real estate described in the grant.

Aircraft: hull & liability policy   Type of business insurance coverage. Self-explanatory.

Alarm valve   Part of automatic sprinkler that makes a noise or activates a signal. The signal may be connected with a fire department.

Aleatory   That which depends on an uncertain event.

Aleatory contract   The parties to the insurance contract realize that the values given up by each party will not be equal.

When such is the fact, it is an "aleatory contract."

Alien carrier An insurer whose domicile is a foreign country. *See* **Alien company.**

Alien company An insurance company incorporated under the laws of a foreign country. For example, in Canada or England. *See* **Alien carrier.**

Alien insurer An insurance company incorporated in one country or state which does business in a foreign country or state.

Alienate To part with title to property. Thus public liability policies cover liability of the insured arising out of a condition or conditions in premises alienated by him, but do not cover liability for damage to the premises themselves resulting from such a condition.

Alienation Where an owner or tenant has the right to dispose of his interests in real or personal property, whether such right is voluntary (e. g. to sell) or compulsory (e. g. a seizure)—that right is a right of alienation.

Alienation clause A special type of acceleration clause that demands payment of the entire loan balance upon sale or other transfer of the title.

Alius dictus A false name.

Allegation A statement of facts set out as a view of the particular individual involved.

Allied lines Those types of insurance associated with property insurance, including perils such as sprinkler leakage, water damage, and earthquake.

All-Inclusive Trust Deed (AITD) *See* **Wrap-around.**

All Lines As it has become known throughout the insurance industry, refers to the writing of life and health lines with the property-liability lines through the same company. The term *all lines* suggests a limitless form of protection whereas in fact there are still a number of lines of protection still not afforded by the so-called *all* lines concept. *All lines* protection does not protect against the full range of loss in suggests.   CIT comment

All Risk refers to the modern package trend of writing so many perils in one contract that enumerating them becomes impossible. Thus, these so-called all risk forms simply identify the perils *not* covered rather than name those included. Herein lies the essential criticism of "all risk" according to several members of the terminology committee. Referring to a contract as *all* risk when in fact it does not cover certain risks is not only confusing to the public but also suggests protection not afforded by the contract. The term *all risk* conveys an erroneous and misleading interpretation by the consuming public and should, therefore, be abandoned for a better, more accurate term. CIT tentative

All risk insurance A name given to a policy which covers against the loss caused by all perils except those which are specifically excluded by the terms of the policy. Ordinary policies, contrarywise, name the peril or perils which are specifically covered in that policy. Insurance protecting the insured from loss arising from any cause other than those causes specifically excluded by name. This contrasts with the ordinary policy, which names the peril or perils insured against (e.g., all-risk insurance). A personal property floater policy which insures personal belongings against loss, theft, or disappearance wherever they may be. On the other hand, a theft insurance policy would protect your property only against theft.

Allocated benefit A provision under which certain expenses usually miscellaneous hospital and medical charges such as x-ray, dressings, drugs, etc, will be paid for at a rate for each as scheduled in the provision. Usually there is also a maximum total that will be paid for all such expenses.

Allotment A body of land which has been divided into small parts; an allotment may be marketed with or without any substantial improvements, such as sidewalks and public utilities having been installed, although the most common practice now is to provide for their installation. In England, an allotment is a small tract of land which is rented to an artisan or laborer for cultivation—a subdivision.

Alluvium Also alluvion. Soil deposited by accretion, the increase in land on a shore or bank of a river due to change in the flow of a stream.

Alteration bond Type of business coverage. Self-explanatory.

Alterations If the meaning, or language, of a policy is changed, an "alteration" is effected. No meaning or language of any policy should be changed except by endorsement signed by the company — if such an alteration is made without the consent of the insurer it will be of no effect. If made by a stranger it is called "spoliation", —and will not effect the contract if the original words can be ascertained with certainty.

Amalgamation   The merger of two or more companies in their undertakings.

Ambiguity   A word is said to be ambiguous where it has a double meaning or can be interpreted in two or more ways. That which is doubtful or uncertain; capable of being understood in more than one sense. Any ambiguity in a policy is always construed against the underwriters.

Amenities   The qualities and state of being pleasant and agreeable. In appraising, those qualities that attach to property in the benefits derived from ownership other than monetary. Satisfactions of possession and use arising from architectural excellence, scenic beauty, and social environment. The nonmaterial attachment to property of certain benefits such as the pleasant or agreeable consideration of the architectural beauty.

American agency system   The system of selling insurance through agents compensated on a commission basis. This is in contrast to the system of selling insurance through salaried company representatives who write insurance for one company only. *See* **Direct writer.**

American Annuitants Mortality Table   Table published in 1918 of mortality rates for males and females as experienced by twenty American insurance companies.

American Bureau of Shipping Register   A list of ships and their descriptions maintained by the American Bureau of Shipping.

American Experience Table   Mortality table developed from the actual experience of the Mutual Life Insurance Co. of New York. Now superseded by the C.S.O. Table.

American Land Title Association (ALTA)   A national association of title insurance companies, abstractors, and attorneys specializing in real property law. The association speaks for the title insurance and abstracting industry and establishes standard procedures and title policy forms.

American Lloyd's   A type of insurance organization permitted in some states. The owners of the organization assume risk as individuals, which, generally limits their full liability.

American Men Table   Mortality table published in 1918 on experience of major companies from 1900–1915. A good table but never widely adopted because of legal technicalities.

Amicus curiae   A friend of the Court.

AMMINET   Automated Mortgage Market Information Network. A nationwide electronic quotation system designed for listing VA, FHA, conventional single-family and multifamily loans, and Government National Mortgage Association securities.

Amortization   The act or process of extinguishing a debt, usually by equal payments at regular intervals over a specific period of time. The liquidation of a financial obligation on an instalment basis.

Amortization schedule   A table showing the amounts of principal and interest due at regular intervals and the unpaid balance of the loan after each payment is made.

Amortized value   The National Association of Insurance Commissioners has ruled that certain premium bonds may be carried at their amortized value rather than the customary current market value.

Amount at risk   This term comprises the amount of insurance effected on any property by a company, irrespective of whether such amount is equal or otherwise to the actual value of the property.

Amount of insurance to value   The term denotes the proportion of the sum insured or "the amount" at risk to the total value of the property.   (See Co-Insurance).

Amount subject   The value which may reasonably be expected to be lost in one fire or other casualty. It depends on the protection and construction of the risk, and the distribution of concentration of values. Estimating the amount subject is a major responsibility of inspectors and underwriters.

Analytic schedule   *See* **Dean schedule.**

Analytic system for the measurement of relative fire hazard
A system for measuring the relative probability of fire loss to property and of determining fire insurance premium rates. *See* **Analytic schedule, Dean schedule.**

Ancillary   Designating or pertaining to a document, proceeding, officer, or office; etc., that is subordinate to, or in aid of, another primary or principal one; as, an ancillary attachment, bill, or suit presupposes the existence of another principal proceeding.

Ancillary benefits   Benefits providing for the payment of miscellaneous hospital charges.

Annualized   The accounting and actuarial technique that reduces data to an annual basis.

Annual mortgagor statement   A report by the lender or servicing agent to the mortgagor telling what taxes and interest were paid during the year and what principal balance remains.

Annual renewal agreement   Clause in which insurance company agrees to renew the covered policy under stated conditions.

Annual report   The summary of pertinent financial information with an accompanying text designed to provide shareholders or policyholders of mutual companies with a summary of the year's activities of the company.

Annual statement   The annual report made by a company at the close of the fiscal year, stating the company's receipts and disbursements, assets and liabilities. Such statement usually includes an account of the progress made by the company during the year. The annual report, as of December 31, of an insurer to the state insurance department, showing assets and liabilities, receipts and disbursements, and other information.

Annuitant   The person during whose life an annuity is payable usually the person to receive the annuity. One who is entitled to receive payment of an annuity from an insurer.

Annuity   The right to give or receive a series of payments of an amount of money. Originally the money was designated on an annual basis. However, today the payments may be made on another but periodic basis. A contract that provides an income for a specified period of time, such as a number of years or for life. A sum of money that constitutes one of a series of periodic payments. A sum of money or its equivalent that constitutes one of a series of periodic payments. Any advantage that may be interpreted in terms of money and answers the requirements of regularity may be considered an "annuity."

Annuity age change   The date of the last previous birthday.

Annuity, cash refund   A life annuity with an agreement that the insurer, on the death of the annuitant, will pay in a lump sum to a beneficiary any amount by which the consideration paid to the insurer exceeds the payments made to the annuitant.

Annuity certain A policy providing income for a stated period of time irrespective of the death or life of the individuals covered. A contract that provides an income for a specified number of years, regardless of life or death.

Annuity certain, life An annuity payable for a specified period in any event, and after that period for as long as the annuitant lives.

Annuity deferred An annuity, commencing more than one year from the payment of a lump sum, or from the commencement of periodic payments, to the insurer.

Annuity due An annuity whose first payment is made at the beginning of each period (i.e., month, quarter, year *et al.*) rather than at the end.

Annuity, group *See* **Group insurance.**

Annuity, immediate life A life annuity commencing one month, three months, six months, or one year after purchase, depending on the frequency of the periodic payments.

Annuity, installment refund A life annuity with an agreement that the insurer will, on the death of the annuitant continue payments to a beneficiary until the total of the payments to annuitant and beneficiary equals the consideration paid to the insurer.

Annuity, joint and survivor An annuity payable as long as any one of two or more persons survives.

Annuity, life An annuity payable as long as the annuitant or annuitants live.

Annuity rent The amount paid to an annuitant under the terms of the annuity.

Annuity, retirement A deferred annuity, the premiums, less loading, for which are accumulated at interest, the accumulation being used to purchase an annuity at a specified age; prior to that age, the annuitant is entitled to a cash surrender value, and in case of death the surrender value is paid to his beneficiary.

Annuity, reversionary *See* **Annuity, survivorship.**

Annuity, survivorship An annuity payable to the annuitant for the period during which he survives the insured.

Annuity Table for 1949 Jenkins and Lew published a table with projection factors to take into consideration reductions in mortality rates.

Ante Date To use a date earlier than the date undertaking is made.

Ante litem motam Before litigation was in contemplation.

Anticancellation laws   State laws that restrict the insurers from canceling insurance policies except for listed specific reasons.

Anti-coercion law   Most state statutes contain a provision prohibiting the use of coercion in the sale of an insurance policy. Normally found under "Unfair Trade Practices."

Anticoercion laws   Laws that prohibit lending organizations from requiring that the borrower obtain insurance from them as a condition for obtaining the loan.

Anticompact laws   Antitrust laws which limit agreements to prevent competition.

Anti-discriminatory laws   Prohibit companies from giving preferential terms of rates not warranted by the rating of the risk.

Anti-Rebate Law   State legislation which prohibits the giving of part of the premium back to the insured.

Antiselection   *See* **Adverse selection.**

Apartment   A complete and separate living unit in a building, usually containing at least four units.

Apartment policy   A type of special multi-peril policy that combines coverages, such as fire, allied lines, liability, burglary, and robbery, associated with the ownership and operation of an apartment house.

Apparent agency   The elements necessary to establish "apparent agency" are acts by the apparent agent or principal justifying belief in agency. There must be knowledge thereof by the apparent principal and reliance thereon by a third party consistent with ordinary care.

Appeals   In many cases where one of the litigants finds the judgement of the lower court to be what they feel is an improper one they may have the case reviewed by a higher court. This action is known as an Appeal. The case is not heard over again but the type written copy of the evidence as given at the trial is reviewed by a higher court and lawyers representing each side submit their brief on their understanding of the facts and the law relating to it. The appeal is usually heard by a panel of judges who may affirm the ruling of the lower court or reverse it or in certain circumstances require a new trial.

Appearance   In Provinces where an action is started in the form of a simple Writ the lawyer defending the action records that he is the lawyer for the defence on this particular cause and this is known as "Filing an Appearance". Further pleadings continue between the respective lawyers.

Applicant A person who fills out and signs a written application for insurance.

Application A questionnaire providing space for information to be used to determine the insurance coverage to be afforded as well as the acceptability of the insurance risk and the amount of premium. A questionnaire which must be filled in, when required, by the person seeking insurance. It gives the company full information about the proposed subject of insurance and the person to be insured, for the purpose of determining whether the company will issue the policy and if so, to have it prepared properly. In hail and accident and sickness insurance it becomes part of the policy. *See* **Daily report.**

Application agent Also called survey agent. Individual not having right to make out his own policy but who must submit the survey or application to his company, which issues the policy.

Appointment Act of authorizing an agent to act for his company.

Appointment papers Documents which the agent compiles and returns to his company. These documents are connected with the agent's appointment.

Apportionable annuity An annuity that provides for a pro rata fractional payment covering the period from the date of the last regular premium payment to the date of death.

Apportionment *See* **Pro rata.**

Apportionment clause A clause found in an insurance policy which distributes the insurance in proportion to the total coverage. Thus, you may have two $1,000 fire insurance policies on a building and one of them provides extended coverage against wind storm and the other does not. In the event of a $100 loss from a wind storm, you would receive only $50 or 50% of the loss. If both policies had provided this extended coverage, you would receive full payment, however, of the loss.

Appraisal An estimate of quantity, quality, or value. The process through which conclusions of property value are obtained; also refers to the report setting forth the estimate and conclusion of value. A survey of property made for determining its insurable value or the amount of loss sustained. The fire insurance policy provides for an appraisal after a loss on demand of either insured or company.

Appraisal clause A clause in an insurance policy which provides that the insured or the insurance company shall have the right to demand an appraisal to fix or determine the amount of damage in terms of money. This would also refer to loss as well as damage.

Appraisal inventory A detailed tabulation of the separate items comprising an assembled property included in an appraisal report and valued by the appraiser.

Appraisal surplus The excess of appraised values over book values.

Appraised value An opinion of value reached by an appraiser based upon knowledge, experience, and a study of pertinent data.

Appraisements The valuations of property by persons selected for the purpose by the parties interested, or under direction of law. Appraisements of the value of salvage after a fire, are provided for under the policy conditions.

Appraiser One qualified by education, training, and experience to estimate the value of real and personal property.

Appreciation An increased conversion value of property or mediums of exchange due to economic or related causes which may prove to be either temporary or permanent. Appreciation is the antonym of depreciation where the latter is used to denote shrinkage in conversion value; also (limited) the excess of appraisal value over book value of property; also the process of developing appraised value by the application of price indices to actual costs or estimated costs of another date and of lower price levels; also as applied to gain in condition of physical property such as in railroad property where roadbeds, for instance, are increased in value by solidification and grassing slopes.

Appreciation rate The index figure used against the actual or estimated cost of a property in computing its cost of reproduction new as of a different date or under different conditions of a higher price level.

Approach The part of a sales presentation which opens the discussion with the prospective insured.

Approved A risk, individual, product, or building that meets the underwriting standards of the company. Usually applied to construction, preventive and protective devices, packing, goods, etc., to indicate that they meet requirements for insurance, or for a reduced premium rate.

Approved, Roof   Usually a roof made of fire resistive material as distinguished from wood.

Appurtenance   Something incident to a principal thing, such as a right of way to land or outhouses in reference to a main building.

Arbitrage   In mortgage banking, the simultaneous purchase and sale of mortgages, futures contracts, or mortgage-backed securities in different markets to profit from differences in price.

Arbitration   If a dispute arises between the insured and the company, or their representatives, in regard to the amount of the loss, the loss can be referred to arbitration. Someone, approved by both parties, is appointed to consider the facts and pass on them. If the parties cannot agree to one person, then each is allowed to appoint someone to represent him, and these two then appoint another acceptable to both. If they do not agree to provisions, the matter must be referred to the Courts. The award brought down by any of these arbitrators is binding and final on both parties.

Arbitration clause   Clause of policy that provides that if the policyholder and the company cannot agree on settlement amount on a claim, they both select a neutral umpire who has the authority to bind both parties to the settlement.

Arbitrator   One chosen to decide a controversy out of Court.

Architect's Inspection Certificate   A document, usually issued by an independent architect, verifying that a certain portion of construction on a project has been completed in accordance with approved plans and specifications.

Architectural specifications   *See* **Plans and specifications.**

Arm's-length transaction   A transaction between a willing buyer and a willing seller with no undue influence imposed on either party.

Armstrong investigation   Study in 1905 that was made in New York on practices of life insurance companies. As a result certain broad changes were enacted not only in New York but in many other states regulating such things as policy forms and provisions which were recommended by the committee.

Arrears   The status of a policy on which the premiums are past due but on which grace period has not yet expired.

Arrest bond   Type of business insurance. Self-explanatory.

Arson   The willful and malicious burning of property; if someone deliberately sets fire to a property, that is arson. If an
individual carries fire insurance the damage will be paid for
under the terms of the policy just as though the fire had
started accidentally; however, if it can be proved that the
insured himself was the arsonist, that is, he started the fire
himself or had someone do it for him for the purposes of
collecting damages, the insurance is automatically voided.

Art glass policy   Type of business insurance coverage. Self-
explanatory.

Arts: all risk policy   Type of business insurance coverage. Self-
explanatory.

As interest may appear   Where the insurable interest in a property
is either unknown or presently unascertainable, the use of this
phrase when attached to "Loss payable to AB", leaves the
whole question of title to the insurance monies to be settled between the insured and the person whose name appears in the Loss
payable clause. In case of dispute, however, there is a danger of
the company being drawn into it, and hence it is a good phrase
to leave out of policy wording. What is better, is to ascertain the
extent of the interest, and its character, and definitely state it in
the policy. In practice, where there are other interests than those
of the named insured, it is usual in the case of loss, for the
company to make the loss check out in the joint names of the
various parties, and paying over to the insured, leave the settlement, or the proportions, to be thrashed out between such
interests. The obligation to endorse the check with the names of
the payees, in order to effect payment, constitutes a virtual
discharge of the liability to all parties. However, there have
been one of two qualifying rulings by the Courts of the United
States in regard to the status of the company in such matters. In
general, however, the practice is satisfactory.

Ash dump   An opening in the fireplace floor, usually placed at
the rear, through which ashes are conveyed to the basement
or outside.

Assailing thieves   Thieves other than officers or crew of a vessel, as found in the ocean marine policies.

Assemblage   The act of bringing two or more individuals or
things to form an aggregate whole; specifically, the cost or
estimated cost of assembling two or more parcels of land
under a single ownership and unit of utility over the normal
cost or current market prices of the parcels held individually.

Assessed value A value set upon real estate by governmental assessors for the purpose of assessing taxes.

Assessment The requirement of a mutual insurance company or a reciprocal exchange that an insured pay an additional amount to meet losses greater than those anticipated. Amounts levied on insureds by insurers collecting a definite advance premium where the insurer's funds prove insufficient to meet its obligation. Amounts levied on insurers for the maintenance of organizations or public services.

Assessment insurance Where the benefit payment is dependent upon the collection of assessments from the policyholders in order to pay the sum required for the losses incurred and where specific premium payments are not fixed in the policy. These are usually associated with fraternity, society, or association that allows the organization to increase the required payments of the insured whenever necessary to meet claims. The claims are known as assessments and are made because of the insufficiency of the initial payment of the insured to cover his proportionate share of losses. It is the opposite from nonassessments.

Assessment rolls The public records of taxable property.

Assessor The designated public official who makes the official estimate of value.

Assets All the available properties of every kind or possession of an insurance company that may be used to pay its debts. These would include real estate, bonds, mortgages, stocks, cash, deferred and unpaid premiums. It would exclude, for example, accounts which are over 90 days due, and office equipment and furniture. The assets of an insurance company include all funds, property, goods, securities, rights of action, or resources of any kind owned by it, less such items as are declared nonadmissible by state laws. These nonadmissible items consist mainly of deferred or overdue premiums.

Assets insurance Coverage for a creditor of his working capital, accounts receivable. Used in credit insurance. *See,* for contrast, **Liability insurance.**

Assigned risk A risk which underwriters do not care to insure but which, because of state law or otherwise, must be insured. The insurance is therefore handled through a pool of insurers and assigned to companies in turn.

Assignee A person, firm, or corporation to which an insurance policy is assigned or transferred.

Assignment   The transfer of the legal right or interest in a policy to another party, generally in connection with the sale of property. In many kinds of insurance it is valid only with the consent of the insurer, in life insurance, usually binding on the insurer only if filed with the insurer. The transfer, after an event insured against, of one's right to collect an amount payable under an insurance contract.

Assignor   The person who assigns a mortgage or insurance agreement.

Assigns   The parties to whom an assignment has been made. Assignments are not valid until approved in writing by the company. The assigns have no right or title to its benefits until such transfer has been effected, and consented to by the company.

Association group   Members of a business fraternal organization or trade association may form a group in order to qualify for group insurance under one master health insurance contract.

Assume   To accept all or part of a ceding company's insurance or reinsurance on a risk or exposure.

Assumed liability   *See* **Contractual liability.**

Assumed liability policy   Type of business coverage. Self-explanatory.

Assumed reinsurance   See Reinsurance Assumed.

Assumption agreement   A written agreement by one party to pay an obligation originally incurred by another.

Assumption certificate   Coverage provided by a reinsurer which guarantees payment to a party or parties not participating in the reinsurance contract.

Assumption fee   The fee paid to a lender (usually by the purchaser of real property) resulting from the assumption of a mortgage.

Assumption of mortgage   Assumption by a purchaser of the primary liability for payment of an existing mortgage or deed of trust.

Assumption of Risk   This is used where one places himself in a situation which he realizes to be dangerous to him. He consents to taking a chance and thereby under certain circumstances frees an employer or others from liability.
The accepting of a risk by an Insurance Company.

Assurance   Considered identical to and synonymous with insurance. *See* **Insurance.**

Assured   An interchangeable word that is the same in meaning as insured.

Assurer   Same as **Insurer.**

At occupation   An underwriting designation for an occupational accident.

Attach   A verb meaning what a policy does at the time it comes into force, that is, when the coverage begins.

Attachment   The act of taking into custody of the law either the person or the property of someone under and by virtue of an order of court.

Attained age   The age an insured has reached on a certain date, based on nearer birthday.

Attest   One who witnesses the signing of a contract or the signatures on a will and such matters can "Attest" as to the fact that these signatures were properly made before him to affirm as genuine.

Attestation clause   A clause following the general provisions of an insurance policy to which the officers of the insurance company subscribe their names to complete the contract. In actual practice, the number of policies that are written by most companies are so numerous that it is physically impossible for the president or secretary of a company to personally write his name, so most of the policies are printed by the insurance company containing the printed signatures of the officers and only the authorized representative of the company actually signs the contract when it is completed and ready to be presented to the policyholder.

Attorney in fact   An individual who has the authority to act for another within the area of the terms of his appointment. *See* **Power of attorney.**

Attractive nuisance   A dangerous place, condition, or object which is particularly attractive to children. In these cases the courts have frequently held that where "attractiveness" exists, the owner is under a duty to take steps to prevent injury to those that may be attracted and the owner may be held liable for failure to do so. Certain types of machinery such as a railroad turntable have been held to be "attractive nuisances."

Auction   A method of selling real or personal property. An auctioneer asks for bids and, upon receipt of the highest bid, completes the sale.

Auctioneer's bond   Type of business insurance coverage. Self-explanatory.

Audit A survey of the insured's records to determine the premium which should be paid the insurance company for the protection furnished. For example, audits have been made in connection with workmen's compensation policies with the premium to be determined on the basis stated in the policy. This term also has a more general meaning from the accounting sense. An examination of the insured's books and records to determine actual exposures for premium computation purposes. Audits are most commonly made in workmen's compensation, manufacturers' and contractors' liability, product liability and reporting form lines, and on automobile fleet, gross receipts, and garage payroll policies, where the premium is based on such items as the insured payroll, gross receipts, values on hand, owned automobiles, or units handled or sold.

Audit bureau *See* **Stamping office.**

Auditor Individual who makes a formal examination and verification of records.

Authentication. The performance of certain acts upon or with reference to a written instrument, for the purpose of rendering it admissible in evidence as being what it purports to be, without other proof that it is such.

Authorization The amount of insurance an underwriter says he will accept on a risk of a given class or on specific property, given for the guidance of agents and in response to requests from producers.

Authorized company A state insurance department licensed insurance company that is permitted to do business in the licensed states. In all other states it would be an unauthorized company.

Authorized Insurer An insurer approved by the state or legally allowed to transact business in the state for the types of insurance for which they may be licensed.

Auto trailers policy Type of business insurance coverage. Self-explanatory.

Automatic cover Provided in many forms of insurance usually for a specified period and limited amount, to cover increasing values, newly acquired and changing interests.

Automatic Coverage Subject to contract terms, coverage of additional property or for other perils by an existing contract without specific request by the insured.

Automatic Loss Reinstatement Reinstatement, without request by the insured or obligee, of coverage of future losses to the extent that its amount has been reduced by payment of a loss.

Automatic premium loan   Contractual agreement by the insurance company to utilize the cash value of the insurance policy to pay a past due premium. This prevents a lapse in coverage. A feature in a life insurance policy providing that any premium not paid by the end of the grace period (usually 31 days) be automatically paid by a policy loan if there is sufficient cash value.

Automatic reinstatement clause   A clause in an insurance policy which provides for automatic reinstatement of the full face value of the policy after payment for a loss. *See* **Reinstatement.**

Automatic reinsurance treaty   *See* **Reinsurance treaty, automatic.**

Automatic restoration   *See* **Automatic reinstatement.**

Automatic sprinkler   A property protection device to prevent damage by fire. The sprinkler head is made of a substance that melts at a low point and releases a spray of water.

Automatic treaty   *See* **Obligatory treaty.**

Automobile Assigned Risk Plan   A program, operative in each state, under which automobile liability insurance is made available to persons who are unable to obtain such insurance in the voluntary market.

Automobile: car and liability policy   Type of personal and business insurance coverage for liability due to car ownership.

Automobile death and disability coverage   Under the private passenger automobile liability policy an extra premium is required for this endorsement which pays a sum in stated amounts for specific injuries or accidental death as well as indemnity in case of total disability.

Automobile fleet   A group of automobiles under the same ownership and management which may, because of the number, justify a discount in the premium on the insurance.

Automobile insurance   Contractual protection against losses connected with use of automobile. The terms of the contract will determine the coverage. Such features as collision, public liability, comprehensive, property damage, theft, fire, lightning, and transportation are covered by many policies.

Automobile insurance, comprehensive   Insurance against any physical loss to an automobile except by collision or upset.

Automobile insurance, drive other cars   Insurance against loss due to claims for damages arising out of maintenance or use of automobiles other than the car or cars described in the policy contract.

Automobile insurance, hired cars   Insurance against loss due to claims for damages arising out of the maintenance or use of motor vehicles hired or borrowed from others by the insured.

Automobile insurance, nonownership liability   Insurance against loss due to claims for damages arising out of the use of motor vehicles not owned or hired by the insured but used in the conduct of his business.

Automobile liability insurance   Indemnity policy for legal liability for bodily injury or damage to others arising from accidents of ownership or operation of an automobile.

Automobile medical payments insurance   Sometimes called basic medical payments. This optional coverage pays for medical expenses of the passengers and policyholder irrespective of responsibility for the accident.

Automobile physical damage insurance   Covers damage or loss to automobile of policyholder.

Autopsy   A post mortem medical examination to determine the cause of death.

Autrefois acquit   A plea in bar to criminal prosecution; that a prisoner has already been tried for the same offsense before a Court of competent jurisdiction, and has been acquitted.

Average   *See* **General average, Particular average.**

Average (rate of return)   The return on an investment calculated by averaging the total cash flow over the years during which the cash flow is received by the investor.

Average adjuster   An individual specializing in marine losses involving general average. *See* **General average.**

Average blanket rate   A rate for a blanket policy, established by multiplying the rate for each location by the value at that location declared by the insured, and then dividing the sum of the results by the total value. *See* **Blanket policy.**

Average clause   A term loosely used to mean pro rata distribution, coinsurance clause. A clause providing that the insurer shall be liable in the event of loss for not more than that proportion of the loss which the amount of the insurance under the policy bears to a specified percentage of the actual cash value of the property insured. *See* also Coinsurance clause; Pro rata distribution clause.

Average distribution clause *See* **Pro rata distribution clause.**

Average rate A rate used in fire insurance to determine the premium for a policy or policies covering more than a single location or more than one type of property. Where several separate risks are insured under a single policy for a single amount of insurance, the rate determined by taking the weighted average of the rates for the various risks insured separately. A rate for a blanket policy established by multiplying the rate for each location by the value at that location declared by the insured and dividing the sum of the results by the total value. *See* **Blanket policy.**

Average risk The average risk is the basis of all insurance work. The whole insurance conception is based on the law of average. In fire underwriting, the "line" is based on the average inherent hazard, and conditions of the risk to be written. A "Below Average" risk is one where conditions surrounding it comprise and embrace hazards not found in the average risk.

The risk "Above Average" is one where the conditions are better than the average, and the fire hazard thereby lessened. Under the operation of schedule rating, the establishment of an "average risk" is given its greatest effect, although to some extent the perception of what is the average, is obscured by the difference that occurs in the rating. An average risk under schedule treatment, would be a risk in accordance with the conditions called for in the establishment of the basic rate.

Average weekly benefits Usually called weekly compensation in workmen's compensation insurance. The amount payable per week for disability or death as prescribed by law. This is usually a percentage of the average weekly wage, subject to a minimum and maximum amount.

Average weekly wage The average rate of remuneration per week, computed as prescribed by law. The several workmen's compensation laws and disability benefit laws vary widely in the methods of computation prescribed.

Aviation clause A clause limiting the liability of the insurer in case death or injury is connected in a specified degree with aviation.

Aviation hazard The extra hazard of accidental death or injury resulting from participation in aeronautics. The tendency is to liberalize the exclusion to cover everything except pilot, crew, instructor, student, or duties aboard requiring descent therefrom.

Aviation insurance Contractual protection against losses connected with airline accidents on domestic scheduled airplanes. Nonscheduled trips and nondomestic flights require higher premium.

Aviation passenger accident insurance   Indemnification for accidental injury during a specific flight or for flights in a certain period.

Avigation rights   *See* **Air rights.**   An agreement between parties to a transaction settling what each shall give and receive.

Avulsion   The sudden tearing away of land by the violent action of a river or other body of water.

B.B.B.   Banker's blanket bond.

B. & C.   Building and contents.

B.B.S.U.   Bid Bond Service Undertaking

B.C.I.   Bureau of contract information.

B.C.P.   Blanket Crime Policy

B.F.U.P.   Board of Fire Underwriters of the Pacific.

B.I.   Bodily injury, also Business interruption.

Bo.   Bonding.

B.P.   Brick protected (classification).

B.P.B.   Blanket Position Bond

Br.   Brick

B.R.   Builder's Risk

Bu.   Burglary.

B.U.   Brick Unprotected

B.V.   Brick Veneered

Baggage policy   Type of business insurance coverage. Also may provide personal coverage.

Bail bond   Guarantees appearance of individual answering a court summons. The bonding company or individual pays the amount of the bond to the court if the summoned individual does not appear when required.

Bailee   One who has temporary possession of property belonging to another. Bailees have different degrees of liability for such property. For example, if your personal property, insured under a personal property floater policy, is turned over to a moving company to be transported, the moving company is the bailee during the time your property is in its hands. Your insurance policy protects you in case of loss or damage but does not protect the bailee.

Bailee's customers' insurance   The bailee insures property of his customers. Laundry and furs in storage are examples of property frequently insured by this type of coverage.

Bailment Delivery of personal property for a particular purpose with the intent that the property will be returned to the person who originally delivered it. Storage of goods, the pledge of securities as collateral are examples of bailments.

Bailor A person who entrusts goods to another.

Balance The residual amount of money due an insurance company from its agent after all credits and charges.

Balance sheet The tabulated listing of the assets and liabilities of a company or individual as of a given date.

Balloon loan A loan in which small periodic payments are made during the term of the loan. These sums are not sufficient to pay the full loan so that at the end of the period there is a need to refinance the loan since the last payment is a balloon or large amount that was not expected to be paid in full. Credit insurance of level term or decreasing term life may be written. The latter is more appropriate for a balloon loan.

Bank burglary and robbery policy Type of business insurance coverage. Self-explanatory.

Banker's blanket bond Type of business insurance coverage. A broad form of bond guaranteeing banks against loss due to dishonest, fraudulent, or criminal acts of their employees, and insuring against loss due to robbery, larceny, burglary, theft, hold-up, forgery, misplacement, and mysterious unexplained disappearance.

Banker's forgery and alteration bond Type of business insurance coverage. Self-explanatory.

Bankrupt A debtor whose estate is vested in a trustee for division among his creditors persuant to an order in the Court.

Bankruptcy Proceeding in a Court for the distribution of property of an insolvent person among his creditors after which he is relieved of all liability to these creditors even though payment into bankruptcy to some of the creditors is less than the full obligation.

Bargain A contract regarding the terms of sale and purchase.

Barratry The illegal handling of a vessel by its crew or officers while at sea. The sinking of a ship for purposes of collecting insurance would be an example of barratry. Act of master or mariners, for some wrongful purpose, causing injury to the owners of a vessel.

Base Wood member carried around the walls of a room and touching the floor.

Base mold Moulding applied at top of base.

Base shoe Moulding applied at junction of base and floor.

Base Premium *See* **Subject premium.**

Basic limits of liability—*See* **Liability limits.**

Basic point One one-hundredth of 1 percent. Used to describe the amount of change in yield in many debt instruments, including mortgages.

Basic premium A percentage of the standard premium used in determining the premium for a workmen's compensation risk utilizing the retrospective rating plan which permits adjustment of the final premium for a risk or the basis of the loss experience of the insured during the period of protection, subject to maximum and minimum limits.

Basic rate The manual or experience rate, from which are taken discounts or to which are added charges to compensate for the individual circumstances of risk.

Basic rent The rent charged in a subsidized housing project and computed on the basis of a maximum subsidy.

Basket provision A provision contained in the regulatory acts governing the investments of insurance companies, savings and loans, and mutual savings banks.

Beauty parlor public liability insurance Indemnification against errors, malpractice, or mistakes resulting in legal action being brought against the proprietor of the beauty parlor.

Bench marks Identification symbols on stone, metal, or other durable matter permanently fixed in the ground, from which differences of elevation are measured as in tidal observations or topographical surveys.

Beneficial interest The interest arising from an insurance policy.

Beneficiary A person who may become eligible to receive, or is receiving, benefits under the plan, other than as a participant. CIT

Beneficiary Change The beneficiary may be changed only if the policy gives such right to the policyholder and if the law permits. In the United States a beneficiary is revocable and the beneficiary's interest may be eliminated in favor of another beneficiary if the policy gives such right to change the beneficiary. If no such right is given, the beneficiary is "irrevocable."

Beneficiary, contingent A beneficiary who is entitled to benefits only after the death of a primary beneficiary.

Beneficiary, irrevocable A beneficiary for whom another may not be substituted by the insured.

Beneficiary, primary   A beneficiary who is first entitled to benefits on the death of an insured.

Beneficiary statement   The statement of a lender that shows the remaining principal balance and other information about the loan.

Benefit of selection   The advantage afforded an insurance company through careful selection of insurance risks and therefore is desirable, as for example, risks that have fully guarded their machinery are more desirable for workmen's compensation insurance than those that have not.

Benefits   Sum of money provided in an insurance policy to be paid for certain types of loss under the terms of an insurance policy.   For example, an accident insurance policy may provide that certain sums be paid for death, loss of limbs or sight, or loss of time.   These specified amounts are the benefits provided by the policy.

Bequest   A gift of personal property in a Will.

Best's Reports   Reports of insurance companies that include their ratings and underwriting results.   Best's is to the insurance industry what Dun & Bradstreet is to general business.

Betterment   An improvement in a property which is considered to add to the investment or capital cost as distinguished from repairs or replacements where the original character or cost is unchanged.

Bicycle floater insurance policy   Type of marine insurance coverage.   Self-explanatory.

Bid   An offering of money in exchange for property for sale.

Bid bond   A guarantee that the contractor will enter into a contract, if it is awarded to him, and furnish such contract bond (sometimes called performance bond) as is required by the terms of the bond.

Bill of lading   There are many types of bills of lading.   All are contracts for transportation between the carrier and the shipper.

Bill of sale   A written instrument whereby one person transfers his title and interest in personal property to another.

Binder   A temporary agreement which obligates the several parties of the contract.   In insurance the insurance company is obligated to pay if the loss insured against occurs before the policy is written.   Thus a person taking an insurance policy on his home will be covered immediately by the insurance representative binding his company if the home should burn before the policy from the insurance company has been received, the loss will be paid exactly as if the policy had been written. A preliminary agreement to provide immediate insurance until a policy can be written, either by an agent or by a company. It should contain a definite time limit, should be in writing, and clearly designate the company in which the risk is bound, the amount and the perils insured against, as well as the type of insurance. A temporary insurance contract pending execution of the policy contract. Except for specified differences, the terms of the binder are by implication those of the contract which is intended to replace it.

Binder, insurance   A written evidence of temporary hazard or title coverage that runs for a limited time only and must be replaced by a permanent policy.

Binding receipts   A receipt given for payment of premium with the application, which binds the company on the contract if the risk is approved as applied for. *See* **Conditional receipt**.

Birth rate   The number of births compared to the total population for a stated period of time and for a specific group or area.

Blackout period   That period of years between the time the last child of a widow reaches eighteen years of age and the time that the widow becomes sixty-two years of age. The blackout refers to Social Security benefits.

Blanket bond   Used in banks and related institutions to cover losses caused by robbery, burglary, or the dishonesty of employees and officers of the financial institution.

Blanket bonds, fidelity, forgery, alterations   Type of business insurance coverage. Self-explanatory.

Blanket contract   An insurance policy in the health field, providing benefits covering dismemberment and accidental death for classes of individuals as distinguished from those individually identified.

Blanket crime policy   Coverage against employee dishonesty and losses, inside and outside a covered premise. It also covers counterfeiting and forgery as well as money order.

Blanket expense policy   A policy or provision which pays all expenses for some type of disability: medical, nursing, surgical, hospitalization, x-ray, etc.

Blanket fidelity bond   Covers losses to an employer by dishonest acts of his employee or employees.

Blanket insurance   Insurance which covers more than one type of property in one location or one or more types of property at several locations. For example, you may have a blanket policy to insure a building and its contents at one location, or you may insure furniture, fixtures, and stock in two or more buildings under a blanket policy.

Blanket medical expense This provision in loss of income policies which allows the insured to collect up to a maximum amount for all hospital and medical expenses without any limitations on individual types of medical expenses.

Blanket mortgage A single mortgage which covers more than one piece of real estate.

Blanket policy Insurance with broad coverage frequently used in burglary and fire insurance. A policy issued to cover a number of individuals such as an athletic team, passengers in a certain airplane, etc. An insurance policy which covers several different properties or exposures under one form, instead of under separate items.

Blanket position bond Protects the employer from loss caused by dishonesty on the part of his employees. The most that is payable for a single embezzlement is the face amount of the bond times the number of dishonest employees involved in the embezzlement.

Blanket rate An insurance rate applied to more than one property or subject of insurance.

Blight A reduction in the productivity of real estate from a wide variety of causes and having a multitude of visible effects on the physical appearance and condition of the property or area affected.

Blighted Area A neighborhood or area within a city composed in general of obsolete structures which reflect lack of acceptable maintenance.

Block A square portion of a city or town enclosed by streets, whether partially or wholly occupied by buildings or containing only vacant lots as defined in the plot.

Block limits The maximum amount of insurance that an insurance company will write in any one city block. This reduces the risk of large losses in case of a fire that burns the entire block.

Block policy A policy covering all the property of the insured (usually a merchant) against most perils, including transportation. It may also cover property of others held by the insured on consignment sold but not delivered, for repairs, or otherwise held. It usually covers both on and off the insured's premises. Examples: jewler's block, camera and musical instrument dealer's, equipment dealer's.

Blue Cross hospitalization   A group hospitalization insurance on a nonprofit basis found in the United States. Plans vary considerably with the local conditions. Typical coverage includes group hospitalization, surgical, as well as medical coverage. Frequently associated with Blue Shield Plan.

Blue Shield Plan   Nonprofit surgical and medical insurance coverage requiring membership in a Blue Cross Plan. *See* **Blue Cross.**

Bodily injury   Injury to the body of a person. The term is usually specifically defined in the policy and these individual definitions have variations.

Bodily injury liability   The responsibility which may arise from injury to life, or health of another individual or individuals.

Bodily injury liability insurance   Protection against loss arising out of the liability imposed upon the insured by law for damages because of bodily injury, sickness, or disease sustained by any person or persons other than employees.

Boiler   A heating plant used to generate steam or hot water.

Boiler and machinery insurance   Contractual protection for the insured against stated damage to property and legal liability for damages caused by accidents of boilers, pressure vessels, or related machinery.

Boiler policy   *See* **Boiler and machinery insurance.**

Bonafide   In good faith.

Bona Vacantia   Goods without an actual owner or which have been abandoned and in which no individual can claim a proper legal title except the government e.g. lost treasures.

Bond   An obligation of the insurance company to protect the insured against financial loss caused by the acts or omissions of another person or persons known as the principal. A fidelity bond on employees would reimburse the insured up to the limits of the policy for the loss caused by dishonesty of the covered employee. Originally it meant any obligation under seal. In a noninsurance sense a bond is a debt instrument consisting of a promise to pay and usually issued on the security of a mortgage or a deed of trust or on the credit of the issuer.

Bond, bail   A bond guaranteeing appearance in court of the principal named in the bond.

Bond, bankers' blanket   A broad form of bond guaranteeing banks against loss due to dishonest, fraudulent, or criminal acts of their employees and insuring against loss due to robbery, larceny, burglary, theft, hold-up, forgery, misplacement, and mysterious unexplainable disappearance.

Bond, bid   A guarantee that a contractor will enter into a contract on which he has bid if it is awarded to him and furnish a contract bond as required by the terms of the contract.

Bond, blanket   A broad bond covering all employees and in the case of financial institutions including insurance against enumerated hazards.

Bond, completion   A guaranty of performance in the form of a fidelity or guaranty company bond upon payment of a premium.

Bond, contract   A guarantee of the faithful performance of a construction contract; it may include the payment of all labor and material bills incident thereto. These two guarantees may be written separately, the first as a performance bond, the second as a payment bond.

Bond, court   A bond required of a litigant as a condition of pursuing his rights in court.

Bond, depository   A bond guaranteeing payment of funds to depositors in accordance with the terms of a deposit in a bank. Not the same as federal deposit insurance.

Bond, fidelity   A promise to make good financial loss due to the dishonesty of employees, a financial guarantee of the performance of an implied obligation.

Bond, fiduciary   A bond executed in behalf of a person appointed by a court to a position of trust; it guarantees performance of statutory duties and proper accounting.

Bond, forgery   Insurance against loss due to forgery or alteration of, on or in checks or other instruments.

Bond, lenders'   *See* **Bond, completion.**

Bond, license   A bond guaranteeing that the person to whom a license is, or is to be issued will comply with the law or ordinance regulating the privilege for which the license is issued.

Bond, maintenance   A bond guaranteeing against defects in workmanship or materials for a stated time after acceptance of work.

Bond penalty   The face amount of a bond, which is the amount the surety must pay for loss.

Bond, performance   *See* **Bond, contract.**

Bond, permit   A bond guaranteeing that the person to whom a permit is, or is to be issued will comply with the law or ordinance regulating the privilege for which the permit is issued.

Bond, position   A fidelity bond covering all persons occupying stated positions.

Bond, public official   A guarantee that a public official will properly account for public funds and will perform such other duties as are prescribed by law. The form of the bond and the performance guaranteed are often prescribed by statute.

Bond, schedule   A bond in which are listed the names or positions of the employees covered as principals.

Bondsman   A surety or a person bound by a bond.

Bond, surety   A guarantee of the performance of an expressed obligation, usually evidenced by a written instrument.

Bonding   Also called surety. Describes a type of firm that writes bonds.

Book cost   The actual cost of assets purchased or acquired.

Book value per share   The value of the company's assets, minus its liabilities, divided by the number of shares outstanding.

Book depreciation   The amount reserved upon books of record to provide for the retirement or replacement of an asset.

Book value   The value of Assets (Stocks, Bonds, Real Estate etc.) as shown in the Company's books.

Books   Under the designation "books" all volumes are embraced whether they are bound or unbound. The word "Book" at law, embraces any aggregation of printed or manuscript sheets, and even a single sheet of paper. If "books" in common meaning of the word are intended to be covered, they should be designated "bound" or "unbound printed volumes". Books, unless specifically so stated, are not included in the term "furniture". "Books of account" of a used character are not insurable.

Borderline risk   A risk on the border between those acceptable to the insurer and those not acceptable. *See* **Accommodation line.**

Bordereau   A memorandum containing detailed information concerning documents that accompany it. An economical procedure of reporting business to the home office, employed in handling the business from some branch offices. Also it is used extensively in passing reinsurance from one company to another under a reinsurance agreement.

Borrower   An individual or company who receives funds in the form of a loan with the obligation of repaying the loan in full with interest, if applicable.

Bottomry   A combination of money lending and insurance on hulls associated with early marine insurance.

Bracing   Wood structural member installed to provide rigidity.

Branch office   A company office for the purpose of supervising business within a certain territory. It is operated under a manager, it is usually headquarters for a number of special agents, claim men, engineers, and auditors, and provides service to agents within its territory.

Branch office system   The method of handling insurance through branch offices of the insurer as contrasted with the general agency system. *See* **Direct writer.**

Breach   The art of breaking, used in such phrases as "breach of peace," "breach of promise," "breach of trust."

Break-even point   In residential or commercial property, the figure at which occupancy income is equal to all necessary expenses and debt service.

Breeder's policy   Type of business insurance coverage especially designed to protect breeders of livestock.

Brick Construction   A building or structure with 75% or more of the exterior walls constructed of masonry having a minimum wall thickness of 8″ for brick, stone or hollow masonry tile 6″ for poured reinforced concrete, or 4″ of hollow masonry blocks faced with 4″ of brick, and with a roof structure of combustible sheathing and/or combustible roof supports.

Brick Veneer Construction   A building with the outside supporting walls constructed of wood or other combustible material and faced with a single layer of brick, usually not more than 4″ in thickness. In many areas brick veneer construction, for fire insurance purposes, is considered the same as frame construction.

Bridge policy, vehicular and rail   Special type of business insurance coverage of bridges. It is an inland marine policy insuring bridges against stated hazards and perils.

Bridging   Wood members used to brace floor joists.

Bridging the gap   A clause that provides coverage for fire damage that may be caused by a windstorm. Some fire policies do not provide coverage if a significant part of a building falls, so a fire resulting after windstorm damage under those policies would not be collectable. The bridging-the-gap clause corrects this situation.

Broad form   *See* **All risks.**

Broad Form Personal Theft Coverage   A form of theft coverage on property, as defined, from a private residence.

Broad Form Storekeepers Insurance For the small storekeeper, a package of nine specific crime coverages, including all risk protection on money and securities.

Broker An insurance broker ordinarily is a soliciter of insurance who does not represent insurance companies in a capacity as agent but places orders for coverage with companies designated by the insured or with companies of his own choosing. Broker is frequently incorrectly used to designate an agent of more than one insurance company.

Brokerage Agency An establishment operated by a broker who conducts his business in behalf of clients seeking to purchase personal or property insurance.

Broker-agent While generally one is either a broker or an agent some individuals maintain two offices, one as a broker the other as an agent. One who is licensed to act both as broker and as agent.

Broker of record Broker designated by the policy as such.

Brokerage The business of a broker.

Brokerage department A department of an insurance company the purpose of which is to aid agents in handling insurance outside of their territory and to aid brokers in the placing of insurance throughout the country.

Bucking arrears Applying advance payments of one policy-owner to another policyowner's arrears. It is a falsification of records and a form of embezzlement.

Budget plan With certain provisions, large policies of insurance may be divided into smaller policies, to expire and be re-newed on consecutive years, the policies being written at pro rata of the long term rates so that the premium payment is spread over several years.

Builder/Sponsor Profit and Risk Allowance (BSPRA) The devel-oper's remuneration for assuming the risks involved in build-ing government-assisted, low-income rental housing.

Builder's risk insurance Insurance against loss to buildings or ships, including machinery and equipment, in course of con-struction, and to materials incidental to construction. With the value of the construction changing during the building process a fixed amount policy would not properly cover the risk. This type of insurance may be written on a reporting form or on a completed value form.

Building and loan associations State or federally chartered sav-ings institutions that may insure members' accounts up to $100,000 through the F. S. & L. Insurance Corp.

Building code Regulating the construction of buildings within a municipality by ordinance or law.

Building efficiency The ratio of net rentable area to gross building area, expressed as a percentage.

Building paper Heavy waterproof paper used over wall sheathing to provide insulation.

Building rate A fire insurance term which refers to the rates on buildings rather than on the contents of the building. *See* **Contents rate.**

Built-ins Cabinets, ranges, and ovens or similar features that are an integral part of a structure.

Bullion Precious metals such as platinum, gold, or silver which are cast in ingots or bars and considered merely as metal.

Bundle of Rights The rights or interests that a person has in property. An individual has the exclusive right to own, possess, use, enjoy, and dispose of real property.

Burden of Proof The burden of proof or onus of proof is the responsibility of putting forth the evidence to support the particular cause. Normally the plaintiff must prove his case, however, as the case progresses the burden of proof may easily shift from side to side from time to time.

Bureau rate (STANDARD RATE) For hazard insurance, and for title insurance in some states, a standard rate established by a rating bureau for all companies writing policies in a specific area.

Bureau, rating An organization that classifies and promulgates rates and in some cases compiles data and measures hazards of individual risks in terms of rates in a given territory.

Burglar alarm A warning device to signal if entry is made by unlawful person or persons. The use of such alarms will permit certain reductions on premiums.

Burglary Breaking and entering into premises of another, with felonious intent, and with visible signs of the forced entry. Since most insurance policies specifically define burglary under their own terms it is wise to be sure that the term burglary in the policy has the meaning for the coverage desired.

Burglary insurance, open stock Insurance against loss of merchandise or equipment by burglary of the insured premises.

Burglary policy Type of business and personal insurance coverage against loss or damage to property by burglary. Commonly used to include burglary, theft, and robbery insurance and often insurance against loss of money or securities due to any cause.

Burglary special coverage insurance   Special endorsements attached to a policy that provide specific types of burglary coverage, such as office burglary, paymaster robbery, and the like.

Burning cost   *See* **Pure loss cost.**

Burning ratio   Ratio of actual fire loss to the total value of the property that could burn. Ratio of loss by fire to insurance in force.

Business   The volume of premiums written. *See* **Line.**

Business insurance   Accident and sickness coverage issued primarily to indemnify a business against loss of time because of the disability of a key employee.

Business Insurance; Partnership Insurance; Corporation Insurance   Insurance concerned primarily with the protection of an insured's business or vocation. Business insurance protects a business againt the loss of its valuable lives or key men; stabilizes the business through the establishment of better credit relations; and provides a practical plan for the retirement of business interests in the event of the death of one of the owners.

Business interruption insurance   Protection for the owner of a business from losses which would be sustained during a period when the business is not operating due to such occurrences as fire or other hazards. The insurance generally provides reimbursement for salaries, taxes, rents, and other necessary continuing expenses plus net profits which would have been earned during the period of interruption within the limits of the policy.

Business interruption insurance, coinsurance form   A form under which losses will be paid only in the proportion that the amount of insurance bears to a stated percentage of the business interruption value.

Business interruption insurance, contingent   Insurance against loss to the insured caused by an accident to property of one other than the insured; e.g., a supplier of raw material.

Business interruption insurance, gross earnings form   A form under which the insured's gross earnings are insured.

Business interruption value   Amount of business interruption insurance necessary in order to provide for payment in full of any business interruption loss within the period of interruption covered by the contract.

Business life insurance trust Agreement where a trustee will collect and distribute the proceeds of a policy of business life insurance.

Buy-back deductible The provision for payment of an additional premium to obtain full coverage in a standard policy that otherwise would contain a deductible figure.

Buy-sell agreement This agreement binds the surviving partners to purchase the partnership interest of the first partner to die at a prearranged price set forth in the agreement and obligates the estate of the deceased partner to sell his interest to the surviving partners.

Buyers' market The period of a contracting demand; prices are on a downward trend.

By-laws Laws made by Corporations, Trading Companies, County Councils, Railway Companies, Public Libraries, etc., under powers granted by Act of Sovereign. By-laws are binding unless they are contrary to the law or unreasonable.

By order of civil authority Action by municipal body such as a fire department in damaging or destroying certain property to prevent greater damage to other property; e.g., cutting a fire brake.

C Casualty.

c% Cents per cent.

C.A. Current Assets

C.A.F. Cost and Freight

C.A.I.G. Canadian Aircraft Insurance Group

C.A.S. Casual Actuarial Society.

Canc. Cancel.

C.B.B. Commercial Blanket Bond

C.B.M.U. Canadian Board of Marine Underwriters

C.B.M.U.A. Canadian Boiler and Machinery Underwriters Association

C.C.I.A. Consumer Credit Insurance Association.

C.D.D.D. Comprehensive Dishonesty, Disappearance and Destruction Policy

C.D.P. Comprehensive dwelling policies.

C.F. Carried Forward

C.F.I. Cost, Freight and Insurance

C.F.I.A.B.   Canadian Federation of Insurance Agents and Brokers

C.F.M.   Cubic Feet per Minute

C.F.M.U.A.   Cotton Fire and Marine Underwriters Assn.

C.H.I.A.   Canadian Health Insurance Association

C.H.I.A.A.   Crop-Hail Insurance Actuarial Association

C.H.U.A.   Canadian Hail Underwriters Association

C.I.   Cost and Insurance; Certificate of Insurance

C.I.A.   Cotton Insurance Association.

C.I.A.C.   Canadian Independent Adjusters Conference

C.I.C.M.A.   Canadian Insurance Claims Managers Association

C.I.F.   Cost, insurance, and freight.

C.I.T.   Commission on Insurance Terminolgy of the American Risk and Insurance Association.

C.L.   Current Liabilities

C.L.U.   Chartered Life Underwriter

Co.   Coinsurance.

C. of C.   Course of construction.

C.O.D.   Cash on Delivery

Comp.   Comprehensive, also compensation.

C.P.   Contract Price; Cost Plus

C.P.A.   Certified Public Accountant

C.P.C.   Commercial Property Coverage

C.P.C.U.   Chartered Property and Casualty Underwriter.

C.R.   Credit Report

C.R.E.F.   College Retirement Equities Fund.

C.S.A.   Canadian Standards Association

C.S.O.   Commissioners 1941 Standard Ordinary Table.

C.S.R.P.   Canadian Sprinkler Risk Pool

C.S.T.   Central Standard Time

C.U.A.   Canadian Underwriters Association

C.U.N.A.   Credit Union National Association.

C.V.L.I.   Cash Value Life Insurance

Cafeteria style benefits   Perks and fringe benefits within a monetary ceiling cost such as dental insurance. They are selected by key employees from a collection of benefits available from an employer. The idea is to provide those benefits which the employee wishes, rather than benefits not as attractive.

Calendar year experience   Experience developed on premium and incurred loss transactions occurring during the twelve calendar months beginning January 1, irrespective of the effective dates of the policies on which these transactions arose.

Call provision   In the mortgage or deed of trust, a clause giving the mortgagee or beneficiary the right to accelerate payment of the mortgage debt in full on a certain date or on the happening of specified conditions.

Camera, all risk policy   Type of floater all risk coverage.

Camera floater   Insurance for camera and related equipment in inland marine form coverage.

Canadian roll-over mortgage   A renegotiated loan where the interest rate and, hence, the monthly payment are renegotiated every five years. No limit is placed on the magnitude of interest rate increases to the borrower.

Cancellable   A contract, terminable by either the insured, or insurer upon notification to the other party in accordance with the provisions of the contract.

Cancellation   The termination of an insurance policy or bond before its expiration by either the insured or the company. The notice necessary before such cancellation becomes effective is almost invariably stated in the insurance contract.

Cancellation, flat   The cancellation of a policy as of its effective date without a premium charge.

Cancellation, pro rata   The termination of insurance contract or bond with the premium charge being adjusted in proportion to the time the protection has been enforced.

Cancellation, short rate   The termination of an insurance contract at the request of the insured prior to the expiration date where the contract provides for a premium larger than the charge applicable for the period. Thus, if the insured cancels the policy before the expiration date, an increased charge is made because of the fixed expenses incurred by the company.

Cancellation evidence   A cancelled policy, or any legal notice of cancellation.

Capacity   Maximum amount of insurance that a company will write on a single risk.

Capital   An accumulation of economic goods used in the production of other goods as compared to something valued because of its immediate enjoyment and consumption. It is the funds invested with the intention that it be a permanent part of a business. The aggregate par value of the stock of an insurance corporation, the amount which must be paid in at the time of formation, and which must be kept unimpaired. Accumulated wealth. A portion of wealth which is set aside for the production of additional wealth. Specifically it is the funds belonging to the shareholders of a business, invested with the expressed intention of their remaining permanently in the business.

Capital charges Sums required to satisfy interest upon and amortization of monies invested in an enterprise.

Capital expenditures Investments of cash or other property or the creation of liability in exchange for property to remain permanently in the business; usually land, buildings, machinery, and equipment.

Capital requirements The total monetary investment essential to the establishment and operation of an enterprise. The appraised investment in plant facilities and normal working capital. It may or may not include appraised cost of business rights such as patents, contracts, and charter.

Capital stock insurance company A company having in addition to surplus and reserve funds, a capital fund paid in by stockholders.

Capital sum The amount specified in an accident policy for payment in the event of the loss of limb or sight of the insured. *See* **Principal sum.**

Capital surplus Paid in surplus, donated surplus and revaluation surplus, that is, surplus other than earned surplus. Surplus not arising from profits of operation but from such sources as sale of capital stock at premium, profit on dealings in a corporation's own stock, donated stock, appraisal valuations, and surplus shown by the accounts at time of organization.

Capitalization The act or process of converting (obtaining the present worth of) future incomes into current equivalent capital value. The amount so determined as referring to the capital structure of a corporation.

Capitalization rate The rate of interest or return adopted in the process of capitalization, ordinarily assumed to reflect factor of risk to capital so invested.

Captive agent Either a "direct writer" or an agent that has agreed to sell insurance for only one company or fleet.

Care, custody, or control exclusion Those clauses in liability insurance that restrict the liability for property in the insured's care, custody, or control.

Cargo Material or goods carried by ship, truck, or airplane.

Cargo certificate An insurance policy covering cargo.

Cargo Insurance Insurance against loss to cargo carried in ships or by other means of transportation. (Trucks, planes, etc.)

Cargo policy Ocean-inland or river-automobile truck insurance against loss to cargo carried by covered means of transportation.

Carpenter cover *See* **Spread loss reinsurance.**

Carpenter plan Plan of reinsurance that utilizes a profit and loss sharing technique.

Carrier An insurance company which "carries" the insurance. It differs from common carrier and contract carrier.

Carrying charge Premium for insurance on property would be a recurring current expense and in accounting would be termed a carrying charge. Expenses such as taxes, insurance, interest on mortgage are carrying charges.

Cash flow The spendable income from an investment after subtracting from gross income all operating expenses, loan payments, and the allowance for the income tax attributed to the income. The amount of cash derived over a certain measured period of time from the operation of income-producing property after debt services and operating expenses, but before depreciation and income taxes.

Cash market A market where mortgages or mortgage-backed securities are bought and sold for immediate or forward delivery. *See also* **Forward delivery.**

Cash-on-cash return The rate of return on an investment measured by the cash returned to the investor based on the investor's cash investment without regard to income tax savings or the use of borrowed funds.

Cash-refund annuity A life annuity with an agreement that the insurer, on the death of the annuitant, will pay in a lump sum to a beneficiary any amount by which the consideration paid to the insurer exceeds the payments made to the annuitant.

Cash surrender value The amount available in cash upon surrender of a policy before it becomes payable by maturity or occurrence of the circumstance insured against.

Cash value *See* **Actual cash value** and **Cash surrender value.**

Casualty insurance The coverage of loss or liability arising from accident or mishap excluding certain types of loss which by law or custom are considered as falling exclusively within the scope of other types of insurance such as fire or marine. It includes, but is not limited to, employees' liability insurance, workmen's compensation insurance, public liability insurance, automobile liability insurance, plate glass insurance, burglary and theft insurance; also personal liability insurance, forgery, power plant, aviation insurance. Many casualty companies also write surety business.

Catastrophe A sudden and severe calamity or disaster. An event which causes a loss of extraordinarily large amount.

Catastrophe hazard The hazard of loss by reason of a simultaneous peril to which all insured in a group or a large number of insureds are subject.

Catastrophe number Number assigned by the National Board of Fire Underwriters to a severe loss of over $1 million to permit special statistical treatment.

Catastrophe policy Also called major medical expense policies. These policies are designed to pay all medical or hospital costs above a certain deductible amount and up to the maximum provided in the policy. The term catastrophe as applied to them is in reference to the economic catastrophe of huge medical expenses. It is not related to catastrophe as used in catastrophe hazard.

Catastrophe reinsurance Agreement whereby a reinsuring company assumes defined losses above a stated amount that result from a catastrophe.

Causa causans The immediate cause; the last link in a chain causation.

Causa sine quo non The remote or distant cause as distinguished from an immediate cause.

Cause of Actions The basis upon which a suit may be brought against another party. There is a distinction between "cause of action" and "right to sue". The "right to sue" is generally conferred by having a cause of action but the right to sue may be taken away by some other statute as for example a statute of limitations. A person may also have a cause of action but no right to sue because the person or body to be sued possibly cannot lawfully be sued. In practice therefore a "cause of action" implies that there is some person in existence who can bring suit and also a person who can lawfully be sued.

Caveat emptor Let the purchaser beware.

Cede To buy reinsurance. To effect reinsurance. *See* **Reinsurance.**

Ceded Reinsurance See Reinsurance Ceded.

Ceding company Insurance company that places reinsurance business of its original risk with a reinsuring company.

Center of influence A person who is influential in forming a good opinion among life insurance prospects for a certain agent or company. Also used as in "center of recruiting influence" to designate a person who is influential in building a good opinion of a specific general agent or manager which aids that general agent or manager to obtain good agents.

Cents per cent Marine rates are usually quoted as so many cents per $100 of insurance, using this expression.

Certificate A statement that a policy has been written for the benefit of one or more individuals. Also used in evidencing reinsurance between companies.

Certificate of authority A paper showing the powers an insurance company grants to a particular agent.

Certificate of Claim A contingent promise to reimburse an insured mortgagee for certain costs incurred during foreclosure of an insured mortgage, provided the proceeds from the sale of the property acquired are sufficient to cover these costs.

Certificate of convenience A temporary license or permit allowing a person to act as an agent. Examples: A person studying for an agent's licensing examination or the executor of a fully licensed agent's estate.

Certificate of Deposit (CD) A written document issued by a bank or other financial institution that is evidence of a deposit with the issuer's promise to return the deposit plus earnings at a specified rate of interest. *See also* **Negotiable Certificate of Deposit.**

Certificate of insurance A statement of coverage taking the place of the policy as evidence of insurance and often transferring the right to collect claims to the holder of the certificate. In group insurance, a statement issued to a member of the group certifying that an insurance contract has been written and containing a summary of the terms applicable to that member. In insurance other than marine or group, a statement that a specified insured and risk are covered to a specified extent, but ordinarily without responsibility on the part of the insurer to notify the certificate holder of termination of the insurance. A document evidencing the fact that an insurance policy has been written and includes a statement of the coverage of the policy in general terms. It is frequently found where there are group plans. Thus a master policy is issued to the company, and certificates of insurance are given to the individuals covered by the terms of the policy.

Certificate of Occupancy Written authorization given by a local municipality that allows a newly completed or substantially completed structure to be occupied.

Certificate of Reasonable Value (CRV) A document issued by the VA establishing maximum value and loan amount for a VA-guaranteed mortgage.

Certificate of Reinsurance A short-form documentation of a reinsurance transaction.

Certificate of Sale A certificate issued to the buyer of real property at a judicial sale.

Certificate of Title A statement furnished by an abstract or title company or attorney to a client stating that the title to a piece of property is legally vested in the present owner.

Certiorari A proceeding to review in a competent court the action of an inferior tribunal, board, or officer exercising judicial functions, when such action is alleged to be without jurisdiction or otherwise illegal.

Cession An exactly stated yielding of a property or right under a reinsurance agreement. A reinsurance. An amount ceded as reinsurance.

Cession number A number assigned by an underwriting office to identify reinsurance premium transactions.

Cestui que trust A person having a beneficial interest in property held in trust.

Cestui que vie The person on whose life insurance is written. The applicant for the insurance is properly called the insured whether the applicant be the person whose life is insured or not. Where the beneficiary applies for a policy and retains all the incidences of ownership. The person (other than the beneficiary) on whose life the policy is issued is not a party to the contract and has no rights in it.

Chain A series of measurements. Care should be taken to distinguish between engineer's chain and surveyor's chain. Engineer's chain is 100 feet. Surveyor's is 66 feet in length.

Chain of title The succession of conveyances from some accepted starting point whereby the present holder of real property derives his title.

Chain stores, multiple locations policy Type of business insurance coverage specially designed for stores having multiple locations, that is, a number of retail stores under the same ownership, under a central management selling uniform merchandise, and following a uniform policy.

Change in occupancy or use If the occupancy, or if the purposes for which the premises are described as being used, is changed, and which increases the risk, the policy is void unless notice is given. The company has the option of (a) cancellation, or (b) charging an extra premium to cover the additional hazard. If the company charges an extra premium the insured must pay "forthwith" (immediately), failing which the policy is no longer in force.

Charge As related to money, charge is a note of a debt or obligation. Where for example a premium is charged it means the obligation has been incurred for the payment of the sum but that it is not yet paid.

Charge in criminal law means a formal accusation.
To "Charge the Jury" is a direction given by a Judge to the Jury in connection with the law applicable to a certain case. Each side usually requests that the Judge give certain instructions in its favour. After the plaintiff and defendants have presented their respective cases and all the witnesses have been heard, but before the Jury retires a Judge addresses the Jury and may at his discretion cover some or all of the points raised by the counsel.

Chargeable In automobile insurance, certain accidents are not considered adverse to the insured's driving record when they occur under specific circumstances (legally parked, struck in rear, other party cited, etc.) or because of minimal claim cost. Accidents not specifically execpted for such reasons are chargeable and become a part of the insured's driving record.

Chart of accounts Numerical designation of each asset, liability, and capital account.

Charter The grant of rights from a state to a business corporation such as the right to incorporate and transact business. It also means the renting or leasing of a ship.

Charter party A written document stating the terms of agreement between the individual or company chartering a ship and the owner of the vessel.

Chartered Life Underwriter (C.L.U.) A designation conferred by the American College of Life Underwriters in recognition of the attainment of certain standards of education and proficiency in the art and science of life underwriting.

Chartered Property and Casualty Underwriter (C.P.C.U.) A designation conferred by the American Institute of Property and Liability Underwriters to one who has completed a course of instructions and passed a series of examinations.

Chattel   Every species of property, movable or immovable, which is less than a life estate in land.

Chattel Mortgage   A mortgage, the collateral for which is personal or movable property, as distinguished from a mortgage on land or buildings.

Chattel, personal   Any item of movable property besides real estate.

Chattel, real   Any item of property which is connected or concerned or annexed with or to real estate.

Check alteration and forgery insurance   *See* **Forgery insurance.**

Childbirth   The bringing forth of a child; travail, labor. Childbirth is usually excluded in accident and sickness insurance written on female risks, except hospitalization insurance.

Chose in Action   A right to recover by way of an action in law. It usually follows a particular cause of action involved as for example a suit on a contract or negotiable instrument.

In some instances, however, following the right is not quite as simple as for example in some subrogation cases the Chose in Action may remain with the insured even though the Insurance Company may be subrogated to the insured's right and may institute and finance the legal proceedings.

Citation   This is a reference to an authority in jurisprudence e.g., in arguing a case reference is commonly made to earlier court decisions on the point involved. To set out where this earlier decision is reported abbreviations are used. Thus Dube vs Norwich Union 1964 — U2DLR(2D) 489 tells where the case is found. This is a citation.

Civil authority clause   Provision in a fire policy which provides that the insured is protected against damages which may be caused by firemen, policemen, or other civil authorities in their efforts to check fire, e.g., in the case of large fires it has been found necessary to dynamite a whole block of buildings to check the spread of a conflagration. A "civil authority clause" protects from losses resulting from such action.

Civil Code   In France, Napoleon had the law of the land as it applied at that time reduced to a written set of rules.

In the Province of Quebec, the Civil Law was also reduced to sets of rules based largely upon those of Napoleon with suitable changes and revisions and brought up to date. The rules are known as the Civil Code of the Province of Quebec.

Civil commotion   Disturbance between large numbers of individuals in a community frequently associated with damage to private and public property. An uprising of people creating a prolonged disturbance. *See* **Riot.**

Civil commotion policy Type of business insurance coverage protecting against loss caused by an uprising of people creating a prolonged disturbance.

Claim A demand by an individual or corporation to recover under a policy of insurance for loss which may come within that policy or may be a demand by an individual against an insured for damages covered by a policy held by him. In the latter case such claims are referred to the insurance company for handling on behalf of the insured in accordance with the contract terms. A demand for payment under an insurance contract or bond. The estimated or actual amount of a loss.

Claim agent Individual authorized by an insuring underwriter to pay a loss or losses.

Claim department Sometimes called loss department. That part of an insurance company that pays and handles claims or losses.

Claim expense Those expenses other than the insurance costs for adjusting claims. They might include the cost of an independent adjuster, legal fees, expert fees, etc.

Claim representative *See* **Adjuster.**

Claimant Individual asserting a right or presenting a claim for a suffered loss. One who makes or presents a claim.

Claims reserve Those amounts necessary to cover future payments or claims already incurred.

Class rate The premium rate applicable to a specified class of risk. *See* **Minimum rate.**

Classification The underwriting or rating group into which a particular risk must be placed. Pertains to type of business, location, and other factors. Classifying persons, property, or operations as a basis for tabulating statistical experience and determining premium rates. The individual class. The hazards of operating an automobile vary with respect to the type of car and the purposes for which it is used. Therefore automobile insurance groups private passenger cars, trucks, taxicabs, and automobiles operated by garages in different classifications to determine premium rates.

Clause A section of a policy contract, or of riders attached to it, dealing with a particular subject in the contract, as the insuring clause or the coinsurance clause. A particular part of a policy or endorsement to that policy.

Clean-up fund   That function of insurance that provides cash to clean up expenses associated with the occurrence of the event insured against. With death there are expenses for funeral and related charges. Insurance provides a means for paying these charges.

Cleaners insurance policy   Type of bailees' insurance coverage specially designed to take care of the particular bailee risks of cleaners.

Cleanout door   Cast iron door provided at bottom of chimney for removing soot and debris in chimney stack.

Clear space clause   A portion of the insurance contract that calls for the insured property to be separated from certain stated other property.

Clear title   A title not encumbered nor burdened with defects.

Clearance fund   *See* **Clean-up fund.**

Clearing account   A bank account used by a mortgage servicer for temporary, short-term deposit of mortgage payments collected for transmittal to investor or for deposit in escrow accounts.

Client   A party whose interest the agent or broker is engaged to protect or advance.

Close   That portion of a sales presentation leading to the signing of the insurance application.

Close out   The issuance of a policy of insurance.

Closed contract of insurance   An insurance contract under which rates and policy provisions cannot be changed. Fraternal insurance companies are not permitted to write this type of insurance.

Closed period   That portion of the term of a mortgage loan during which the loan cannot be prepaid.

Closing   The conclusion or consummation of a transaction. In real estate, closing includes the delivery of a deed, financial adjustments, the signing of notes, and the disbursement of funds necessary to the sale or loan transaction.

Closing Costs   *See* **Escrow costs.**

Closing Costs (borrower's)   Money paid by the borrower to effect the closing of a mortgage loan. This normally includes an origination fee, title insurance, survey, attorney's fees, and such prepaid items as taxes and insurance escrow payments.

Closing statement   A financial disclosure giving an account of all funds received and expected at the closing, including the escrow deposits for taxes, hazard insurance, and mortgage insurance for the escrow account.

Cloud on the title An outstanding claim or encumbrance which, if valid, would affect or impair the owner's title; a mortgage or judgment.

Cloudburst insurance policy Type of insurance coverage protecting against loss directly associated with a cloudburst.

Clubs Trade term for certain marine mutual insurance associations.

Cluster zoning A type of zoning ordinance proscribing residential or unit density for an entire area. The developer is permitted to concentrate or disperse the density within the area in accordance with flexible site-planning criteria. This differs from a traditional zoning ordinance that allocates density zoning on a lot-by-lot basis, prescribing the same maximum density for all single-structure lots within the zoning district.

CMS Rating Committee Combined Marine Surcharges Committee of the Institute of London Underwriters. This committee maintains statistical records and established British marine insurance rates.

Code A number assigned to each classification for statistical purposes.

Codicil Change in a will made in writing.

Coding The process of translating alphabetical and numerical information into a concise numerical form for statistical or internal recording.

Cognitor An agent appointed to act for another in an action.

Coin collection insurance policy Type of insurance coverage protecting stamp and coin collections.

Coinsurance A provision in an insurance policy requiring the insured to contribute a fair and just share of the total premiums out of which losses are to be paid. The inclusion of this provision, whether mandatory or optional, usually gives the insured lower rates than would otherwise apply. In many parts of the country it is not generally used in policies covering dwellings and their contents or unprotected property, as no rate credit is allowed. It provides for the full payment, up to the amount of the policy, of all losses if the insured has insurance at least equal to the named percentage of the value of the property covered and in some cases in any event. The loss payment in the case of most partial losses is reduced, proportionately, if the amount of insurance falls short of the named percentage, e.g., 80% coinsurance (or average) clause:

Value $10,000

Insurance   8,000
Loss   2,000

Insured collects full amount of loss because his insurance is equal to 80% of the value.

Value $10,000
Insurance   6,000
Loss   2,000

Insurance is for only $6,000 or ¾ of $8,000 the named percentage of value, so insured collects only ¾ of the loss, or $1,500. However, had the loss been $8,000 instead of $2,000 the insured would have collected 6,000/8,000 of $8,000 or $6,000, the full face amount of the policy. Thus the coinsurance provision is of no effect if the amount of the loss equals or exceeds the coinsurance percentage of the value of the property covered. The average clause and the contribution clause are different versions of the same provision, with only slight and highly technical differences. Insurance people commonly refer to either of them as co-insurance.

Coinsurance clause Provision in policy whereby the property owner is to carry insurance up to an amount determined in accordance with the provisions of the policy. This usually is a stated percentage of the value of the property, in return for which he pays a lower premium.

Coinsurer One who shares the loss sustained under an insurance policy or policies. Usually applied to an owner of property who fails to carry enough insurance to comply with the co-insurance provision and who therefore suffers part of the loss himself. An insured or insurer liable to share losses under a coinsurance arrangement. *See* **Cosurety.**

Cold storage lockers insurance Type of business insurance designed to protect the operator of cold storage lockers from the peculiar risks of that activity.

Collateral Accompanying as a side or secondary fact, or acting as a secondary agent; subsidiary; indirect. Related to or not strictly a part of the main thing or matter under consideration. Sometimes specifically pertaining to a security given by a third party, to answer for the death or default of another, as contemplated in the Statute of Fraud, as a collateral promise or undertaking.

Collateral assignment The assignment of a policy as security for a loan; the creditor receives proceeds or values as his interest may appear.

Collateral bond   Additional security for a loan.

Collection book   An Industrial agent's record showing the amount of money collected on each policy, the week of collection, and the policy period covered.

Collection commission   A commission paid to an agent. Represents a percentage of the premiums attributable to a particular agent.

Collection fee   Compensation for an industrial agent earned as a result of his collecting policy premiums on which he receives no commission.

College of Insurance   Educational institution in New York formed in 1962 that has been chartered by the Board of Regents of New York State. It is a degree-granting institution for individuals studying in the field of insurance.

College Retirement Equities Fund   Organization that introduced the variable annuity. It sells fixed and variable annuities only to college staff members. C.R.E.F. is a separate body under the Teachers Insurance and Annuity Association.

Collegia   Ancient Roman society that was influential in developing the idea of life insurance and pensions.

Collision, convertible   A policy for which the insured pays a smaller premium but is required to make an additional payment on the occasion of his making first claim under the policy. Losses which may occur thereafter are paid in full up to the extent of the coverage.

Collision coverage   Automobile insurance against loss or damage to the automobile resulting from collision witih another object or from action of the automobile.

Collision deductible   *See* **Deductible coverage clause.**

Collision insurance   Insurance against loss to insured property caused by striking or being struck by an object; including loss caused by upset.

Collision of the load   Motor transit of merchandise clause that refers to insured material that extends beyond the limits of the vehicle and thus is in greater danger.

Collision policy   *See* **Collision insurance.**

Collusion   An agreement between two or more persons to defraud another of his rights by the forms of law, or to obtain an object forbidden by law. For example, if the insured gives incorrect statements of the facts of an accident in order to permit a guest in his car to recover damages, he is guilty of collusion and thus would void the coverage afforded by the policy.

Color of title   An appearance of title founded upon a written instrument which, if valid, would convey title.

Combination   Applied to a company or agent handling both industrial and ordinary life insurance.

Combination Agency   An agency that sells all the policies issued by a life insurance company, including the small, weekly-payment policies.

Combination automobile policy   Insurance contract combining coverages under policies of automobile physical damage and automobile liability.

Combination Company   A life insurance company whose agents sell both Weekly Premium and Ordinary life insurance.

Combination plan reinsurance   A form of combined reinsurance which provides that in consideration of a premium at a fixed percent of the ceding company's subject premium on the business covered, the reinsurer will indemnify the ceding company against the amount of loss on each risk in excess of a specified retention subject to a specified limit and, after deducting the excess recoveries on each risk the reinsurer will indemnify the ceding company against a fixed quota share percent of all remaining losses.

Combination Policy   An insurance policy made up of the contracts of two or more companies in which there are at least two kinds of insurance each provided by a different insurer.   CIT

Combination residence insurance   A homeowners' policy that includes a number of coverages in one policy, including personal injury liability, loss of use, fixed-glass breakage, personal holdup, burglary, theft and larceny, water damage and explosion of fixtures, tornado, windstorm, and cyclone. Other coverages may also be added.

Combined Annuity Mortality Table   Table published in 1928 for use in writing group annuities and which used the "four year set back" for mortality of men compared to women. It assumed men on the average die four years before women.

Combined ratio   The total of the loss ratio and the expense ratio.

Commercial blanket bond   Bond issued for stated amount on all regular employees of the covered company insuring against loss from employees' dishonest acts.

Commercial forgery policy   Contract of insurance to protect one who accepts checks in payment for services or goods.

Commercial insurance   Accident and sickness insurance intended primarily to be sold to workers in commerce and business as contrasted to industrial workers. The commerce and business workers are exposed to little or no primary occupational hazards, but industrial workers are. It is to be distinguished by being intended to be paid on an annual basis though more frequent payments are usually allowed by option. The payments are remitted to an agency or home office and generally are not called for as is found in industrial policies.

Commercial Multiple Peril Policy A package type of insurance for the commercial establishment, that includes a wide range of essential coverages.

Commercial property floater Insurance coverage for property that may be used in several locations.

Commercial property form Endorsement of a standard fire policy to increase coverage to all risk.

Commercial report *See* **Credit report.**

Commission A payment for the performance of specific duties, generally a percentage of another sum such as the selling price of the policy. A percentage of the premium paid to an agent or broker by the insurer or to a reinsured by a reinsurer. Insurance agents and brokers are usually compensated by being allowed to retain a certain percentage of the premiums they produce. Such an allowance is known as commission.

Commission, contingent A commission, the amount of which is dependent on the profitableness or some other characteristic of the business written by an agent or reinsurer.

Commission of authority Document outlining the delegated powers of an agent granted by the insurance company.

Commissioner of Insurance The state official charged with the enforcement of the laws pertaining to insurance in the respective states. Sometimes called Superintendent of Insurance or Director of Insurance.

Commissioner's disability table Developed by the Health Insurance Association of America. The table is used for valuation of liabilities and many companies use information from it for rate-making purposes.

Commissioner's industrial extended term monetary table This table is used where additional mortality margins are necessary for the computation and valuation of industrial extended term insurance.

Commissioner's standard industrial mortality table A table originally developed in 1941 for the calculation of minimum reserve and surrender values for industrial life insurance policies. Effective in 1968 and 1961 a table of the same title superseded the 1941 table for all new business. This table is used as a standard for the computation and valuation of non-forfeiture values involved in industrial policies.

Commissioners values Annual list of securities published by the National Association of Insurance Commissioners. The values shown on the list are the ones that may be reported by insurance companies on their balance sheets.

Commissioners 1941 Standard Ordinary Table Mortality table prepared by the Guertin committee appointed in 1938 by the National Association of Insurance Commissioners. Called the CSO or C.S.O. Table, it has been established by law in most states as the basis for legal minimum standards for the calculating of nonforfeiture values and policy reserves.

Commitment fee Any fee paid by a potential borrower to a potential lender for the lender's promise to lend money at a specified date in the future. The lender may or may not expect to fund the commitment.

Commitments A promise or pledge by an insurance company to accept certain risks.

Common accident An accident in which more than one person is injured.

Common areas Land or improvements for the benefit of all tenants and property owners. Shopping-center parking lots and residential parks and playgrounds are common areas, as are all spaces within a development that can be used by all the tenants in that development.

Common carrier An individual or corporation which offers its services, for a fee, to the public for carrying persons or property from one place to another.

Common carrier's legal liability policy Type of business insurance coverage designed to protect the carrier from liability associated with the business.

Common disaster clause A clause that provides alternative beneficiary in event both the insured and the original beneficiary die at the same time in an accident.

Common Law Canadian like American and British law derives its force and authority from the universal consent and practice of the people over the years. Certain aspects of the law are written into statutes. The underlying principles and usages and rules of action which do not rest for their authority on this statutory or legislative law are to be found in principles set forth by decisions of the courts over the years.

Many rules were promulgated in feudal times. During the reign of Henry II (beginning 1154 AD) the King's Courts became organized and common law began to evolve. The Courts met frequently and when one court made a decision in connection with a certain issue that decision was followed by the other Courts and became the law unless modified by statute or by gradual evolution.

This has been followed by the courts of all the Colonies and in due course after the revolution by the United States of America.

Common law defenses Pleas which would defeat an injured workman's suit against his employer (and which are still effective in the absence of Workmen's Compensation or Employers' Liability legislation). They are: (1) contributory negligence on employee's part, (2) injury caused by fellow servant, (3) assumption of risk by the employee in the course of his work.

Common law liability The responsibility for injuries or damage imposed upon a party because of his actions, by that part of the law based upon custom and usage as established by the courts, as distinguished from liability under statutes passed by a legislative body. Such law is known as statutory law. Liability of one party to another, other than liability which is covered under a specific legislated law.

Common property Land generally, or a tract of land, considered as the property of the public in which all persons enjoy equal rights; a legal term signifying an incorporeal hereditament consisting of a right of one person in the land of another, as common of estovers, of pasture, of piscary, property not owned by individuals or government, but by groups, tribes, or in formal villages.

Common Tools Doctrine Where tools are so simple that their mechanism, structure and defects, if they have any, are obvious to the workman and the master then upon this account the workman assumes the risk attending the use of them.

Commulation The exchanging of one thing for another. As applied to insurance; generally the exchange of installment benefits for a lump sum payment.

Commulation rights The beneficiary of a life insurance policy has the right to receive in a single payment the remaining unpaid installments of the proceeds or values of the policy.

Community apartment project The multiple ownership of an apartment in which each owner is a tenant-in-common with the right to occupy an apartment in the project.

Community property In some states, a form of ownership under which property acquired during a marriage is presumed to be owned jointly unless it was acquired as separate property of either spouse.

Community rating A means of determining subscribers fees by averaging the charge for the insurance among all insureds according to medical and hospital costs in the community. No differentiation is made among the insureds in terms of individual risks assumed by the insurer.

Commutation clause A clause which provides for estimation, payment, and complete discharge of all future obligations for reinsurance loss or losses incurred regardless of the continuing nature of certain losses.

Commutation rights The privilege of a beneficiary to receive in one payment those unpaid payments which remain under an insurance policy's options.

Commuted value An amount reflecting the current value of a number of payments that will be made. Time preference values are higher for more current receipts.

Company An association of persons, whether incorporated or not, for the purpose of carrying on some business.

Company license The license issued by an appropriate governmental agency in most states. A license today to engage in the insurance business is in perpetuity; however, it may be revoked or canceled for good reason.

Comparables An abbreviation for comparable properties used for comparative purposes in the appraisal process. Facilities of reasonably the same size and location with similar amenities. Properties which have been recently sold, which have characteristics similar to property under consideration, thereby indicating the approximate fair market value of the subject property.

Comparative negligence A method of assessing and facilitating recovery of damages if one's negligence was less than the negligence of the other party. Thus damages may be diminished into portions to the degree of negligence.

Compensating balance A demand deposit at times required by a commercial bank as a condition for extending a line of credit or a bank loan.

Compensation award An order to pay compensation sometimes in instalments, for a number of periods, either definite or indefinite, as the character of the injury requires.

Compensation insurance *See* **Workmen's compensation insurance.**

Competency The fitness or ability to contract. The insurance company must have the charter and permission of the state to write business. The other party to the insurance contract must have the mental faculties to be able to contract. Infants and enemy aliens would be examples of individuals that may not be competent to contract for insurance.

Competitive state fund A state fund writing insurance in competition with private insurers.

Complaint or Declaration In some Provinces it is the first formal pleading starting an action against the third party. It is a concise plain statment of the elements upon which he bases the cause of action.

Completed operations A form of liability insurance which covers accidents arising out of operations which have been completed or abandoned, provided the accident occurs away from the premises owned, rented, or controlled by the insured.

Completion bond A bond guaranteeing the construction of an improvement in connection with which and prior to the completion of which, a mortgagee or other lender advances money to the owner.

Compliance inspection report A report given to a lender by a designated compliance inspector indicating whether or not construction or repairs have complied with conditions established by a prior inspection.

Composite rate A special single rate based upon a measure of exposure which reasonably reflects the variations in the insurable hazards covered for a particular insured. Bases of exposure to which the composite rate is applied include, but are not limited to, payroll, sales, receipts, and contract cost.

Composition roof Roof of asbestos shingles, asphalt shingles, or other similar type of material. The type of roof becomes a rated factor in determining the rate of a fire insurance policy.

Compos mentis Of sound mind.

Compound interest Interest payable on the interest of a debt and on accrued interest from the time such interest fell due.

The interest paid on the principal sum plus the interest on the interest as it falls due and, remaining unpaid, is added to the principal.

Comprehensive coverage   In automobile insurance it is protection against any loss or damage to an automobile except by collision or by upset. If an insured automobile is parked near a building which is being painted and it is damaged by paint splashed on it, the loss would be covered by comprehensive coverage but not under the terms of a specific coverage policy. In other types of policies it is insurance that covers under one insuring agreement, all hazards within the general scope of the contract except those specifically excluded. Sometimes it is insurance under one policy, against a variety of named perils.

Comprehensive Crime Endorsement   Under SMP, providing up to five separate optional crime coverages, including Employee Dishonesty, loss of Money and Securities against destruction, disappearance or wrongful distraction, Money Orders and Counterfeit Currency, Depositors Forgery.

Comprehensive dishonesty, disappearance, and destruction insurance   A broad form of insurance available to business risks covering optionally one or more of eight separate types of loss: loss caused by dishonesty of employees, loss of money or securities from within the premises, loss of money or securities while being conveyed by a messenger outside the premises, loss of securities from a safe deposit box, loss caused by forgery of outgoing instruments, loss caused by forgery of incoming instruments, loss of merchandise caused by burglary, and loss of merchandise or equipment caused by theft.

Comprehensive dwelling policy   *See* **Package policy on homes and dwellings.**

Comprehensive General Liability   Liability coverage for all premises and operations, other than personal, for all general liability hazards, unless excluded.

Comprehensive health insurance   A health insurance policy that incorporates the coverages of major medical and basic medical expense policies into one policy.

Comprehensive medical insurance   Insurance including a basic and a major medical health coverage. Typically, it has a low deductible figure as well as a participation clause and high maximum benefits.

Compromise An agreement between two or more persons of a dispute, something less than the full amount claimed.

Comprehensive Personal Liability Insurance A type of insurance that reimburses the policyholder if he becomes liable to pay money for damage or injury he has caused to others. This form does not include automobile liability, but does include almost every activity of the policyholder except his business operations.

Comptroller The title of the chief accounting officer in some insurance companies.

Compulsory insurance Any form of insurance which is required by law. In Massachusetts and New York, for example, automobile liability insurance is compulsory for all owners of automobiles.

Concealment The withholding of material facts regarding the nature of an insurance risk or loss. Withholding essential information from the insurer in negotiating an insurance contract or in making a claim.

Concurrent insurance Where two or more insurance policies which cover the same property in the same manner and subject to identical conditions though they may differ in amount, or policy dates. *See* **Noncurrency.** If the insured has a policy covering the entire contents of a building and another policy covering only a stock of merchandise in that building, the insurance is not concurrent because the property covered by the two policies is not identical.

Condemnation The legal taking of private property for the public use and interest. The taking of such property must be through the exercise of due process of law.

Condition precedent A requirement which must be satisfied by a claimant in order to establish liability on the part of the insurer.

Condition Subsequent Not met as frequently as "condition Precedent", it is of course of conduct which will defeat or put off rights in existence. Thus, in an insurance contract the insured somewhere in proceedings may fail to co-operate with the insurance company in defending the law suit and the company then may under certain circumstances and conditions consider its obligation under the insurance contract to defend the insured as terminated.
to the others society.

Conditional binding receipt A provision in an insurance receipt providing that if the premium accompanies the application, the coverage will be in force from the time of application.

Conditional commitment   A commitment (most often used with FHA loans) on a specific property for a definite loan amount with specific terms for some future unknown purchaser of satisfactory credit standing.

Conditional receipt   A receipt for the first premium on an insurance contract. The insurance takes effect only on acceptance or approval of the application, under one form, as of the date of acceptance or approval, under the other, as of the date of the application.

Conditional sales contract   A contract for the sale and delivery of property to a buyer, with the seller retaining the title thereof until the conditions have been fulfilled. *See also* **Sales contract.**

Conditional sales floater   Contract of insurance covering property that has been sold on installment or conditional sale.

Conditional Vesting   That form of vesting in a contributory plan under which entitlement to a vested benefit is conditional upon the nonwithdrawal of the participant's contributions.   CIT

Conditionally renewable   The insured in this form of health insurance policy may renew the contract until a stated date or age is reached. The insurer may decline to renew the policy only if certain conditions specified in the contract exist.

Conditions   Provisions of an insurance policy which along with the insuring agreement and exclusions complete the contract. One condition might, for example, be how the insurance contract may be terminated. An event or other fact that determines the liability or nonliability of an insurer, e.g., a hostile fire under a contract of fire insurance. A clause in an insurance contract that defines such an event or other fact as its legal consequences. A clause in a liability insurance contract providing that the insured may not incur certain costs except at his own expense.

Conditions and restrictions   A common term used to designate restrictions on the use of land and providing penalties for failure to comply. Commonly used by land subdividers on newly plotted areas.

Condominium   A form of ownership of real property. The purchaser receives title to a particular unit and a proportionate interest in certain common areas. A condominium generally defines each unit as a separately owned space to the interior surfaces of the perimeter walls, floors, and ceilings. Title to the common areas is in terms of percentages and refers to the entire project less the separately owned units.

Condominium declaration The basic condominium document that must be registered to the originating property owner prior to the conveyance of the first unit sold. This declaration thoroughly describes the entire condominium entity, including each unit and all common areas, and specifies essential elements of ownership that permanently govern its operation.

Confidential risk report A report on physical and moral hazards established through investigations.

Confining sickness Sickness which confines the insured to his home, which is usually defined to include hospital.

Confirm To make valid by a formal assent or ratification. To corroborate or give a new assurance.

Conflagration A highly destructive fire. A fire extending beyond a single risk and over a wide area. Sometimes defined in terms of amount of loss.

Conflagration area Space in which a highly destructive fire has been or could be. An area subject to the conflagration hazard.

Conflagration hazard The chance of occurrence of a highly destructive fire.

Conjugal rights The rights which a husband and wife have, each to the others society.

Consequential damage The impairment of value which does not arise as an immediate result of an act, but as an incidental result of it. The impairment of value to private property caused by the acts of public bodies or caused by the acts of neighboring property owners. The term "consequential damage" applies only in the event no part of land is actually taken. The damage resulting from the taking of a fraction of the whole, that is, over and above the loss reflected in the value of the land actually taken is commonly known as severance damage.

Consequential loss That loss not directly caused by the damage to the property but which arises from the result of such damage. A fire may damage refrigeration equipment, and the nonoperation of the refrigerator causes spoilage. Such spoilage is a consequential loss of the fire. Standard fire and some other policies cover only against direct loss resulting from the peril insured against. Indirect losses, as a consequence of physical damage to the property covered are not infrequent.

Conservators Bond   Probate bond by guardian who is handling the subject estate.

Consideration   The price or subject matter which induces a contract. It may be money, commodity exchange, or a transfer of personal effort. In appraising, usually the actual price at which the property is transferred. In insurance, the consideration may be the statements made on the application and payment of premium.

Consignee   The agent to whom materials are delivered.

Consignee insurance   Type of business insurance coverage that protects the consignee from those particular risks associated with receipt of materials.

Consignment   The act of an individual or company of delivery or transfer of goods to an agent to be cared for or sold.

Consignor   The sender of goods or materials.

Consolidation of Actions   If more than one action is pending in the same Court concerning the same matter the Court may order them to be joined together into one action.

Consortium   The companionship of a wife. A husband may collect damages for the value of his wife's services lost due to some accidents.

Conspiracy   A "conspiracy" is a corrupt or unlawful combination or agreement between two or more persons to do by concerted action an unlawful act, or do a lawful act by unlawful means.

Constant   The percentage of the original loan paid in equal annual payments that provide for interest and principal reduction over the life of the loan.

Constant payment   A fixed or invariable payment, a continually recurring payment.

Construction bond   Type of business insurance coverage that protects the insured from those particular risks associated with construction.

Construction contract   An agreement between a general contractor and an owner-developer stating the specific duties the general contractor will perform according to blueprints and specifications at a stipulated price and terms of payment.

Construction costs   A broad definition of all costs incurred in bringing a building to completion, not including land acquisition costs nor finance and sales costs.

Construction loan A short-term interim loan for financing the cost of construction. The lender makes payments to the builder at periodic intervals as the work progresses.

Construction loan agreement A written agreement between a lender and a builder and/or borrower in which the specific terms and conditions of a construction loan, including the schedule of payments, are spelled out.

Construction loan draw The partial disbursement of the construction loan, based on the schedule of payments in the loan agreement. Also called **takedown**.

Constructive damage Is another term sometimes used instead of Consequential Damage (q. v.).

Constructive notice Information presumed to have been delivered to everyone by virtue of its appearance in the public records.

Constructive performance A particular set of circumstances in which conduct by one of the parties in a contract shows intention to complete the contract. Courts will generally force completion of the contract if the other party or parties reliance upon this conduct is to their detriment.

Constructive total loss Under United States marine law when the cost of repair exceeds 50 percent of the repaired or salvaged value. When an insured peril so damages property that, while not completely destroyed, it is not worth repairing.

"Contained in . . ." This phrase confines the liability of the insurer or company to the definite locality, or building in which the risk is to be covered. It is however, a common practice to transfer or keep moving some kinds of property — such, for instance, clothing in use, a horse on a road, or a vehicle at a repair shop. These conditions are, and have been adjudged by the Courts to be incidental to the intended uses of the property, and therefore, fully covered within the policy terms even when the words "contained in" would appear to confine them. To meet this ruling, and to confine the coverage to the location named, the practice is to insert the word "while" and make the phrase read "while contained in". In England, the situation is met by inserting the words "and not elsewhere" in the policy. Notwithstanding, there are in many localities, permissions given to attach a certain percentage of policy value to goods of a personal character (which are covered at the risk location), while in hotels and other publicly frequented places.

Contents Articles found in a building which are not part of the building.

Contents rate   A fire insurance term which refers to the insurance rate on the contents of the building rather than the building themselves.

Contestible clause   Section of insurance contract that states conditions under which the policy may be contested or voided. Such factors as fraud or material misstatement would be grounds for invoking this clause.

Contiguous   Adjoining.

Contingent annuity   An annuity calling for payment of benefits contingent upon an uncertain event occurring.

Contingency Reserve   That portion of funds which mutual life insurance companies segregate from surplus to provide for unforseen expenses.

Contingency surplus   *See* **Contingency reserve.**

Contingent   Depending upon the happening of some future event.

Contingent beneficiary   Person or persons named to receive proceeds in case the original beneficiary is not alive. An individual who is entitled to benefits only after the death of a primary beneficiary.

Contingent business insurance   Protection for a business firm that has an insurable interest in the continuous production of another business such as a major supplier or customer.

Contingent commission   *See* **Commission, contingent.**

Contingent fees   Remuneration based or conditioned upon future occurrences or conclusions, or results of services to be performed.

Contingent fund   A fund established by an insurance company to cover possible liabilities that may be the result of a chance happening.

Contingent Insurance   Type of indemnity generally not covered by standard policies such as reappearance of lost deeds, securities or future birth of children.

Contingent liability   The liability imposed upon an individual corporation or partnership because of accidents caused by persons (other than employees) for whose acts the first party may be responsible through the operation of applicable laws.

Contingent use and occupancy   Coverage against loss caused by interruption of business by insured perils or hazards.

Contingent Vesting   That form of vesting under which entitlement to a vested benefit is conditioned upon the circumstances surrounding the employee's termination of service or his conduct at the time of an after separation of employment.   CIT

Continuity of coverage   A clause attached or contained in a fidelity bond which takes the place of another bond and agrees to pay the losses that would be recoverable under the first bond except that the discovery period has expired. This would be in a case where losses have been caused by a dishonest employee and have not been discovered, though they had occurred at various times stretching over a period of time, that time being a period under which several bonds had been issued. This may involve a chain of several bonds, each one superseding a prior obligation. Those losses will be covered if the chain of bonds is unbroken and each has included continuity of coverage clause.

Contract An agreement entered into by two or more parties by the terms of which one or more of the parties, for a consideration, undertakes to do or to refrain from doing some act or acts in accordance with the wishes of the other party or parties. A contract to be valid and binding must be entered into by competent parties, be bound by a consideration, possess mutuality, represent an actual meeting of minds, and cover a legal and moral act.

Contract bond A guarantee of the faithful performance of a construction contract and the payment of all labor and material bills incident thereto. In those situations where two bonds are required, one to cover performance and the other to cover payment of labor and material, the former is known as a performance bond and the latter as a payment bond.

Contract carrier A transportation company which carries the goods of only certain customers and not the public in general as is the case of a common carrier.

Contract for deed An agreement by the seller to deliver the deed to the property when certain conditions have been fulfilled, such as the completion of certain payments and provision of insurance. It has similar features to a mortgage.

Contract of adhesion The insurance contract is a contract of adhesion since there is no bargaining basis between the insurance company and the insured.

Contract of sale A contract between a purchaser and a seller of real property to convey a title after certain conditions have been met and payments have been made. *See* **Sales contract**.

Contract rent Actual rent as called for in a rental or lease agreement without regard to estimated rental value in the open market. *See also* **Economic rent** and **rent**.

Contractors, bonds; Contractors, compensation policy; Contrac-

tors, equipment floater policy; Contractors, equipment insurance policy; Contractors, liability policy; Contractors, protective policy All types of insurance used by contractors.

Contractual liability Liability over and above that which would be imposed by law which a person assumes under the terms of a contract. For example, manufacturers in selling their products may agree to protect the purchaser against claims which may arise out of the use of the products.

Contractual liability insurance Provision of protection against claims which may arise as the result of contractual liability. For example, a manufacturer with a sidetrack on his premises may have signed an agreement with the railroad company assuming liability of the railroad for accidents occurring on the sidetrack. Contractual liability insurance will cover claims based on such contracts.

Contra preferendum Any ambiguity in a contract must be interpreted against the person who drew the contract, since he had the opportunity of making it clear. Since insurance contracts are made up by the insurance companies, any ambiguity would be interpreted in favour of the Insured.

Contribution An insurance carrier's payment or obligation to pay all or part of a loss. The amount payable by an insurer under an insurance contract that is one of two or more contracts covering the same loss. The act of contributing. *See* also **Apportionment.**

Contribution clause *See* **Coinsurance clause** and **Average clause.** Both clauses are similar in effect.

Contribution to salvage expenses If, in order to salvage property which is endangered by burning, expense is incurred, the conditions of the policy make it obligatory on the part of the company to contribute pro-rata to the expense of such salvage operations.

Contributions The payments made specifically by covered persons, employers, or both on behalf of covered persons to meet all or a portion of the costs of a social insurance system. CIT tentative

Contributory Plan of insurance in which part of the premium is paid by the employee and part is paid by employer or union.

Contributory negligence The lack of care on the part of the individual which helped cause the accident. Thus if at a railroad crossing the signal of a passing train is on, and the individual drives his automobile onto the track and is struck by the train, the individual would be considered guilty of contributory negligence.

Control of a line Authority given to an agent or broker by policyholder that permits the agent or broker to place the insurance where he sees fit.

Control provision Generally applies to life insurance contracts covering minors. Ownership control is exercised by someone other than the minor who is the insured.

Controlled business The insurance that cannot be written because of other competitive practices. For illustration: captive insurance companies are used by a number of firms; the insurance they write is controlled business.

Convention blanks Forms for detailed reporting on condition of insurance companies provided by the National Association of Insurance Commissioners.

Convention values Values at which Commissioner of Insurance permits certain securities to be carried on insurance companies' books. Also known as commissioner's values. The values are used during very abnormal business conditions, such as in periods of panic and severe depression.

Conventional loan A non-F.H.A. or V.A. loan on property whose principal usually is not extinguished by periodic payments if it is a nonamortized conventional loan.

Conversion The wrongful use or disposition of property by a person or institution who is in lawful possession of it, though not having title thereto. A broker or insurance agent who is given a sum of money for a particular purpose and used it for his private advantage would be guilty of the crime of conversion.

Conversion privilege Right of individual covered by a group-term life insurance policy to purchase other stated types of insurance without a physical examination when he terminates his association with the insured group.

Conversion value Value created by changing from one state, character, form, or use to another.

Convertible collision Automobile insurance permitting the policyholder to pay part of full normal premium. In the event of a claim he must pay the remaining part of the premium. The coverage discourages the submission of small claims.

Convertible insurance Insurance that the insured has the right to convert to insurance of another form. The right to convert a term policy or the term portion of a combination policy into a permanent form of insurance without evidence of insurability. Also often applied to a change from any form of contract to another form.

Convertible term   A provision whereby a more permanent form of insurance may be elected without a medical examination, if the request is made within the specified time and an additional premium is paid.

Convertible term insurance   Term insurance providing the right to exchange for a permanent plan of insurance without evidence of insurability.

Convey   The act of transferring title to another.

Conveyance   The means by which title to real estate is transferred. A written instrument that passes an interest in real estate from one person to another including land contracts, leases, mortgages, etc.

Cooperative   A form of multiple ownership of real estate in which a corporation or business trust entity holds title to a property and grants the occupancy rights to particular apartments or units to shareholders by means of proprietary leases or similar arrangements.

Cooperative insurance   Refers to mutual associations such as fraternal, employee, industrial, or trade union groups. The profit motive is not the factor in this type of insurance but rather the accomplishment of some social end or goal.

Coordinating factors   The services needed to coordinate those of labor, capital, and land, e.g., costs of taxes, insurance, and public utility services.

Coordination of Benefits (COB)   A technique of integrating benefits where there is more than one health insurance plan. The insured's benefits from all the sources are not to exceed 100 percent of the allowable medical expenses.

Cooriginator   In bonding, where the clients of more than one surety company join for a specific contract. Such surety is known as cooriginator for its client's share.

Corner influence   The effect of street intersection upon adjacent property. The cause of a different value for real estate adjacent to a corner, as compared with property away from the corner.

Corporate surety   Insurance provided by a surety company as compared to surety provided by an individual. The writing of bonds by a corporation as obligor.

Corporation   A fictitious legal entity. A group of persons grouped together creating a body of that group which has a legal status very distinct from the individual persons.

Corporation Insurance   See Business Insurance.

Corporeal   Pertaining to a right or group of rights of a visible and tangible nature.

Correction notice   *See* **Rating Bureaus.**

Corridor deductible   The amount of loss which must be suffered and paid by the insured not withstanding the amounts payable under contracts for basic hospital and medical expenses before the coverage of major medical expense benefits comes into effect.

Corroboration   Evidence supporting a cause. Frequently the evidence of independent witnesses.

Cost   Amount paid or charged. The amount necessary to produce or reproduce.

Cost approach to value   A method in which the value of a property is derived by estimating the replacement cost of the improvement, deducting therefrom the estimated depreciation, then adding the value of the land as estimated by use of the market data approach. Also called physical indication of value.

Cost certification   A condition often placed in the contract requiring a certification of cost by the architect, contractor, or owners; must sometimes be audited by a third party.

Cost, insurance, and freight   A selling term reflecting that the price includes charges for handling costs, insurance, and freight to delivery to a foreign port. The buyer must pay any additional charges from that point.

Cost of reproduction, new   The normal cost of exact duplication of a property with the same or closely similar materials, as of a certain date or period.

Cost overrun   The amount of money required or expended over and above budgeted costs, including such items as labor, interest, materials, and land.

Cost-plus contract   A construction contract in which the contract price is equal to the cost of construction plus a profit allowance to the builder, as opposed to a fixed-price contract.

Cosurety   One of a number who jointly insure a particular bond. One of two or more sureties on the same bond.

Cotton insurance policy   Type of full marine or buyers transit insurance coverage.

Counsel Legal advice; also a lawyer or lawyers engaged to give such advice, or to conduct a cause in court.

Counter Claim or Cross Action In a case where the plaintiff files a law suit against the defendant, based upon his cause of action it is frequent that the defendant feels he has a cause of action against the plaintiff. Thus in the same law suit the defendant may file a counter claim of cross action for his claim against the original plaintiff. Both claim and counter claim would be heard at the same time. The defendant in the original action by the original plaintiff will be known as the cross plaintiff and the plaintiff will be known at the cross defendant.

Counterfeit currency coverage A bond that protects the insured against loss through the receipt in good faith of counterfeited or altered United States currency or coin.

Counterman The underwriting employee in an insurance company office or agency, who accepts and acts on applications submitted to him by insurance buyers and, more often, by brokers. He has authority to act at once on most applications brought to his counter.

Countersignature Signature of licensed agent or representative on a policy necessary to validate the contract.

Countersignature law Statute regulating the countersigning of insurance policies in a particular state. A law requiring that all insurance contracts covering property or persons in a state be countersigned by a representative of the insurer located in that state, usually a licensed resident insurance agent.

Country damage Marine cargo insurance description of damage to baled cotton due to improper handling.

Coupon policy Also called guaranteed investment policy. A type of policy sold by some nonparticipating companies as a competitive offering. Typically it is a 20-payment life policy with attached coupons. Each coupon is redeemable in cash at the end of each policy year. Since the coupon is guaranteed it has a selling feature over dividends.

Coupon rate The annual interest rate on a debt instrument, or the annual interest rate on any indebtedness. In mortgage banking, the term is used to describe the contract interest rate on the face of the note or bond.

Court bonds All bonds and undertakings required of litigants to enable them to pursue certain remedies of the courts.

Covenant An undertaking or promise of legal validity by which two or more parties by deed in writing, signed and delivered, and sometimes sealed by one of the parties, pledges himself to the other that something either is done or shall be done or stipulates the truth of that fact.

Covenant Not To Sue A contract or agreement entered into by a party who has cause of action against two or more persons by which the party agrees not to sue one of the wrong doers liable to such action. It is the equivalent of a release with a reservation of Remedies (right to sue) against other wrong doers who are not a party to the particular covenant.

Cover An insurance contract.

Cover note Written statement by agent informing insured that coverage is in effect, used in lieu of a binder but differing in that the binder is prepared by the insurance company while the cover note is prepared by the broker or agent.

Coverage The guarantee against specific losses provided under the terms of a policy of insurance. Coverage is frequently used interchangeably with the word "protection." The extent of the insurance afforded under an insurance contract. Often used to mean insurance or insurance contract. It is used synonymously with the word "insurance" or "protection."

Crash: aviation policy Type of business insurance coverage whose title is self-explanatory.

Credibility The degree of reliability or accuracy found in forecasting. Typically it is predicated on statistical data covering the frequency of past events.

Credit insurance Two different types of insurance. 1. Issued by insurance companies on accounts receivables. Claim payment is made if the account receivable proves uncollectable. The receivable must fall in a mutually agreed upon category. The category is frequently tied to a formula of relationship to the debtors Dun and Bradstreet rating. 2. A type of insurance more properly called credit life insurance. *See* that term.

Credit life insurance Life insurance issued by a life insurance company on the lives of borrowers to cover payment of loans (usually small loans repayable in instalments) in case of death. It is usually handled through a lending office and is written on either a group or an individual basis.

Credit rating A rating given a person or company to establish credit worthiness based upon present financial condition, experience, and past credit history.

Credit report A confidential report made by an independent individual or organization who has investigated the financial standing, reputation, and record of an applicant for insurance. *See* **Moral hazard.**

Creditor A person to whom a debt is owing.

Creditor's position That portion of the market price of a property which is represented by or can be obtained through a first mortgage.

Cremation certificate A trustee's sworn statement that a stated security or securities or documents were destroyed.

Criss-Cross insurance *See* **Buy-sell agreement and partnership insurance.**

Criticism Suggestions made by a rating or auditing bureau to an insurance company. *Also see* **Stamping office.**

Cromie rule Guide for adjusters to apportion losses between nonconcurrent policies.

Crop insurance Protection against loss from such risks as hail.

Cross-examination One of the three stages in the examination of a witness, the other two stages being Examiner-in-Chief and Re-examination.

Cross purchase agreement Plan of partnership insurance that has each partner individually buying and maintaining enough insurance on the life or lives of other partners to fund the purchase of the others equity.

Crown Privilege An absolute right to prohibit certain evidence being given into Court on the grounds of it being against "Public Interest" e.g. Official secrets, etc.

Crude death rate The ratio of total deaths to total population occurring during a stated period of time.

CSO The Commissioners Standard Ordinary Mortality Table of 1941 based on experience from 1930-40. It was prepared by the Committee of the National Association of Insurance Commissioners and is in widest use today.

Cubage (cubic feet) An appraisal method using the cost approach. The front or width of a building is multiplied by the depth of the building and by the height, figures from the basement floor to the outer surfaces of the walls and roof. The total cubic measurement is then multiplied by a cost factor to obtain the appraisal figure.

Cubical content The cubic content of a building is the actual space within the outer surfaces of the outside or enclosing walls and contained between the outer surfaces of the roof and the finished surface of the lowest basement or cellar floor.

Cul de sac A street with a dead end, usually with adequate space at the end where vehicles may turn around.

Cumulative collusive excess coverage Reinsurance in which the seeding company may reduce its exposure data of policy. The actual time and date in which the insurance underwriter assumes liability.

Cumulative liability When one bond is canceled and another issued to take its place and the first bond has a discovery period, the surety company is exposed to the possiblity of a loss equal to the aggregate sum of the two bonds. For instance, an employee of the insured could take an amount equal to the full penalty of the first bond while the first bond is in force and also steal the full amount of the second bond during its currency, and the whole loss could be discovered before the discovery period under the first bond has elapsed. Unless required by statute to afford such cumulative liability the surety company generally attaches a superseded suretyship rider. This not only picks up liability for undiscovered loss under the prior bond, but, in the case where both the bonds are written by the same company, bars the possibility of an accumulation of losses as between two bonds.

Curios insurance policy Type of business insurance designed particularly to protect dealers in curios.

Current assets Quick or liquid assets such as cash, accounts receivable, merchandise inventory, and other moving or readily convertible assets that may be converted within a period of one year or less.

Current disbursement The most expensive means of funding a pension plan. Sometimes referred to as "pay as you go." Distribution and funding of pension benefits when they come due.

Current Future Service Benefit The amount of pension benefits payable for each period (usually one year) of extra participation beyond the minimum requirement.

Current liabilities Short term debts and obligations that must be paid within a period of one year.

Current Service Benefit That portion of a participant's retirement benefit that relates to his credited service in a contemporary period (usually a year). CIT

Curtain wall Modern fire-resisting construction in which the wall does not support a load but rather serves mostly as a partition.

Curtesy The widower's common law right in certain states in his deceased wife's real estate. This right has been amended materially by statutory provisions in most states.

Curtilage Area of land occupied by a building, its yard, and outbuildings, actually enclosed or considered enclosed.

Custodial accounts Bank accounts used for deposit of funds belonging to others. *See* **Escrow account.**

Custodian One who has care or custody, as of some building, a keeper. Property with custodians are less risky and thus entitled to lower insurance rates.

Custody Responsibility for a property, as when the mortgagee turns a foreclosed property over to VA. This is a specialized VA term that may, but does not necessarily, include the legal right to physical possession of the property.

Customhouse bonds Bonds required by the United States Government in connection with payment of duties or to produce bills of lading.

Cut-off A termination provision in a reinsurance contract. The reinsurer is not liable for loss due to occurrences taking place after this date.

Cut rate Premium charge below a scheduled rate. Nonscheduled insurance companies premiums are at times called cut rate.

Cyclone insurance *See* **Windstorm.**

Cy-Pres Doctrine When a person expresses something in a document (e.g. a will) and for some reason the precise intention expressed therein cannot be carried out, a court would interpret the document "Cy-Pres" and order the matter to be carried out as nearly as possible to the original intentions.

D. A. Plan Deposit Administration Plan.

D. &. B. Dun and Bradstreet, Inc.

D.B.A. Doing business as:

D.B.L. Disability Benefit Law.

D.D.D. Comprehensive dishonesty, disappearance, and destruction policy.

D.H. Double hydrant (found on fire insurance maps).

D.I. Double indemnity.

D.I.S.C. Disability insurance sales course.

D.I.T.C. Disability Insurance Training Council.

D.L.P. Date of Last Payment

D.N.R. Do not renew (a policy).

D.O.B. Date of Birth

D.O.C. Drive others' cars.

D.P.P. Deferred Payment Plan

D.R. Daily report.

D.S.T. Daylight Saving Time

Dupl. Duplicate

Daily report An abbreviated copy of pertinent policy information, identical copies of which are usually prepared so that the insurance company's home office, branch office, interested agents, and brokers may each have one. A daily report of an expired policy is, after review, often used as an application for the renewal policy.

Damage from strikers insurance policy Type of business insurance coverage that protects from loss caused by sabotage by strikers.

Damages The estimated reparation in money for injury sustained.

Damper control Built-in metal plate to regulate draft in furnace or fireplace.

Data processing The transferring of data into punched cards, magnetic tape, or other electronic devices for recording and reporting of daily transactions and the maintenance and updating of records.

Date of inception of the policy Actual date and hour of commencement, at which time the underwriter's liability starts.

Date of subscription to the policy The actual hour of commencement, and the time at which the liability of the underwriter ceases, should be embodied in every policy. Generally speaking, all policies have some hour of the day specified as the expiration of the contract, unless, under the laws of the territory governing the insurance, there is provided a definite hour on which insurance contracts shall cease to attach. It is always best to specify the hour of commencement and the hour of termination in a policy wording, if only for the reason that it is emphasized.

Days of grace Period of time in which premiums may be paid following the premium due date and still have the policy remain in force. In life insurance policies most states permit one month or thirty-one days.

DDD policy A package policy providing blanket fidelity, forgery, and broad form burglary coverage by specific insuring agreements.

Dead end main   The last part of a pipe which may be plugged by sediment because water does not flow through it. In the event of fire it may be stopped up and thus is not rated as desirable for fire insurance evaluation of risk.

Dean schedule   A system for analyzing relative fire hazards considering location, exposure, and such factors used as objective standing in determination of fire insurance rates in certain states. Formula for evaluation of fire hazard by relationship of exposure, occupancy, construction, and other related factors.

Death benefit   The amount stated in the policy to be paid upon proof of death of the insured. The sum payable as the result of the death of the policyholder. *See* **Principal sum.**

Death Claim   When a policyholder dies, the person entitled to the proceeds must complete certain death forms giving due proof of the death and establishing the claimant's right to such proceeds. When filed with the company, the company is said to have a death claim.

Death Rate   The proportion of persons who die within a year. Usually expressed as so many per thousand.

De bene esse   To act provisionally or in anticipation of a future occasion.

Debentures   Certificates of obligation and promise to pay; commonly, loans to limited companies issued on the general credit of the company without any specific pledged security and bearing a fixed rate of interest, the principal being repayable after a number of years.

Debit   Collection of premiums of industrial type insurance. A group of industrial policies assigned to an agent for collection and servicing.

Debit agent   The same as a debit man. The former is preferred since it is not sexually discriminatory.

Debit man   Collector of premiums for industrial insurance.

Debit Systems   Premiums which are collected on a weekly or monthly basis.

Debris removal clause   A clause often added to a policy or included in the policy form under which the company assumes liability for the removal of debris resulting from damage to the property covered by the insured peril.

Debt coverage ratio   The ratio of effective annual net income to annual debt service.

Debt service   The periodic payment of principal and interest earned on loans.

Debtor   A person owing a debt to another.

Debtor's position   That portion of the market price of property which is in excess of a prime first mortgage, or mortgagable interest; the equity holder's position.

Decedent   One who is dead.

Decentralization   Dispersion from a center, as the outward growth or movement of a retail center.

Declaration   A statement by the applicant for insurance, usually relative to underwriting information. Sometimes, as in most casualty policies, this is copied into the policy. That part of an insurance policy which contains information regarding the insurance risk on the basis of which the policy is issued. The information in the declaration is usually obtained from the application.

Declaratory Judgement   The result of a suit brought by one party against another party solely for the purpose of ascertaining the rights of the party or the opinion of the court in a point of law. An actual controversy must exist between the parties. For example two or more insurance companies might have wordings in their policy which are not consistent. The judgement might set forth the relative liability of each company with respect to a loss. Similarly the companies may wish to know whether they are obliged to defend an insured in a loss involving "Loading and Unloading", according to its particular insuring agreement. Such a matter could be decided by an action and declaratory judgement.

Declination   Action by an insurance company rejecting an application.

Decreasing Term Insurance   Term insurance of which the death benefit decreases in steps from the date the policy comes into force to the date the policy expires.

Decreation term   Term life insurance in which the coverage amount is reduced during the period of the term.

Decree   The judgment of a court of equity.

Decrement   Quantity lost by gradual diminution or waste.

Dedicate   To put aside one's private property for some public purpose, such as to make a private road public.

Dedication   The donation of land by the owner for some public use and its acceptance for such use by authorized public officials.

Deductible   This is the amount of a loss which the insured has to pay, it operates in several different ways. A windstorm loss of

$150.00 with $50.00 deductible would mean that cost of re-repairs being $150.00 the insurance company would pay everything beyond the $50.00 deductible paid by the insured or $100.00 whereas the insured would pay $50.00 of each loss irrespective of the amount of the loss.

Deductible clause Provision that specifies an amount to be deducted from any loss or makes the company liable only for the excess of a stated amount. This clause is used largely on risks where many small losses are to be expected, such as scratches and dents to automobile bodies. *See* **Franchise and deductible coverage.**

Deductible coverage clause Provision that in return for a reduced rate the insured will assume losses below a specified amount. For example, an automobile insurance policy having collision protection may have a $50 deductible collision clause. Thus an accident which costs $100 to repair would have the insurance company pay $50 and the assured ·pay the deductible amount of $50. An accident which costs $200 would find the insurance company paying $150 of that loss.

Deductible liability ˙ insurance A method of coverage under which the insured agrees to contribute up to a specified sum, per claim or per accident, toward the amount paid to claimants as damages. Insurance on this basis is written at re duced rates.

Deed A written instrument which conveys certain rights in real property. The written instrument may be a quit claim deed, trust deed, or warranty deed, for example.

Deed in lieu (of foreclosure) The instrument conveying real estate to the mortgagee after a default by the mortgagor without going thru the process of foreclosure.

Deed of reconveyance The transfer of legal title from the trustee to the trustor (also called the borrower) after the trust deed debt is paid in full.

Deed of trust Same as trust deed.

Deed, quit claim Quit claim deed.

Deed restriction A limitation placed in a deed to limit or restrict the use of the real property.

Deed, warranty Warranty deed.

Defalcation Embezzlement of money.

Defamation A form of misrepresentation. Many state laws provide penalties for verbal or printed circulation of materials calculated to injure any insurance company's business or reputation, or for the abetting of such acts. Also see Twisting.

Default Failure of a defendant or plaintiff to appear at the required time to defend or prosecute an action or procedure, or the failure to do what is required by duty or law; thus the failure to meet an obligation.

Default point *See* **Break-even point.**

Defeasance A clause that provides that performance of certain specified acts will render an instrument of contract void.

Defect of record An encumbrance on a title that is made a part of the public record. Some recorded defects are judgments, mortgages, other liens, or easements.

Defence A defendant answers to a Plantiff's statement of claim, in which he denies the truth or validity of the complaint.

Defendant The party sued or called to answer in any suit, civil or criminal, at law or in equity. Individual who has a lawsuit brought against him by a plaintiff.

Deferred annuity An annuity providing for the income payments to begin at some future time or date such as in a specified number of years or at a specified age.

Deferred Dividend Policy This term is applied to various forms of policies on which dividends are not paid annually but are postponed for several years. Such contracts are seldom issued today. Most of the old form deferred dividend policies provided that, if the insured died or discontinued his polcy before the dividend due date, his share of the accumulations from surplus would be forfeited to the company.

Deferred-interest mortgage A mortgage instrument by which the borrower pays a lower interest rate than under fixed-rate mortgages and so has lower fixed mortgage payments. The borrower is required to reimburse the lender for accumulated interest deferred over the life of the loan, plus a fee, either by refinancing after a set time period or when the property is sold or transferred.

Deferred maintenance Existing but unfulfilled requirements for repairs and rehabilitation.

Deferred payments Money payments to be made at some future date.

Deferred Premium File The electronic tape file maintained by a company office and used to record and report subsequent premium payments when due.

Deferred Vesting That form of vesting under which rights to vested benefits are acquired by a participant commencing upon the fulfillment of specified requirements (usually in terms of attained age, years of service and/or plan membership). CIT

Deficiency judgment The difference between the indebtedness sued upon and the sale price, or market value of the real estate at the foreclosure sale.

Deficiency Reserve This supplemental reserve is required by most state insurance laws when the gross premium charged by a life insurance company for a particular class of policies is less than the net premium. The net premium in this case being the one used to calculate the company's policy reserves.

Defined contribution plan Also called a **money-purchase plan.** Under this pension plan an individual's account is maintained for each participant. The benefits are based solely on the amount contributed either by the individual or the company, plus any earnings and forfeitures, minus the expense of maintaining the plan.

Degree of risk The probability that actual experience will differ from statistically expected experience.

Delay clause A mandatory policy provision in life insurance policies designed to protect the companies against losses that might develop as the result of excess demands for cash during an economic crisis. The clause allows the company to withhold payment of the cash surrender value for six months.

Delayed payment clause Similar to "Delay Clause." In this case payment to the beneficiary of a life insurance policy is delayed. Normally occurs in common disaster situations.

Delcredere agent Agent who indemnifies his principal in the event of loss to the principal because of the extention of credit to a third party by the agent.

Delinquency ratio Ratio of past-due loans to total loans serviced, expressed in a percentage.

Delivery The transfer of the possession of a thing from one person to another.

Delivered business Those policies whose applicants have been medically examined, and the policies have been made out and delivered to the policyholder but have not as yet been paid for. See distinction between delivered, examined, paid, placed, issued, and written business.

Delivery of goods Delivery, under a contract of sale, must be actual. In such a case the title to the goods passes from the vendor to the purchaser, whether the goods remain in, or be removed from the vendor's care. When, however something requires to be done after a sale is negotiated such for instance as making, measuring or counting, and which must be done before the goods are laid aside, the contract is incomplete so far as the purchaser is concerned, and the title remains with the vendor and the risk is his. In such a case the sale is "conditional", and the same term applies to all property which is not complete and ready to hand over to the buyer. "Delivery of goods is constructive or symbolical; when the sale contract is completed by handing over a key to the room in which the property is contained, or by an order on a warehouseman, or by simply counting, marking or otherwise setting the goods aside, whereby the control without the custody of goods is given. The risk follows the title in all cases, unless otherwise provided." (Griswold)

Delivery of policy The receipt by the insured of the insurance contract. Actually delivery is determined by the intent of the parties and does not necessarily require the physical policy. A conditional receipt or binding receipt or at times verbal acknowledgement will provide coverage.

Delivery Receipt A receipt signed by the policyowner stating that he has received his policy.

Demand note A note that is due whenever the holder demands payments.

Demise To convey an estate to another for life, for years or at will; surrendering the right of occupancy to a tenant; the quitting of the property.

D.S.P.; demisit-sene-prole Died without issue.

Demolition clause The standard fire policy excludes liability for any loss to the insured property caused by "ordinance or law regulating construction or repair." Insurance against such loss may ordinarily be provided by the demolition clause and an additional premium.

Demolition Insurance If there is a loss due to the peril insured against by the policy, this insurance covers further loss due to demolition of any part of a building not damaged by primary peril, if the demolition is required by law or ordinance. In some territories it may include loss due to increased cost of repair or reconstruction of the damaged portions, similarly required.
From a liability viewpoint, demolition insurance protects an insured who is engaged in the business of demolishing buildings and structures.

Demurrer Allegations that the pleadings of the other party show no good cause of action.

De Novo New

Density   The ratio between the total land area and the number of residential or commercial structures placed upon it. Local ordinances usually regulate density.

Dental insurance   Insurance which provides benefits for dental care. Coverage varies depending upon which company is chosen and the conditions under which the policy is undertaken.

Dentist's liability insurance   Type of business insurance protection designed specifically for dentists.

Dependency Period Income   One of the basic uses for life insurance. Income for the family during the years until the youngest child reaches maturity.

Dependent   Also spelled dependant. A person who relies on someone else for support or existence.

Depondant   Also depondent. An individual making a sworn deposition. A person who gives written testimony under oath.

Depose   To state under oath. To bear witness. To testify.

Deposit administration plan   A type of pension plan, usually under a master group annuity contract, providing for the accumulation of contributions in an undivided fund out of which annuities are purchased as the individual members of the group retire. An insured pension arrangement. Periodic contributions of the employer are not allocated to the purchase of annuities for a particular employee until he is ready to retire. A feature of the plan is that the employer may hire his own independent actuarial consultants.

Deposit premium   The premium deposit required by the company on those forms of insurance subject to periodical premium adjustment. Also called provisional premium. *See* **Audit** and **Advance premium.**

Deposition   A statement made under oath. Most commonly the statement of a witness in a judicial proceeding.

Depositor's forgery bond   Type of business insurance protection against loss due to forgery.

Depository bond   *See* **Bond, depository.**

Depreciation   Loss in value. The difference between the replacement cost new and present value. The difference between the values as of two different dates. Also, loosely used, the amount charged against income to offset future depreciation and to recover the capital invested in a wasting asset.

Depreciation allowance   The accounting charge made to allow for the fact that the asset may become economically obsolete before its physical deterioration. The purpose is to write off the original cost by distributing it over the estimated useful life of the asset. It appears in both the profit and loss statement and the balance sheet.

Depreciation insurance Insurance under which there is payable in case of loss, the difference between the actual cash value of the loss to the property insured and the cost of replacing or rebuilding it in like size and of similar construction. *See* **Replacement cost insurance.**

Depth table Tabulations of factors or coefficients purporting to represent the rating of value per front foot between a lot of a selected standard depth and of other lots of greater or lesser depth. Factors for computing the front foot value of lots of different depths by comparison with a standard.

Descent The passage of real estate upon the death of the owner, to his heirs at law.

Destruction, money, securities, records insurance policy Type of business insurance coverage. Self-explanatory.

Detached Building unconnected in any way with other buildings.

Deterioration Impairment of condition. One of the causes of depreciation and reflecting the loss in value brought about by wear and tear, disintegration, use in service and the action of the elements. Deterioration results in depreciation, that is, loss in value.

Developer A person or entity who prepares raw land for building sites, and sometimes builds on the sites.

Development loan A loan made for the purpose of preparing raw land for the construction of buildings. Development may include grading and installation of utilities and roadways.

Deviating insurer An insurer which offers rates different, and generally lower, than those of other companies or rate-making organizations.

Deviation Ship's course or port other than one described in the marine insurance policy. A departure from the voyage described in the insurance contract. Use of a premium rate other than the standard rate filed with a state insurance department.

Deviation policy An insurance contract that differs from a standard policy.

Deviation rate A premium charge that differs from a scheduled bureaus rate. *See* **Cut rate.**

Devise Gifts of real property by the means of a last will and testament.

Diagnostic coverage   Accident and sickness policy that provides expenses up to a stated amount for the expense of x-ray examination, or other laboratory tests.

Dictum   Correctly known as Obiter Dictum, an observation made by a judge in connection with legal points made during the course of a trial, but having no particular reference to the subject matter before the judge at that particular time. It is not binding as a precedent.

Dies insurance   Type of business insurance. Coverage is self-explanatory.

Difference in conditions   A rider which expands insurance written on a named period basis whereby all risks subject to exclusion are incorporated into the coverage. *See* **Rider.**

Direct   That which is proximate as opposed to remote.

Direct Action   The right of an individual to bring a suit against someone who is not directly the wrong doer. In insurance cases any right of an injured third party to sue an insurer direct. Generally there is no right of "direct action" against the insurer without first obtaining a judgement against the "insured." Some states, however do allow this right in certain circumstances.

Direct Cause   The active, efficient cause that sets in motion a train of events which brings about a result without the intervention of any force started working actively from a new and independent source.

Direct damage   Loss caused by the immediate hazard or peril as compared with indirect damage, which is contingent upon the immediate peril.

Direct damage earthquake insurance   Coverage to insure part or all of a deductible which is frequently found in earthquake insurance policies.

Direct loss   One which is the immediate consequence of the peril insured against. Direct losses include damage to the owner's property, damage to the property of others, loss of life, or injury to persons as the result of accidents.

Direct Mail   Letters sent out by the Agency Department, or an agency, designed to assist the agent in securing prospects for insurance.

Direct placement   The selling directly of a security issue to a financial institution such as an insurance company and by-passing the middle man-investment banker, by the issuer of the securities. Insurance companies have purchased many direct placements.

Direct rated deposit administration plan *See* **Immediate participation guarantee plan.**

Direct reduction mortgage A mortgage that requires a fixed payment of principal each period. The total payment will vary, as the interest portion will reduce with each payment.

Direct Selling System A distribution system under which the insurer negotiates contracts with the insured only through the insurer's employees. CIT

Direct writer An insurance company which sells its policies through salaried employees or agents who represent its exclusively, rather than through independent local agents or insurance brokers. The insurer that contracts with the insured as distinguished from the reinsurer.

Direct written premium The premium collected without provision for sending part of it to a reinsurer.

Directed Verdict It is generally the responsibility of a judge to decide all matters of law and the responsibility of a jury to decide matters of fact. If there is no conflicting evidence then there is really nothing for the jury to decide. In such cases the judge then declares what the law is and orders the jury to find accordingly.

Directors & Officers Liability Insurance Insurance that affords protection against liability claims resulting from poor judgment, illegal acts. etc.

Disability Takes several forms and would depend upon the terms of the individual policy. Major areas are Partial, which is found under accident and health insurance; Permanent Partial, which is found under workmen's compensation insurance; and Permanent total disability, which is found under workmen's compensation insurance; also Temporary partial, which is under workmen's compensation, and Temporary total disability, which is also under workmen's compensation; also Total disability, which is under accident and health insurance.

Disability benefit A feature added to a life insurance policy providing for waiver of premium and sometimes payment of monthly income upon the furnishing of proof that the insured has become totally and permanently disabled.

Disability benefit law A statute which imposes upon an employer the legal liability to provide nonoccupational weekly benefits to employees who sustain accidents or sickness outside of employment.

Disability Clause (Waiver) A benefit provision forming part of a life insurance policy providing for certain benefits in the event of total and permanent disability from accident or sickness. A benefit providing for the waiver of premiums only is called a Waiver of Premium Disability clause.

Disability Income   A disability benefit usually provided by a rider attached to a regular life insurance contract providing for a monthly income and waiver of premiums in the event of total permanent disability after a fixed waiting period.

Disability Income Insurance   A form of health insurance that provides periodic payments when the insured is unable to work as a result of illness, disease, or injury.   CIT

Disability insurance   Coverage which generally provides non-occupational weekly benefits payable to employees for accident or sickness not within the scope of workmen's compensation laws.

Disability insurance, group   *See* **Group insurance.**

Disability insurance sales course   An institutional level training course in accident and sickness insurance, developed by the International Association of Accident and Health Underwriters.

Disability, partial   Under accident and health insurance disability, which from the date of an accident or immediately following a period of total disability prevents the insured from undertaking a part of the duties of his occupation. The exact degree of such inability which must exist in order to constitute partial disability depends upon the terms of the individual policies.

Disability pension   A pension paid to a disabled individual.

Disability, permanent-partial   Under workmen's compensation insurance it is a condition which actually or presumptively results in partial loss of earning power. *See* **Schedule injury.**

Disability, permanent-total   Under workmen's compensation insurance it is a condition which actually or presumptively is considered the equivalent of a complete and permanent loss of earning power. Many compensation laws specify that certain injuries, such as total loss of sight, loss of both hands or both legs shall constitute permanent total disability regardless of the injured's ability to do some work.

Disability, temporary-partial   Under workmen's compensation insurance it is a condition which results in a partial loss of earning power but from which recovery can be expected. Workmen's compensation laws generally provide for compensation for temporary partial disability on the basis of a percentage of the difference between the employee's wages before the injury and what he can earn in his disabled condition.

Disability, temporary-total Under workmen's compensation insurance it is a condition which disables the employee from working, but from which complete or partial recovery can be expected, enabling him to return to employment.

Disability, total Under accident and health insurance it is a condition, caused by either injury or sickness which wholly, necessarily, and continuously prevents an insured from performing any and every duty pertaining to his occupation.

Disabling injury An injury which causes loss of working time beyond the day or period on which the injury occurs.

Disappearing deductible requires the insured to pay the full amount of the loss up to the amount of the deductible after which the the insurance company assumes full responsibility for the full amount. In the instance illustrated above, since the amount of the loss exceeds the deductible, the insurance company would pay the full $150.00.

Disbursements Marine term for expenses for certain labor and supplies which will be lost if a ship is sunk. The payment of monies on a previously agreed-to basis. Used to describe construction loan draws.

Disclaimer A denial of liability for cause, e.g. to deny coverage under a policy on grounds that a statutory condition had been breached.

Disclosure Revealment of material data generally required by a regulatory agency. TIL (Truth in Lending) calls for interest rate to be stated as A.P.R. (annual percentage rate.)

Discontinuance A legal procedure to voluntarily discontinue a legal suit. It of course may be reinstituted if other steps are not taken to support it and remove the basis for the cause of action.

Discounted Premiums Premiums paid in advance by means of an equivalent lump sum payment in lieu of the frequency called for in the policy. Such single payment is less than the sum of the premiums discounted, and the company normally allows discount at a rate of interest which depends on company practice.

Disintermediation The flow of funds out of savings institutions into short-term investments whose interest rates are higher. This shift normally results in a net decrease in the amount of funds available for long-term real estate financing. Also describes the market condition that exists when this shift occurs.

Discounting for mortality *See* **Advance discounting for mortality.**

Discounting for severance *See* **Advance discounting for severance.**

Discovery The right of discovery, is the right by which a party to some proceedings, actually commenced or contemplated before Civil Court, is enabled, before the determination of any matter of consequence in those proceedings, to exhort an oath from another party to those proceedings, (1) all his knowledge, remembrance, information and belief concerning the matter so in question; (2) the production of all documents in his possion, or power relating to such matters.

Discovery period The time allowed the insured after termination under certain bond and policy provisions to discover a loss which occurred during the period covered by the contract and would have been recoverable had the contract continued in force. This period varies from six months to three years where a company can fix the period of time to be allowed. It may be governed by statute and in certain bonds the period is indefinite because of statutory requirements.

Discretion Freedom in the exercise of judgment.

Discrimination State laws in many cases prohibit undue discrimination. That is the handling of like risks in different ways. Actually the nature of underwriting is based upon discrimination of the good risk from the poor risk. What is prohibited is treating any of a given class of risk differently from other like risks.

Dishonesty, disappearance, and destruction insurance *See* **Comprehensive dishonesty, disappearance, and destruction insurance.**

Dismemberment Loss of a hand or foot through or above the wrist or ankle joints, or the entire and irrevocable loss of sight. *See* **Capital sum.**

Dismemberment Insurance A form of health insurance that provides payment in the event of the loss by bodily injury of one or more body members or the sight of one or both eyes.

Dismissal A word used by a judge in making the final ending of a particular suit. It may not be a final judgement on the particular controversy particularly as to facts but it is an end to the particular proceedings and may be for entirely a different reason such as for example that the court does not have jurisdiction over the parties to the suit. If the order of dismissal is "without prejudice" then another suit may be brought at a later date on the same cause of action. If the order carries the words "with prejudice" then the plaintiff is forever barred from restitutions in a law suit based on that cause of action.

Dispossess To deprive one of the use of real estate.

Dissent In Appeals where the facts are heard by a panel of judges the majority may find for one ruling whereas one or more of the judges may disagree. The majority judgement of course rules but the dissenting judge or judges freqently set out their reasons for feeling the decision should have been otherwise.

Distrain To seize goods by distress.

Distress The taking of goods from another under legal right to obtain satisfaction for a wrong committed.

Distribution clause *See* **pro rata distribution.**

Disturbance The hindering of an owner of a property in the enjoyment of it.

Diversification Spreading of risk. It may be accomplished by several different techniques such as geographically, by type of risk, by type of coverage, or by insuring more risks that are separate exposures.

Divided coverage Division of insurance that would normally be covered by one insurance policy, between two or more companies. Some states do not permit this for workmen's compensation insurance. It has a slightly different meaning regarding burglary, whereby grouping of property by classes in an insurance policy with a separate maximum amount of payments stipulative for each class to cover the loss or damage sustained within that specific class. Thus the insurance company would pay up to a certain amount for the theft of jewelry, up to another amount for the theft of household furnishings.

Divided coverage, burglary Grouping of property by classes in an insurance policy, with a separate maximum amount of payment stipulated for each class, to cover the loss or damage sustained with that class. A burglary policy, written under divided coverage would specify that the company would pay up to a certain sum for the theft of jewelry, silverware, and furs, up to another amount for household furnishings.

Dividend   In a mutual or participating company, it is the return to the policyholder out of the earnings of the company. In a stock or nonparticipating insurance company it is the division of the profits among the stockholders of the company. A refund of part of the premium on a participating life insurance policy. It is a share of the surplus earned apportioned for distribution and reflects the difference between the premium charged and the actual experience.

Dividend accumulation   A policyholder's dividends which are left with the insurance company and will draw compound interest.

Dividend addition   An additional amount of paid-up insurance (added to the face of the policy) purchased with a policy dividend.

Dividend options   Clauses in a policy that give the insured alternatives in his use of his dividends, such as to receive them by check, have them accumulate and draw interest, or use them to purchase additional insurance.

Dividend Reinvestment   (1) Technique whereby a policy-holder's dividend is used to purchase additional coverage. (2) Option available to shareholders of some companies whereby dividends on stocks are used to purchase additional stock of the company. Often this involves no brokerage fee and at times may even be at a modest discount from the current market price.

Divisibility   The privilege, under an insurance contract covering two or more items, of treating the insurance as though a contract had been written separately on one or more of the items.

Divisible contract clause   A clause which provides that a violation of the conditions of the policy at one insured location will not void the policy at all locations.

Division wall   A partition, meeting stated standards of construction that separates the structure into two areas so that the fire in one area will have less chance to spread into other areas.

Documentary evidence   Evidence in the form of written or printed papers.

Documentary stamp   A revenue stamp issued for the payment of a tax on documents, as deeds, checks, or wills.

Dog   Slang expression to describe a risk that no insuring company would be apt to accept.

Domestic carrier In a given state, an insurer domiciled in that state. *See* **Domestic company.** An insurance company incorporated under the laws of the state in which it is doing business.

Domestic insurer or company Same as **Domestic carrier.**

Domicile The place where one has his true, fixed, and permanent home, and to which, whenever he is absent, he has the intention of returning.

Domiciled company A company whose head office is in the same state as the person referring to it.

Dominus litus The principal in the suit.

Double indemnity Feature of some policies that provides for twice the face amount of the policy to be paid if death results from stated but generally accidental causes. A provision under which the principal sum in an accident policy, and sometimes other indemnities, are doubled when accident is due to certain causes. In a life insurance policy a provision that the face amount payable on death will be doubled if death is a result of an accident.

Double insurance Two or more insurances on the same risk.

Double (or Triple) Protection Policy A combination policy that adds level term coverage to a basic whole life policy: if the insured dies during the term coverage period, the term payment to the beneficiary is usually made in a lump sum. The amount of term coverage must be equal to the amount of whole life coverage to make the protection double. (Term protection must be twice the amount of the whole life coverage to make the total protection triple.)

Dower A widow's legal right in the real estate of her deceased husband. Originally this was a common law right. At present it varies according to the various statutory provisions.

Draft Negotiable instrument frequently used by insurance companies to pay claims. Instead of ordering a bank (as in a check) to pay, it orders itself, the insurance company, to pay.

Dram Shop Act A common reference to laws of certain states and provinces which hold taverns and bars liable for losses to third parties if such losses result from the activities of the person who sold liquor by such taverns. Taverns have been held liable for support of families who have met with accidents after having over indulged in a tavern.

Dread disease policy Insurance (subject to a maximum amount) providing discretionary, blanket repayment of expenses incurred for treatment of specified diseases such as cancer, polio, etc.

Drive In Claims Service   Automobile insurer's facility to which an insured may bring his damaged auto in order to facilitate the adjusting of claims and the settlement of damages.

Drive Other Cars (DOC)

Broad Form   A coverage of insurance intended to cover the insured's legal liability for Bodily Injury and Property Damage Liability under certain conditions while driving borrowed or furnished automobiles for business purposes.

This coverage is referred to as Broad Form DOC.

Limited Form   A coverage of insurance intended to cover the named insured's or spouse's legal liability for Bodily Injury and Property Damage Liability under certain conditions while driving borrowed automobiles for nonbusiness purposes.

This coverage is referred to as "Use of other automobiles" in the policy. It is also known as DOC Lt. Form.

Driver training credit   A deduction in the premium on a policy because the insured has taken driver education classes.

Drop at (date)   Instructions not to renew a policy as of a certain date.

Druggists Liability Coverage   Liability coverage for products, (including drugs) which are prepared, sold, or handled by a drug store.

Dry season charge   *See* **Standing timber insurance.**

Dry valve   Automatic sprinkler under air pressure. When the sprinkler is activated by heat from fire the air is first released and this permits water to flow through the pipes. By having air in the pipes the problem of freezing and bursting pipes is reduced and thus the chance of water damage.

Dual interest policy   A policy providing protection to two or more individuals or companies, such as a finance company and the purchaser of the property being financed by the finance company.

Dual Life Stock Company   A stock company issuing both nonparticipating and participating life insurance contracts. *See* **Stock Life Insurance.**

Duplex   A single structure designed with two separate housing units.

Duration of Risk   The period of time for which the risk is to run.

The period should be distinctly stated in the policy.

Duress The compulsion under which a person acts through fear of personal suffering. A contract obtained by means of duress exercised by one party over another is voidable.

Dwelling package policies A family of policies for owner-occupied premises, combining at a substantial discount, various broad real estate and personal property coverages and also comprehensive personal liability.

Dwelling unit The living quarters occupied, or intended for occupancy, by a household.

E.C.E. Extended cover endorsement.

ECOA Equal Credit Opportunity Act. Law that makes it illegal for a creditor to discriminate in granting of credit.

E. & O. Errors and omissions.

E. & O.E. Errors and Omissions Excepted.

E.D.T. Eastern Daylight Time

E.K.G. Electrocardiogram

E.O.M. End of Month

E.P. Earned premium.

E.S.T. Eastern Standard Time

E.T. Eastern Time

E.T.A. Estimated Time of Arrival

E.U.A. Eastern Underwriters Association.

Early retirement A clause in an annuity policy to cover the participant who retires before a stated retirement date; in the case of his/her early retirement the amount of annuity is proportionately reduced.

Earned premium That part of an insurance premium which pays for the protection the insurance company has already given on a policy. Thus insurance on which a premium has been paid one year in advance, will at the end of six months be half earned by the insurance company.

Earned reinsurance premium *See* **Aggregate excess loss re-insurance.**

Earnest A sum paid as part of the price of property sold, or of money due upon an agreement, for the purpose of binding the bargain. *See* **Earnest money.**

Earnest money Money which is paid as an evidence of good faith or intent to complete a transaction and may be forfeited by the willful failure to complete the transaction.

Earnings   Money derived from personal services, that is, salary, wages, and commissions.

Earnings and Profits   If a person has an insurable interest in productive property, he may insure the prospective earnings arising therefrom. Such interests must be covered specifically as such. The forms of policy under which insurances of such risks can be effected are those termed "Use and Occupancy" and "Profit Insurance."

Earthquake insurance   A contract to indemnify against loss caused by earthquake damage.

Easement   The right to use or enjoy certain privileges that appertain to the land of another, such as the right of way, the right to receive air and light by reason of an agreement of record with the owner of adjacent property.

Economic life   Period through which a building may be profitably utilized; period during which a building is more valuable in use than for salvage.

Economic obsolescence   Impairment of desirability or of useful life arising from economic forces, such as changes in optimum land use, legislative enactments which restrict or impair property rights, and changes in supply-demand relationships. Loss in the use and value of a property arising from the factors of economic obsolescence is to be distinguished from loss in value from physical deterioration and functional obsolescence.

Economic rent   A philosophic concept of the true value of a property as compared with the contract rent which would be expressed in monetary units and might not be necessarily indicative of the true value, being possibly either over or under the economic rent.

Economic value   The valuation of property based on its earning capabilities.

Educational Insurance   Insurance proceeds arranged to provide a child with a given income during the educational period.

Effective date   The date on which an insurance policy or bond goes into effect and from which time protection is furnished.

Effective gross income   Normal annual income, including overtime, that is regular or guaranteed. It may be from more than one source. Salary is generally the principal source, but other income may be significant and stable, and thus qualify.

Effective gross income (property)   Stabilized income that a property is expected to generate after a vacancy allowance.

Effective gross revenue Total income less allowance for vacancies, contingencies, and sometimes collection losses, but before deductions for operating expenses.

Effective rate The actual rate of return to the investor. It may vary from the contract rate for a variety of reasons. Also called **yield**.

Effects Property, goods and chattels, including clothes and documents.

Egress The act of going out; exit. It is used with **ingress** to describe the right of access to land.

Eianoi Ancient Greek society that was influential in developing the idea of life insurance.

Ejectment The name of an action wherein the plaintiff seeks to recover from the defendant the possession of real property, with damages for the unlawful detention of the same.

Elective benefits Those conditions which may be chosen by the insured in settlement of his claim as alternate to another form of compensation. Thus on an accident policy the terms may be upon a certain damage that payment may be for a period of the disability or a lump sum payment may be elected. The optional benefits.

Electric motors and equipment insurance policy Type of business insurance coverage. Title is self-explanatory.

Electrical exemption clauses Several different paragraphs in fire insurance policies limiting coverage to electrical machinery damage by electric current. A clause attached to a fire insurance contract stating that, in the event of electrical injury or disturbance to electrical appliances, including wiring, caused by artificially generated electric currents, the insurer shall be liable only if fire ensues and then for the damage by fire only.

Elevator Collision Coverage Coverage for damage to an elevator and any property thereon.

Elevator Liability Coverage Liability coverages against claims arising from the ownership, maintenance, or use of elevators or hoisting devices.

Elevator liability insurance policy Type of business insurance against loss due to claims for damages arising out of the ownership, maintenance, or use of elevators or other hoisting devices.

Eligibility period The interval of time following immediately upon the date of eligibility when members entitled to group insurance may apply for such insurance without providing evidence of insurability.

Eligibility period   The period during which a person is qualified for a particular form of insurance.

Eligibility requirements   The requirements which must be met or surpassed in order to become eligible for a particular variety of insurance.

Elimination period   Waiting period of time after the beginning of a disability for which no indemnities are payable. Waiting periods usually apply only to sickness benefits. Do not confuse with probation period.

Embezzlement   Defalcation of money. The fraudulent use of money or any other property which has been entrusted to one's care.

Embezzlement insurance policy   Type of business insurance coverage protecting one from losses caused by embezzlement by one's employees or staff.

Emergency benefits   *See* **Identification benefits.**

Emergency Fund   One of the basic uses for life insurance. A reserve death benefit fund provided by the insured to protect his family against sudden large, unbudgetable expenses such as accidents, operations, etc. The increasing loan values of life insurance policies also constitute, and often are referred to as, an emergency fund for the insured while he is living.

Eminent domain   The power of a sovereign body to appropriate for public use certain private property. The most common forms of the exercising of this power are in the condemnation of private property for streets, roads, railroads, public utilities.

Employee   One who performs services for another under a contract of hire, acting under the direction and control of the person by whom he is hired. Workmen's compensation laws sometimes contain special definitions of the term. *See* for contrast **Independent contractor.**

Employee benefits   Advantages besides salary or wage that an employee may have through his employment. Sometimes called fringe benefits. In the insurance area these benefits may include pension plans, group life insurance, group health, hospitalization, medical care, accident, and sickness coverage.

Employers Non-Ownership Liability Coverage   Liability coverage with respect to non-owned automobiles, as defined.

Employer's liability insurance   Protects an employer against the claims for damages which arise out of the injuries to employees in the course of their work. A workmen's compensation policy insures the employer against liability under state compensation laws. Employers liability insurance provides protection in cases not covered by the compensation law.

Encroachment The act of trespassing upon the domain of another. Partial or gradual invasion or intrusion. Encroachment of low value district upon high class residential section.

Encumbrance Any outside interest in or right to property founded on legal grounds, such as a mortgage, lien for work and materials, or a right of dower or curtesy. It diminishes the interest of the person owning the property, but does not prevent conveyance of the fee by the owner thereof. Mortgages, taxes, judgments are encumbrances known as liens. Restrictions, easements, reservations are encumbrances though not liens.

Endorsement Special circumstances frequently require that a policy be altered. Such alterations are effected by attaching to the policy a form bearing the terms necessary to make the change. A provision added to a policy, usually by being written in on the printed page. It may also be in the form of a rider. No endorsement is valid unless signed by an executive of the company and attached to and a part of the policy.

Endowment annuity insurance A contract of insurance combining features of a deferred annuity of the retirement type plus decreasing term insurance of the excess of the face amount over the cash value. Developed as retirement contracts in employee pension plans under the pension-trust system.

Endowment insurance Type of life insurance that pays upon the death of the insured within covered period or at the end of the covered period if individual is still alive. If the policyholder dies during the endowment period, payment is made to a beneficiary.

Enemy alien A citizen or company whose nation is at war with the nation of the other party. Contracts of insurance between enemy aliens are held to be against public policy and are void.

Engineer An employee of an insurance company or rating bureau, trained in the technicalities of his field such as fire, workmen's compensation, public liability, automobile fleet,

with the major purpose of assisting insureds in loss prevention and obtaining rating and underwriting information.

Engineering service   *See* **Loss prevention service.**

Engines, all types, insurance policy   Type of business insurance. Title is self-explanatory.

Entirety of the policy   Where the policy is issued for a single premium (such as a blanket or floater policy) but covers a number of separate items or subjects, a breach of condition in
any part of the property covered will void the insurance on the
whole of the property. It is customary in such cases, to insert
a condition in the policy offsetting this principle, the condition
reading to the effect that "breach of contract in one part of the
premises will be held to attach to that part only, and will not
prejudice other parts in which no breach had occurred."

Entity plan   *See* **Partnership entity plan** and a comparison with
cross purchase agreement.

Enure or inure   Refers to serving the benefit of a person. This
clause in an insurance policy provides that if, for example,
household goods insured under a residence and outside theft
policy should be stolen while in transit, the insurance shall
not enure to the benefit of the trucking or moving company
transporting the property although the insurance company
will pay for the loss sustained.

En ventre sa mere   Unborn child.

Environmental Impact Statement (EIS)   A statement required by
many federal, state, and local environmental and land use
laws. It contains a analysis of the impact that a proposed
change may have on the environment of a specific geographic
region.

Environmental Protection Agency (EPA)   Federal regulatory
agency created to coordinate governmental efforts to protect
the environment by abating and controlling pollution on a
systematic basis. EPA is primarily responsible for adminis-
trating laws regarding air, noise, and water quality.

Equal Credit Opportunity Act (ECOA)   A federal law that requires
lenders and other creditors to make equal credit available to
all without discrimination based on color, race, religion,
national origin, age, sex, marital status, or receipt of income
from public assistance programs.

Equipment   That portion of fixed assets other than real estate;
usually qualified as office equipment, automotive equipment,
etc. To be distinguished from assets that are included under

the category of fixtures by virtue of their attachment to realty, either in a physical sense or by legal interpretation.

Equipment floater insurance Type of inland marine broad protection. Type of coverage depends upon type of equipment. *See* above definition.

Equitable Lien Is a right in equity to have a fund or specific property applied in full or in part to the payment of a debt.

Equity The interest or value which an owner has in real estate over and above the mortgage against it. System of legal rules administered by courts of chancery.

Equity annuities Term formerly used for variable annuities. The annuity is based on investments mostly in common stocks which are not guaranteed as to income or liquidation value but are expected or intended to provide a hedge against the impact of inflation on the purchasing power of the fixed annuities.

Equity of redemption The common law right to redeem property during the foreclosure period. In some states the mortgagor has a statutory right to redeem property after a foreclosure sale.

Equity participation Partial ownership of income property, given by the owner to the lender, as part of the consideration for making the loan.

Equity rate Rate applied to very large risks that have had outstandingly good or bad records of claims so that the ordinary rates would not truly represent the risk.

Equivalent level annual dividend The average of an annual policy dividend which may be projected during a stated time frame. The critical factor is the assumption of a specific rate of interest.

ERISA Employee Retirement Security Act: federal legislation concerning pension and profit sharing plans.

Erosion The action on land of such natural causes as wind, running water, or ice causing a wearing away of elements of the land.

Error in name An error in name, or in designation of place, occurring in an insurance policy, is unimportant if there be no possibility of mistaking the identity of the person insured, and exact location of the risk as these are matters of primary importance and should be always furnished by the agent.

Errors and omissions Mortgagees generally require insurance on mortgaged property. If they fail to procure such insurance the security of the mortgage may be impaired. Errors and omissions insurance provides for indemnity to the mortgagee if, by reason of error or omission in the operation of its customary procedure in procuring insurance, it happens that a damaged or destroyed building is found to be without insurance.

Errors and Omissions Insurance Insurance against losses of others resulting from failure, through error or unintentional omission on the part of the policyholder.

Insurance against loss due to failure, through error or unintentional omission, to have insurance in force.

Escalator clause A clause providing for the upward or downward adjustment of rent payments to cover specified contingencies, such as the provision in a lease to provide for increases in property tax and operating expenses.

Escheat The returning of property to a sovereign because of the failure of the owner; thus a property obtained from public domain providing for certain improvements such as digging of a well within so many years. If at the end of those years the well is not dug the property would escheat or return to the government. Property may also escheat to the state by reason of lack of heirs.

Escrow The placing of a deed or other instrument or money in the hands of a disinterested person, frequently a bank or trust company, for delivery upon the performance of certain conditions or the happening of certain contingencies. A transaction in which a third party, acting as the agent for both buyer and seller, carries out instructions of both and assumes the responsibilities of handling all the paperwork and disbursements of funds.

Escrow account A segregated trust account in which escrow funds are held.

Escrow agent The person or organization having a fiduciary responsibility to both buyer and seller (or lender and borrower) to see that the terms of the purchase/sale (or loan) are carried out. Synonyms: **escrow company** and escrow depository.

Escrow analysis The periodic examination of escrow accounts to determine if current monthly deposits will provide sufficient funds to pay tax, insurance, and other bills when due.

Escrow company A corporation established to act as an escrow agent.

Escrow contract A three-party agreement of the buyer, seller, and the escrow agent (holder) specifying the rights and duties of each.

Escrow costs All the costs to the buyer and seller individually that are associated with the sale or financing of real property. These include, but are not limited to, prorating of agreed items such as taxes, rents, the cost of title insurance policies, the cost of credit reports, recording fees, and escrow fees. Synonyms: **closing costs,** settlement costs.

Escrow fees Fees charged by the escrow holder for services.

Escrow overage or shortage The difference, determined by escrow analysis, between escrow funds on deposit and escrow funds required.

Escrow payment That portion of a mortgagor's monthly payments held by the lender to pay for taxes, hazard insurance, mortgage insurance, lease payments, and other items as they become due. Known as **impounds** or **reserves** in some states.

Established fund A welfare and sick benefit fund established by contributions of employees of a given company or by the company.

Estate A right in property. An estate in land is the degree, nature, or extent of interest which a person has in it.

Estate in reversion The residue of an estate left in the grantor, to commence in possession after the termination of some particular estate granted by him. Not to be confused with remainder estate.

Estate plan An adequate estate plan would include several types of insurance so that upon death of the insured his beneficiaries would obtain the maximum benefits.

Estate Settlement What the deceased owed is subtracted from what he owned, and the remainder is transferred to another party or parties. If the deceased had a will and named an executor, the executor pays all debts and distributes the proceeds of the estate. If the will does not name an executor, the court will appoint an administrator to handle the executor's duties.

Estate shrinkage A decrease in the total value of the estate caused by expenses at the time of the death of the owner, such as funeral expenses, debts, taxes, and the cost of administration.

Estate tax *See* **Federal estate tax.**

Estimated premium A provisional premium subject to final adjustment on ascertainment of the necessary facts.

Estoppel   A rule of evidence which precludes a person from denying the truth of some statement earlier made by him, or by others in cases where the person's conduct has led the innocent person to believe the statement to be the truth.

The statement may be made even by some other person and if for example it is made in front of the individual and the individual does not deny it and by his conduct leads the innocent party to believe the statement to be true, he is held to the statement.

If A owns a pen and stands by and watches B sell that pen to C, claiming that it belonged to B, A cannot later reclaim the pen, arguing that it was his pen.

In addition to this, estoppel can be created by a Judgement or by deed.

Estoppel certificate   An instrument which shows the unpaid principal balance of a mortgage and the rate and amount of interest thereon.

Estovers   Materials or supplies that a tenant is permitted to take from the custody of the landlord in order to make necessary repairs and prevent constructive eviction. It would include such things as tools, necessary fuel, and certain repair materials.

Et ux   And wife.

Eviction   The depriving by due process of law of a person or persons from the possession of land in keeping with the judgment of the court.

Evidence   That which tends to prove or disprove any matter in question.

Evidence of insurability   Evidence (medical examination records, etc.) considered necessary by the insurer which establishes a potential insureds qualification or nonqualification for the particular insurance in question.

Examination   Audit of an insurer's records, transactions, methods, and assets by a state insurance department or by internal or external auditors or accountants.

Examination in chief   One of the three stages in the examination of a witness. The purpose of this is to place the witness's version of the facts before the Court and or Jury, and in this examination, a witness must not be asked leading questions — that is, questions indicating the answer desired. The other two stages in the examination of witnesses are "cross-examination" and "re-examination."

Examination of title The review of the chain of title as revealed by an abstract of title or public records. *See also* **Title search.**

Examination under oath Clause in some policies that permit the insurance company to obtain under oath statements on claims and related facts from the insured. Perjury charges may thus be brought for false claims.

Examined business Those applications that have been signed by the applicant and the applicant has received a medical examination but has not paid any premiums. *See* distinction between delivered, examined, paid, placed, issued, and written business.

Examiner An insurance underwriter who reviews applications and risks to determine whether his company should write coverage on the risk. Also a member of the insurance department of a state that examines the records of insurance companies to see that they are complying with the law.

Excepted city Specifically listed big cities that are not subject to the prevailing rates of commissions.

Excepted period The time after the beginning date of a policy during which sickness benefits will not be payable. The purpose of the period is to eliminate sickness actually contracted before the policy went into force. Not to be confused with waiting or elimination period.

Exception In legal descriptions, that portion of land to be deleted or excluded. The term is often used in a different sense to mean an objection to title or encumbrance on title. *See* **Encumbrance.**

Excess cover for catastrophe A form of reinsurance in the event of loss above a stated amount.

Excess floater insurance Insurance against losses that may exceed specified insurance. The insured may otherwise lose due to such factors as distribution clauses in existing policies, coinsurance, or averaging.

Excess insurance A policy or bond covering the insured against certain hazards, which applies only to loss or damage in excess of a stated amount. The risk of initial loss or damage, so excluded in the excess policy or bond may be carried by the insured himself or may be insured by another policy or bond, which is known as primary protection. Also that portion of a line that exceeds the company's net line or retention is known as excess insurance.

Excess interest The difference between the minimum rate of interest contractually guaranteed on dividends or proceeds left with the company and the interest actually credited.

Excess limit A limit higher than the basic limit established as a general policy of the underwriters of a company.

Excess line broker An agent who places a surplus line. *See* **Surplus Line.**

Excess of lien reinsurance That liability beyond which an insurance company will have primary retention.

Excess of loss reinsurance Reinsurance that indemnifies the ceding company for the excess of a stipulated sum or primary retention in event of loss.

Excess per risk insurance *See* **Excess of loss reinsurance.**

Excess policy Insurance that does not apply until other insurance has been exhausted. It is typical that a certain amount of insurance is required and the claims will be paid by the specific insurance. The rates for excess insurance are lower than the specific rates.

Exchange A rating organization, as the New York Fire Insurance Rating Organization.

Excluded Articles Those articles which are excluded by the policy conditions unless otherwise specified elsewhere in the policy.

Excluded period *See* **Excepted period** and **Probation period.**

Exclusion Provision of part of the insurance contract limiting the scope of the coverage. Certain causes and conditions, listed in the policy, which are not covered.

Exclusive agency *See* **Exclusive listing.**

Exclusive Agency System A distribution system operating through agents under agreements which limit representation to one insurer, or several insurers under common management, and which reserve to the insurer the ownership of policy records and expiration data. CIT

Exclusive listing This agreement provides that the broker shall be the sole agent of the owner.

Ex contractu Arising out of a contract.

Exculpatory clause A clause in a contract holding one party harmless in the event of some default. For example, the provision in a note that the debtor will not be held personally liable in the event of a default.

Ex delicto Arising out of a tort.

Execute To complete or finish. In real estate deeds, to sign, seal and deliver.

Execution A judicial order directing an appropriate officer of the court to enforce a judgment against the property or person of the judgment debtor in order to attempt to satisfy the judgment.

Executor The person appointed by the court to carry into effect, or execute, the provisions of a will. The court usually appoints the person named in the will for that purpose, if one is named.

Executor's deed A deed given by an executor.

Executrix A woman appointed to perform the duties of an executor.

Exempt Free from burden or liability.

Exempt property Real estate that is not subject to property taxation. Religious, educational, and charitable organizations generally hold exempt property.

Ex gratia payment Settlement of a claim which the insurance company does not think it is legally obligated to pay, to prevent an even larger expense of defending itself in the courts. Strike suits or threats of suit may result in an ex gratia payment.

Exhibitions insurance Type of business insurance coverage pointed to the special needs and liabilities of those putting on exhibitions.

Ex officio By virtue of his office. A Secretary of State may be ex officio chairman of the insurance commission.

Ex parte Application, motions, etc., made by one party, only in the absence of other parties, to the suit. An ex parte statement, is a statement previously made by one party only.

Expectation of life The average number of years of life remaining for persons of a particular age according to a certain mortality table.

Expected morbidity The expected occurence of injury or sickness within a given risk category during a specific period of time.

Expected mortality The mortality, or deaths, anticipated on the basis of the figures in the mortality table used.

Expediting charges Funds expended to replace or repair damage to prevent even larger claims. Repair to a roof in time to prevent rain damage to the interior would justify overtime payments to the roofer.

Expense account Record of money spent by an officer or employee in advancement of the company for which reimbursement will be made by the company.

Expense allowance   Compensation paid to insurance agents in excess of prescribed commissions. Sometimes called **expense reimbursement allowance.**

Expense constant   A flat amount added to the premium of a risk below the experience rating size. Designed to offset the fact that the expense loading on the smaller risk does not yield enough money to cover the minimum cost of issuing and servicing a policy. This term is found in a workmen's compensation policy. The charge is supposed to equate the cost to the insurance company of issuing and servicing the policy of a very small risk.

Expense loading   The practice in rate making denoting the amount which is added to the pure premium to provide for the expense of the insurance company.

Expense ratio   The percentage of premiums obtained by dividing the premiums into the expenses. The percentage of the premium used to pay all the costs of acquiring, writing, and servicing business.

Expense reimbursement allowance   *See* **Expense allowance.**

Expense reserve   An incurred but unpaid expense liability.

Expenses   The cost to the insurer of conducting its business other than paying losses.

Expenses incurred   Expenses paid and expenses to be paid in respect of a given unit of insurance.

Expenses paid   The amount of money that has been disbursed by the insurer for conducting its business other than paying claims.

Experience   The loss record of an insured or of a class of coverage. Classified statistics of events connected with insurance, of outgo, or of income, actual or estimated. *See* **Policy year experience** and **Calendar year experience,** or **Experience, policy year.**

Experience, policy year   The experience under policies written during a twelve month period following the anniversary of their date of issue.

Experience modification   Rate adjustment based upon experience rating. *See* **Experience rating.**

Experience rating   Rating or rate making based on an individual or specific company's record for the purpose of determining the rate to be charged for that specific risk. A plan, available in certain lines of casualty insurance, which is applicable to risks that meet qualifying tests. This plan provides that manual rates (average rates that reflect the experience of large groups of similar risks) shall be increased or decreased in accordance with the actual past experience of such risks. *See* **Merit rating.**

Experience refund A form of profit sharing in life reinsurance agreements. The reinsurer returns a certain portion of the reinsurance profit to the ceding company each year.

Experienced mortality The actual mortality experienced by a company over any given period. The number of death claims for a stated interval of time.

Expiration The date upon which a policy will cease to cover, unless previously canceled.

Expiration card Record, generally kept in tickler form, of date on which policies of customers terminate.

Expiration date The date on which the insurance policy ceases to protect the policyholder. Not only is the date mentioned but the hour of the day and the time 12:00 noon standard time is the usual time for fire and burglary 12:01 A.M. standard time is common for liability policies.

Expiration notice Slip or letter advising the customer, broker, or agent that a policy will terminate in the near future.

Expiry Termination of a term policy at the end of the term period.

Explosion A violent bursting with noise. Several legal decisions have interpreted the term differently.

Explosion insurance Type of business insurance coverage against loss of property caused by explosion; does not cover explosion of steam boilers, pipes, or certain kinds of pressure vessels.

Export Goods shipped outside a country. To ship goods outside a country.

Exposure (1) State of being subject to the possibility of loss; (2) Extent of risk as measured by payroll, gate receipts, area, or other standard; (3) Possibility of loss to a risk being caused by its surroundings; (4) Surroundings producing No. 3. CIT

Express covenants Those parts of a contract that are created by specific words of the parties which are declaratory of their intention.

Expropriation The act or process whereby private property is taken for public purpose or use, or the rights therein modified by a sovereignty or any entity vested with the necessary legal authority, e.g., where property is acquired under eminent domain.

Extended coverage A clause in an insurance policy or of an endorsement of a policy which provides extra or additional coverage for other hazards or risks than those provided for under the basic provisions of the policy.

Extended coverage endorsement An endorsement extending the fire policy, usually to cover loss with certain exceptions caused by windstorm, hail, explosion (except by steam boilers), riot, civil commotion, aircraft, vehicles, and smoke.

Extended medical payments insurance Clause of automobile medical payments insurance.

Extended term insurance A form of insurance available as a nonforfeiture option. It provides the original amount of insurance for a limited period of time. On failure to pay premiums, insurance for the face value of the policy, plus dividend additions or accumulations, and usually less the amount of indebtedness, for the term for which the cash value used as a single premium will pay.

Extended wait A particular form of health insurance. The re-insurer pays disability benefits after a predetermined number of monthly payments have been made by the ceding company.

Extension Continuation past original maturity date; continuation of a commitment.

Extra expense Extra funds needed to continue a business uninterruptedly, after damage. Applied to dwellings, it is called additional living expense coverage, and is available through extra expense insurance, and additional living expense insurance.

Extra Expense Insurance Provides reimbursement to insured for the expenses reasonably incurred to maintain operation of the business when described property is damaged by a peril covered by the contract, if operation can be maintained only by incurring such extra expense. This insurance is normally used by businesses where continuity of operation regardless of cost is a practical necessity, as for example, banks, dairies, contract laundries. Written either as a separate policy or as an addition to a base policy.

Extra percentage tables The most common method used for the insurance of substandard risks. All substandard risks are divided into broad groups and the average rating for each will be progressively higher than that for the standard class.

Extra premium An additional amount added to the basic premium which may be required because the risk covered is unusually hazardous.

Extra premium removal If the cause of the extra premium is eliminated in that the rated medical impairment no longer exists, or there has been a change from a hazardous occupation to a nonhazardous one, it is prudent to seek the reduction of the amount of the premium that is attributable to the risk. Such a reduction is extra premium removal.

Extra time; overtime Working extra or overtime is an increased hazard, and if intended to be covered, must be specifically mentioned in the policy wording, and the company's consent obtained, with or without an extra charge.

F Fire.

F. & A. Fire and allied lines.

F.A.P. Family auto policy.

F.A.S. Free alongside.

F.C.A.S. Fellow of the Casualty Actuarial Society.

F.C. & S. Free of capture and seizure clause.

F.D. Fire Department

F.D.I.C. Federal Deposit Insurance Corporation.

F. & F. Furniture and fixtures.

F.G.A. Free of General Average

F.H.A. Federal Housing Administration.

F.H.L.B.B. Federal Home Loan Bank Board.

FHLMC Federal Home Loan Mortgage Corporation.

F.I.A. Full interest admitted.

F.I.A. Factory Insurance Association.

F.I.A. Fellow of the Institute of Actuaries.

F.I.C.A. Federal Insurance Contributions Act.

F.I.F.O. First In, First Out

F.I.I.C. Fellow, Insurance Institute of Canada

F.I.R.A.A. Fire Insurance Research and Actuarial Association

F.L.M.I. Fellow of the Life Management Institute.

F.M. Factory Mutuals

F.N.M.A. Federal National Mortgage Association; Fannie May.

F.O. Federal official.

F.O. Foreign to occupation.

F.O.B. Free on board, a term of sale.

F.O.C. Free of Charge

F.O.M. Fault of management.

F.P. Faithful performance.

F.P. Frame protected (classification).

F.P.A. Free of particular average.

F.P.M. Feet Per Minute

F.P.S.   Feet per Second

F/S   Financial statement.

F.S.A.   Fellow of the Society of Actuaries.

F.S.L.I.C.   Federal Savings and Loan Insurance Corporation.

F. & T.   Fire and theft.

F.T.C.   Federal Trade Commission.

F.U.   Frame unprotected (classification).

F.U.A.   Farm Underwriters Association

F.Y.I.   For Your Information

Face   The first page of a life insurance policy.

Face of policy   The first page of an insurance policy.

Face amount   The amount stated on the face of the policy that will be paid in case of death or at maturity. It does not include any amounts added through dividend additions, double indemnity or other special provisions. Same as face value.

Face of policy   The front or first page of the insurance policy. It customarily includes the name of the insurance company as well as certain insuring clauses. Commonly used to mean the amount in dollars of insurance provided.

Facility of payment clause   A provision of an accident and health or life insurance policy that provides that the insurer may, under stated conditions, pay insurance benefits to persons other than the insured, the designated beneficiary or the estate of the insured.

Facility plan   An industry or state-required plan so that a market is assured for poorer risks.

Factory Mutuals   A group of mutual insurance companies that specialize in writing policies on factories and related manufacturing facilities.

Facultative   A term used in reinsurance—the reinsuring company may exercise its "faculty" (prerogative) to accept or reject the risk offered.

Facultative certificate of reinsurance   A document formalizing a facultative reinsurance cession.

Facultative Obligatory Treaty   A reinsurance contract under which the ceding company may cede exposures or risks of a defined class that the reinsurer must accept if ceded.

Facultative reinsurance   One of several types of reinsurance contracts. A reinsurer retains the right of rejecting any business ceded to it, but this rejection must be prompt notification to the ceding company.

Facultative reinsurance treaty See **Reinsurance treaty, facultative**

Fair market value A legal term variously interpreted by the courts but in general connoting a price obtainable in the market which is fair in view of the conditions currently existing.

Fair plan Stands for Fair Access to Insurance Requirements Plans. A state requirement in a number of states to ensure that property in such areas as slums will be insured. It is a type of assigned risk pool to cover property that normally would be unattractive to insurance companies.

Fair value Value that is reasonable and consistent with all of the known facts.

Fait accompli An accomplished fact.

Fallen building clause A provision found in some fire insurance policies, it stipulates that if any material part of the building which is insured falls or collapses from causes other than from fire or explosion, the fire insurance becomes void.

False pretense Refers to any untrue statements or representations made with the intention of obtaining property or money.

Family automobile policy Contract of insurance providing larger coverage than the combination automobile policy, providing liability coverage, physical damage, and medical expense coverage.

Family expense policy An accident and sickness policy, or an accident only policy covering all the members of one family.

Family Income A type of life insurance. It is usually an ordinary life policy combined with a term policy which face value decreases monthly over a fixed period. If the person dies before the term policy expires his family gets a monthly income from the term policy until the expiration date. The family is paid the face amount of the ordinary life policy in a lump sum or installments.

Family income insurance Insurance that provides an income (usually $10 monthly per $1000 of insurance) to the beneficiary to the end of a specified period from the inception of the insurance if the insured dies within that period. The face amount of the insurance is paid at the end of the income period or when the insured dies after the end of the period.

Family Income Rider (A Life term) A rider of decreasing term insurance written in combination with Term of Age 70 or higher premium plans. This form of contract provides a higher face value of protection at a level premium during a policyholder's younger years, when he may not have available the higher premiums required for a permanent form of insurance.

Family Maintenance (Family Protection) Contract   A contract similar to the family income contract. It combines ordinary insurance and term insurance, but without the decreasing insurance feature. It provides for payment beginning at the death of the insured of an income for a fixed period of 10, 15, or 20 years, as selected, running from the date of death and not from the date of issue as in the family income contract, with payment of the principal sum of the ordinary insurance at the end of the fixed period.

Family maintenance insurance   *See* **Family income insurance.**

Family Plan Policy   An all-family plan of protection, usually with permanent insurance on the father's life, and with mother and children automatically covered for lesser amounts of protection—usually term—all included under one premium. The policy has been offered with numerous variations and features.

Family protection automobile coverage   Contract of insurance providing protection in the event damage is caused by a motorist that is financially irresponsible or has no liability insurance.

Fannie Mae   *See* **Federal National Mortgage Association.**

Farm equipment and liability insurance   Type of business insurance coverage specifically designed to cover owners of farm equipment.

Farm Mutual   A mutual insurance company concentrating on farm property.

Farmer's comprehensive personal liability insurance   A modified comprehensive personal liability policy covering risks associated with farming.

Farmer's Home Administration (FMHA)   A government agency established under the Farmer's Home Administration Act of 1946 to provide financing to farmers and other qualified borrowers who are unable to obtain loans elsewhere.

FAS price   An amount charged an importer which includes such expenses as insurance, warehousing, trucking, lighterage up to the loading tackle of the ship. All risk of ownership rests with the seller up to the loading on the vessel.

Fatal Accidents Act   (In some areas known as "Lord Campbells Act") Is an act which provides compensation for the families of persons killed by accident.

Fault of management   *See* **Unsafe.**

Feasibility study A study or analysis that determines whether a project, proposed or existing, successfully meets desired objectives.

Federal crime insurance Insurance offered by the Federal Insurance Administration, an agency of the U.S. government. It covers burglary, larceny, and robbery losses.

Federal Crop Insurance Corporation Insurance of growing crops by an instrumentality of the United States Government. No element of compulsion is involved.

Federal Deposit Insurance Corporation An instrumentality of the U.S. government that insures deposits in insured banks under certain restrictions as to maximum amounts per account. The premium is paid by the bank as a small percentage of all deposits, although insurance is only on that portion of the deposits below $100,000 per account. The U.S. Congress is considering merging the FDIC and the FSLIC.

Federal estate tax The Internal Revenue code specifies the conditions for including life insurance proceeds in the gross estate of the deceased for purposes of estate tax.

Federal flood insurance Insurance offered by the federal government in those localities meeting specific requirements. The insurance protects against flood and mud slides.

Federal gift tax The Internal Revenue Service requires the individual concerned taxpayer to obtain a statement of the value of life insurance gifts from his insurance companies. These prescribed forms are then processed as required by the Internal Revenue Code.

Federal Home Loan Bank Board (FHLBB) A regulatory and supervisory agency for federally chartered savings institutions. It oversees the operations of the Federal Savings and Loan Insurance Corporation and the Federal Home Loan Mortgage Corporation.

Federal Home Loan Mortgage Corporation (FHLMC) A private corporation authorized by Congress. It sells participation sales certificates secured by pools of conventional mortgage loans, their principal and interest guaranteed by the federal government through the FHLMC. It also sells Government National Mortgage Association bonds to raise funds to finance the purchase of mortgages. Popularly known as **Freddie Mac.**

Federal Housing Administration (FHA) A division of the Department of Housing and Urban Development. Its main activity is the insuring of residential mortgage loans made by private lenders. It sets standards for construction and underwriting. FHA does not lend money, nor plan, nor construct housing.

Federal Insurance Contributions Act Tax on employees and employers based on wages. Paid to Collector of Internal Revenue to meet Social Security payments.

Federal National Mortgage Association A secondary mortgage market for F.H.A. and G.I. insured mortgages.

Federal official bonds Contracts under which the surety company will reimburse the government for dishonest acts of the bonded federal official.

Federal Savings and Loan Insurance Corporation An instrumentality of the U.S. government that insures (deposits) shares and accounts in insured savings and loan, building and loan, and banks for cooperatives for that portion of the deposits below $100,000 per account. The U.S. Congress is considering merging the FSLIC and the FDIC.

Federal Tort Claims Act Permits the United States to be sued for damage to property or personal injuries under circumstances such that if the federal government were an individual it would be liable. Previous to this the concept of sovereignty that a government cannot be sued without its permission was in effect.

Federal Unemployment Insurance Tax Dual state and federal tax based on merit rating to provide insurance benefits for unemployment of covered individuals.

Fee Depending on the contexts, it may either be a remuneration for services or an inheritable estate in land.

Fee simple The highest and best estate by which an owner is entitled to the entire property with unconditional power of disposing of it during his life. The property descends to his heirs and legal representatives should he die without a will. At times the term is used to refer to this estate. Fee simple absolute is also a synonym for fee simple.

Fee simple limited An estate less than fee simple under which the owner has rights only so long as certain conditions prevail. When those conditions do not prevail the estate is terminated. Important in cases of insurable interest.

Fee tail An estate limited to a particular class of heirs of the person to whom the property or estate is granted.

Fellow of the Institute of Actuaries A designation for an individual who has been examined and become a member of the Institute of Actuaries. See that term.

Felony A major crime such as murder, arson, or rape for which a statute provides a harsher penalty than for a misdemeanor.

Feme covert   A married woman.

Feme sole   An unmarried woman, including widows and those divorced.

FHA loan   A mortgage insured by the Federal Housing Administration usually with constant periodic payments which pay the interest and amortize the principal during its term.

Fiat   Historically the "King could do no wrong".
In modern times, the Sovereign (government) is still considered "to do no wrong", while acting in a Governmental function and cannot be sued without consent. A Fiat is a decree or order or warrant usually by a Judge or public officer after suitable hearing, which permits the process of the suit to be started.

Fidelity bond   A form of insurance which protects the covered employer against loss due to dishonesty of his employees. A bond which will reimburse an employer for loss up to the amount of the bond sustained by an employer named in the bond by reason of any dishonest act of an employee covered by the bond. Blanket fidelity bonds embrace groups of employees. *See* **Bond, fidelity.**

Fiduciary   A person who occupies a position of special trust and confidence, e.g., in handling or supervising the affairs or funds of another. Involving the exercise of confidence and trust.

Fiduciary bond   *See* **Bond, fiduciary.**

Field   Geographic area or territory covered by agent, agency, or company. Also used to refer to type of insurance written such as marine field.

Fieldman   An individual employee working away from the head or home office in the territory served by his company.

Fieri Facias   A Writ of execution directing a sheriff to whom it is addressed to levy against goods and chattels (only) for the purpose of realizing a judgement debt. It is commonly known in brief as a Writ of Fi fa.

Filing company   An insurance company which files risk information with an insurance bureau.

Finance   As a noun, the system by which the income of a company is raised and administered. As a verb, to conduct financial operations or to furnish money. Deals with methods for supplying capital needed to acquire, develop, and operate real property.

Financed insurance   The use of borrowed funds to pay life insurance premiums. The funds are generally provided from the cash value of the policy.

Financial guaranty   A type of bond in which the insurer guarantees that it will pay a fixed or determinable sum of money.

Financial responsibility clause   Clause found in some insurance policies and it states that the policyholder is protected under the terms of any state. This is exemplified in those states which have a financial responsibility law. In case of an automobile accident the driver may be required to post a bond or make a deposit to cover any personal injuries or property damage which might result. The financial responsibility clause in a policy assures the holder that he complies with the state legal requirements.

Financial responsibility law   A statute requiring motorists to furnish evidence of ability to pay damages, either before or after an accident. The law requires an operator or owner of a motor vehicle to give evidence of financial ability to meet claims for damages in order to be licensed to drive a motor vehicle or to have his vehicle registered. May be compulsory on all registrants in certain states.

Financing package   The total of all financial interest in a project. It may include mortgages, partnerships, joint venture capital interests, stock ownership, or any financial arrangement set up to carry a project to completion.

Financing statement   Under the Uniform Commercial Code, a prescribed form filed by a lender with the registrar of deeds or secretary of state. It gives the name and address of the debtor and the secured party (lender), along with a description of the personal property securing the loan. It may show the amount of indebtedness.

Finder's fee   That sum of money that is paid to the individual for finding or establishing the contact that makes a financial transaction possible. A large borrower may pay a finder's fee to an individual that knows of an insurance company that is willing, able, and does lend funds to the borrower.

Fine arts floater insurance policy   Type of business insurance coverage on fine arts works against all risks on a valued basis.

Fine Arts Insurance (Floater Policy)   Type of business insurance coverage on fine arts loss against all risks on a valued basis. Usually written by inland marine underwriters.

Fine print   The unfortunate confusion in nomenclature of policies that grant coverage in one part of the policy and exclude the coverage in another part of the contract in the fine print. At one early period, before 1920, some policies used different size print, however, in many cases today limitations are set in larger or boldface type, so the situation has actually become reversed.

Finished stock Merchandise which has been completely processed.

Fire The courts have held that fire must be combustion sufficient to produce a spark, flame, or glow, but not an explosion, and must be hostile, as opposed to friendly, i.e., not in the place where it is intended to be, as in a furnace, stove, or fireplace. It must be accidental and must be the proximate cause of the damage.

Fire department service clause In a fire insurance policy this clause provides reimbursement for the insured for fire department charges where such charges are made because of the location of the property. This generally is found where the property is outside the corporate limits of a city or town and the fire department of that corporation charges for sending fire fighting equipment outside the limits. When a fire insurance policy has this clause the insurance company will reimburse the holder for such charges.

Fire, friendly Fires which do not exceed the limits assigned, such as found in a stove, furnace, or kerosene lamp. A fire which is not outside the place where it was intended to be. *See* **Fire.**

Fire, hostile All fires which occur where they are not intended to be. *See* **Fire.**

Fire insurance Contract prescribed by each state subject to modification by endorsements insuring against direct loss by fire, lightning, and other defined causes.

Fire legal liability A policy which provides liability protection for negligent acts of the insured involved in the destruction of property under his control.

Fire limits The limit of an area of fire protection.

Fire maps A map showing the location and distribution of a particular insurers fire insurance contracts in a given area. By avoiding heavy concentration in a given area the risk of catastrophic loss is greatly reduced.

Fire mark A medallion or sign on a building indicating which insurance company had insured the building. It was used in the early days of insurance when municipalities did not have fire departments and individual fire insurance companies had their own fire fighting equipment. The mark helped identify a property for the company and their firemen would concentrate their attention in protecting so identified properties.

Fire marshal　A public official charged with the prevention and investigation of fires.

Fire resistant　Construction according to certain standards designed to resist fire and thus reduce its spread.

Fire wall　A divisional wall that separates a property into two fire areas. *See* **Division wall.**

Fire, Wind & Theft　A form of automobile coverage for those specified perils. In some instances may be provided singly or in combinations.

Fireproof (fire resistive)　The term fireproof is a misnomer. Fire occurring in an adjoining building or in the combustible contents of a building may cause damage to any structure. Therefore no building can accurately be termed fireproof. The term fire-resistive is a better description of modern incombustible construction.

First loss earthquake insurance　*See* **Direct damage earthquake.**

First mortgage　The senior mortgage, thus having precedent over all other mortgages. Mortgage which has precedence over all other mortgages.

First party insurance　Any insurance covering the insured's own person or property.

First party release　The agreement between the insured and the insurance company that provides a release according to the terms of the policy.

First policy year　This phrase in a statute eliminating suicide of insured after such year as a defense. This means year for which policy, annually renewed, was first issued.

First surplus treaty　A reinsurance contract on the amount of coverage above which an insurance company wishes to assume. It is generally handled on a pro rata basis.

Fiscal year　Any 12-month period used for financial reporting and preparation of balance sheets, profit and loss statements, and other financial summations.

Five point policy　A term in trade use denoting an automobile policy, under which just one company provides insurance for the casualty coverages of bodily injury liability, property damage liability, and medical payments, and the physical damage coverages of comprehensive (of fire and theft and collision).

Fixed annuity Fixed payments are provided throughout the period of the annuity.

Fixed benefit The dollar amount of this benefit does not vary.

Fixed charges The regular recurring costs or charges required in the holding of a property or for the guarantee of the unimpairment of capital invested therein, as distinguished from the maintenance of the condition or utility of the property and other direct expenses of operation.

Fixed-dollar annuities An annuity under which the amount of each payment is stated in a fixed amount, such as $100 per month.

Fixtures Appurtenances which are affixed to the building or land and generally in such a way that they cannot be moved without causing damage to either the property or themselves. Fixtures have variable definitions under the state laws.

Fixtures and fittings Those articles that are attached and appear to be a permanent part of the property however at times they are used to refer to articles of furniture and equipment which are not permanently attached. Thus shelves, showcases, counters are customarily regarded as fixtures and fittings, though some of these may not be permanently attached.

Flat cancellation When liabilities have not existed thereunder, policies may be canceled free of any charge to the insured. Such terminations are known as flat cancellations.

Flat commission Remuneration paid to an agent on the basis of a straight percentage of premium for all types of risks and policies as compared to a graded scale of separate percentages for different types of policies.

Flat maternity benefit A hospital-reimbursement stipulated benefit. Payment for the maternity confinement is not the actual cost of the confinement, but the amount or formula noted in the policy.

Flat rate Has two meanings. A rate used when no coinsurance clause is attached to the policy, or the rate from which the credits for coinsurance are deducted. In some states the term is called the gross rate. Sometimes used for judgment rates. *See* **Judgment rates.**

Fleet of companies Many insurance companies are affiliated with others under the same management. These groups, which usually include fire, marine, casualty, and surety companies, are called fleets.

Fleet policy An insurance contract covering a number of automobiles. The automobiles may be specifically designated or provision may be made for automatic coverage of all automobiles owned by the insured, on a reporting basis. To be eligible for such coverage, all automobiles must be owned by a single insured.

Floater policy A policy under the terms of which protection follows movable property, covering it wherever it may be; e.g., a policy on tourist's baggage.

Flood insurance Contract of protection for damage caused by overflowing or rising water. Obtainable under fire and marine contracts as an incidental feature to a more comprehensive coverage. Straight flood insurance alone is a very rare coverage.

Floor loan A portion or portions of a mortgage loan commitment that is less than the full amount of the commitment. It may be funded upon conditions less stringent than those required for funding the full amount. For example, the floor loan, equal to perhaps 80 percent of the full amount, may be funded upon completion of construction but before occupancy, but substantial occupancy of the building may be required for funding of the full amount of the loan.

Floor plan insurance Protection taken out by finance companies on equipment such as automobiles or electrical appliances which they have financed for retail dealers. The articles are in the possession of the dealer but are collateral for the loan by the finance company.

Flotsam Goods lost at sea if floating and unclaimed belong to the Sovereign a phrase commonly used in Marine Insurance and more fully covered in Merchant Shipping Acts.
Loss of property or right as a penalty e.g. a breach of warranty a creative forfeiture which would deny the insured the right of recovery under his contract.

Flowage A colloquial term in lumber areas to designate lands flooded by artificial or natural dams originally for the purpose of creating storage areas for floating logs; an artificial lake or a bog land.

Flywheel insurance Insurance covering direct loss or damage to property, as well as loss of life or bodily injuries to individuals due to the breaking, bursting, or explosion of the flywheel. Additional coverage may be written covering loss to the insured of profits or income.

Following the fortunes A clause generally found in reinsurance contracts stating that the reinsurer is bound to the same fate as the ceding company.

For account of whom it may concern Clause protecting rights of individuals or companies not described in the policy that have an insurable and enforceable interest in the insured property.

Forbearance The act of refraining from taking legal action despite the fact that a mortgage is in arrears. Forebearance is usually granted only when a mortgagor makes a satisfactory arrangement by which the arrears will be paid at a future date.

Forced sale The act of selling property under compulsion as to time and place. Usually a sale made by virtue of a court order, ordinarily at public auction.

Forced sale value Amount that may be realized at a forced sale. That price that could be obtained at immediate disposal. An improper use of the word value. The term forced sale value is used erroneously to designate forced sale price.

Forcible entry and detainer The name of an action for the prompt recovery of the possession of real property in certain cases.

Foreclosure The forced transfer of property ownership by order of court as a means of satisfaction of an unpaid obligation such as a mortgage or property taxes that are unpaid.

Foreign carrier In a given state, an insurer domiciled in another state, or in some states an insurer domiciled in a foreign country. *See also* **Alien carrier** and **Foreign company** for technical correct position.

Foreign company Incorporated or organized under the laws of some other state or territory of the United States, such as a company organized under the laws of Louisiana doing business in Texas. This corporation is a foreign company in Texas. It would be an alien company if it were incorporated in Canada doing business in Texas. The term may also be applied to a company writing or soliciting business in the jurisdiction in which it is not admitted to transact business, in which cases such companies are also referred to as nonadmitted. Technically an insurance company chartered in a foreign country is described as an alien company while a company chartered in another state than in which it is doing business is a foreign company.

Foreign insurer An insurer incorporated in a different state from which it is authorized to do business.

Foreign to occupation   Underwriting designation for an accident foreign to occupation, that is, as opposed to the A.O. (at occupation).

Forfeiture   The alienation for fault or crime. The loss of a right. The reversion to a sovereign of private or real property such as in the satisfaction of unpaid taxes.

Forgery   In general, any false writing with intent to defraud. It is defined by statute in the various states.

Forgery bond   Type of business insurance coverage. Title is self-explanatory.

Forgery insurance   One of two types of policies: commercial forgery policy, which is used by firms other than banks; and depositors' forgery policy, which is used to protect the insured and his bank.

Form   A descriptive form attached to a policy setting forth the nature of the property covered, the location, and other pertinent data. It may grant certain privileges or impose certain obligations on the insured.

Forthcoming bond   A bond typically used by a defendant to obtain a release of attachment.

Forthwith   This term strictly means immediately.

Fortuitous circumstance (or cause)   A chance happening. An accident caused by an unforeseen happening. *See* **Inevitable accident.**

Foundation exclusion clause   Part of fire insurance policy that excludes the value of the foundation and insurance on it. This exclusion has bearing on the coinsurance part of the policy.

Foundation wall   Masonry wall below ground supporting building.

Foundering   The sinking of a ship.

Fractional premium   A proportionate amount of the regular premium usually used when a change in premium-paying date is desired and the portion of the premium year between the old date and the new must be settled.

Frame   Lumber construction.

Franchise   If a loss is higher than a stated percentage, then the entire loss is paid by the insurance company. A minimum percentage or amount of loss which the insured must incur to be indemnified under an insurance contract. If the minimum is reached, the entire loss is covered. Franchise clauses differ from deductible clauses. *See* **Coinsurance, deductible and wholesale.**

Franchise bond Bond usually required by a municipality when granting a franchise. The bond guarantees that the grantee will construct a utility and have it ready for operation within a specified time.

Franchise clause Marine policy feature providing that no claims below a stated amount are to be paid by the insurance company but if the claims are above that amount the entire amount will be paid. This clause discourages the submission of small claims that cost more to process than the actual settlement amount.

Franchise deductible often found in automobile policies and home owner's policies a formula whereby the deductible applies in small losses and is gradually reduced as the size of the loss increases so that in the larger losses the insurance company pays the loss in full.

Franchise insurance Accident and health insurance under contracts sold to individuals under an agreement with an employer for access to his employees and usually for deduction of premiums from payroll or written on individual members of an association, the employer or association remitting the premiums to the insurer.

Fraternal insurance A system of cooperative protection furnished by a fraternal order to its members on a nonprofit basis.

Fraternal Insurance Counsellor A designation awarded to fraternal life underwriters, associated with societies that are members of the National Fraternal Congress; who complete the prescribed course of study, pass the F.I.C. examination, and who meet the standard requirements set up by the Fraternal Field Managers' Association. Fraternal life underwriters are eager to attain this designation—official recognition of their ablity as life underwriters.

Fraud Deception or artifice used to deceive or cheat. In insurance it is understood to be related to misrepresentation and concealment. Proof of willful fraud is grounds for voiding a policy.

Fraud bond Type of business insurance protection against loss caused by fraud.

Fraudulent Misrepresentation A false statement made knowing it to be false and intending another to act on it to his detriment, or made carelessly or recklessly without regard to whether it is true or false.

F.R.E. Program   The initials F.R.E. are used to designate those risks "Filed without Referral to the Examiner."

Freddie Mac   *See* **Federal Home Loan Mortgage Corporation.**

Free alongside (F.A.S.)   Sellers quoted price which includes delivery of material to the loading facility of the ship. *See* **FAS price.**

Free of capture and seizure clause   A clause exempting claims caused by damage or capture by enemies of the nationality of the insured. Called the F.C. & S. clause.

Free of particular average clause   A part of a marine insurance contract excluding particular average from coverage, often with the exception of loss incurred under specified circumstances.

Free on Board (FOB)   Phrase meaning that the seller assumes costs of placing goods purchased from him on board truck, ship, train, plane, or other carrier at the point named. Transportation costs beyond that point are paid by the purchaser.

Freehold   The tenure of real property by which an estate of inheritance or for life is held, or the estate itself; thus it may be either in fee simple, fee simple limited, or in fee tail.

Freezing insurance policy   Type of business insurance coverage protecting against loss caused by a drop in temperature below freezing.

Freight insurance   A marine insurance purchased by the owners of the transporting vehicles or vessels or owner of the product.

Freight insurance policy   Type of business insurance protection against loss caused to freight.

Friendly fire   *See* **Fire.**

Fringe benefits   *See* **Employee benefits.**

Front end earthquake insurance   *See* **Direct damage earthquake.**

Front-end money   Funds required to start a development and generally advanced by the developer or equity owner as a capital contribution to the project.

Front foot   The measure of twelve inches in length of the frontage of real estate upon a thoroughfare.

Front foot cost   The cost of a parcel of real estate expressed in terms of twelve inch units of the real estate's frontage.

Frontage   The property line abutting the most important adjacent property, usually a street, a lake, river, or ocean.

Frustration clause   Provision of marine contract that makes it impossible to claim for a lost voyage that could not be completed because of orders of a government authority if the goods are recovered.

Full age The period of life at which a person becomes legally capable of transacting business, or of becoming contractually responsible, usually at twenty-one years of age.

Full coverage Any form of insurance which provides for payment, without deduction, of all losses occasioned by hazards covered. Insurance against the full amount of any loss up to the amount of the insurance, without deductions. *See* **All risks insurance.**

Full interest admitted Clause of marine insurance policy that establishes agreement of the insuring company that the insured has right to payment in case of loss. In this clause the insurable interest is agreed upon. *See* **Honor contracts.**

Full-Paid Additions See Dividend Additions.

Full Preliminary Term Some states permit the use of a minimum reserve basis other than the level net premium basis in order to enable the companies to use a large portion of the first year's premium for expenses. The full preliminary term basis allows the full first-year premium, less the charge for mortality, to be used for expenses, and the reserve is then accumulated from a higher net premium for the subsequent years.

Full preliminary term reserve plan Method of computing reserves by new companies that assumes that a policy has no reserve at the end of the first policy year. At the end of the second year of the policy one year reserve will be established. In this way the surplus of the company is not called upon to the same extent and the new company may write more policies.

Full reporting clause Sometimes called the honesty clause. Provision of penalty on the insured if he revealed and reported less than required on his policy application.

Full Vesting That form of immediate or deferred vesting under which all accrued benefits of a participant become bested benefits. CIT

Fully insured status A term commonly pertaining to social security benefits (Old Age, Survivors, and Disability Insurance). Whether a person is currently or fully insured depends upon the number of quarters of coverage he or she has. Those with forty quarters of coverage are fully insured. There are certain exceptions to this rule however. For specific details contact a local Social Security Administration office.

Functional obsolescence The reduction in the value of a real estate property because that property does not possess the technological features of more efficient or newer property.

Funded pension plan   A systematic method used by the insurer to accumulate the amount or fund which will be needed to meet the claims of the plan. A plan may be funded by purchasing insurance annuity contracts from insurance companies. This is known as an insured plan. Or it may be funded by depositing funds with a trustee, frequently a bank. In which case it is known as a self-administered or uninsured plan.

Funded Trust   See Life Insurance Trust.

Funding Agency   An organization or individual that provides facilities for the accumulation of assets to be used for the payment of benefits under a pension plan, or an organization that provides facilities for the purchase of such benefits.   CIT

Funding Instrument   Agreements or contracts governing the conditions under which a funding agency performs its function.

Funding Medium   The character of the asset structure used by a funding agency in fulfilling its obligations as set forth in the funding instrument.   CIT tentative.

Funeral Directors Malpractice Coverage   Liability coverage with respect to claims arising from malpractice or error in the insured's practice as a funeral director.

Fungible   Interchangeable, such as a certain type and grade of wheat stored in a public elevator. Thus a claim may be settled by tendering the same amount, type, and grade but not necessarily the original material.

Fur floater insurance policy   Type of insurance coverage on fur. An all risk marine coverage.

Furnace explosion   A violent bursting with noise of the fire box of a furnace. This type of happening is covered by fire insurance. Explosion policies, while an explosion of the boiler would come under a boiler explosion policy.

Furniture and fixtures   Phrase signifying inclusion of items in the contents of a structure for sale, and not including merchandise or products in the course of manufacture.

Furriers' customers insurance   Coverage under an inland marine policy for a furrier storing garments for customers.

Future advance   Disbursement of funds subsequent to the execution of a mortgage. Obligatory future advances, found in construction loans, normally take preference over another encumbrance that is recorded prior to disbursing the next construction loan advances. Optional future advances are found in open-end mortgages and do not take preference over another encumbrance recorded prior to the disbursement of the advance.

Future Service Benefit   That portion of a participant's retirement benefit that relates to his period of credited service after the effective date of the plan.   CIT

G.A.   General agent.

G.A.B.   General Adjustment Bureau.

G.A.M.C.   General Agents and Managers Conference.

G.C.   General Cover

G.C.T.   Greenwich Civil Time

G.L.   Gross Line

G.N.M.A.   Government National Mortgage Association.

G.T.C.   Good Till Cancelled

G.I. Insurance   U. S. Government, National Service Life Insurance, Servicemen's Gratuitous Indemnity.

Gambling   Creation of a risk of loss as compared with insurance, which eliminates the risk of loss.

Gap financing   An interim loan to finance the difference between the **floor loan** and the maximum permanent loan as committed.

Garage liability insurance   Also called garage keepers insurance. A policy covering the special hazards of keeping a commercial garage.

Garment contractors' floater   Coverage under an inland marine policy for makers of garments while the garments are in the possession of a subcontractor.

Garnishee   The order attaching some money for a creditor, in the hands of the Garnishee (person who has the money belonging to the debtor), by the Garnishor.

Garnishment   Legal notice to appear in court. Also a legal warning to persons or companies holding another's property that it is thus attached and should not be delivered to the owner but should be accounted for in a court. In some cases money or settlement under an insurance policy is subject to garnishment.

General agency system   Method of handling insurance through general agents, as contrasted with the branch office system.

General agent, casualty   Individual who may solicit business from the public and has a commission contract with an insurance company. The contract will state whether he has an exclusive territory or not.

General agent, fire Individual having an exclusive territory and in charge of supervision of agents in that territory. The general agent does not sell insurance to the general public directly.

General Assembly. The body charged by the constitution with the duty of enacting statutory laws for some states.

General average In maritime law and marine insurance, "a sacrifice to avert a common peril." It means losses suffered through expenses voluntarily incurred and sacrifices intentionally made by a master of a ship of a part of a ship's cargo to preserve the rest from destruction. Since they were for the benefit of all, these losses and expenses must be shared proportionately by each of the interests involved. However, a policy of insurance may be had to provide coverage for such a risk.

General average contribution The amount which an interest in a marine venture must contribute as its share in making good a general average sacrifice.

General average sacrifice A voluntary sacrifice by the master of a ship of all or part of an interest in a marine venture for the purpose of saving the remainder of the venture.

General cover *See* **Reporting form.**

General cover contract A form of insurance designed to assure adequate protection on stocks of goods which fluctuate in volume and price. It is frequently associated with companies that have many establishments.

General liability insurance *See* **Liability Insurance.**

General mortgage bond A written instrument representing an obligation secured by a mortgage but preceded by senior issues.

General provisions Those provisions in addition to the regular insuring and benefit provisions and to the standard or uniform provisions, which define and limit the coverage. Also called additional provisions.

General-writing mutual A mutual insurer with a broad offering of insurance.

Geographical limitation A specification in a policy that coverage is limited to those risks occurring or acquired within certain geographical limits.

German Alliance Insurance Co. vs. Lewis, Superintendent of

Insurance, State of Kansas Review of decree, sustained a demurrer and dismissed bill in suit restraining enforcement of statute which would regulate insurance rates on fire policies.

G. I. Bill of Rights The popular term for those privileges that veterans possess under the Servicemen's Readjustment Act of 1944 as amended.

G.I. Loan Colloquial term given to a mortgage loan guaranteed by the Veterans Administration.

Gift tax An excise tax levied by the federal government and many states on the gift or transfer of property. Most taxes on gifts are progressive and have minimum exemptions.

Gimmicks Used critically to refer to certain clauses or coverages found in some policies. The inference is that the policyholder is not obtaining the value or coverage that a more informed individual would by being aware of the limitations of the "gimmicks."

Ginnie Mae *See* **Government National Mortgage Association.**

Girder A heavy wood or steel structural member supporting joists, beams, partitions, or other structural members.

Give The transferring to another, a yielding or bestowing. One of the important words in deeds of conveyance of real estate.

Glass insurance Sometimes called plate glass insurance. It provides insurance for broken glass. In many cases the company replaces the actual glass rather than making a cash settlement of the claim.

Golf liability insurance The insured is provided protection against any accidents he/she causes to the public while playing golf.

Golfer's insurance Covers legal liability for personal injury to others caused by the golfer insured, and covers his golf equipment.

Good will A business asset which has been defined judicially as "the probability that customers will return." It is made up of such intangible items as the reputation, patronage, trade name, good public relations, and drawing power of a business concern. Although not insurable, because exact valuation of it is impossible, good will frequently is arbitrarily priced and sold when liquidating a commercial enterprise.

Goods The word "goods" applies to inanimate objects only, and usually does not include "fixtures." It is always best to specify the nature of character of the goods desired to be covered.

Goods-in-process insurance Type of business insurance coverage. Title is self-explanatory.

Governing classification Pertains to the main operation of an employer where several different functions are performed. The main operation of an employer, the one which carries the largest payroll, and is used as a basis for determining workmen's compensation insurance rates.

Government National Mortgage Association (GNMA) A mortgage association partitioned by congressional legislation on September 1, 1968, into two continuing corporate entities. GNMA has assumed responsibility for the special assistance loan program and the management and liquidation function of the older GNMA. GNMA also administers the mortgage-backed securities program that channels new sources of funds into residential financing through the sale of privately issued securities carrying a GNMA guarantee. Popularly known as **Ginnie Mae.**

GNMA futures market A regulated central market in which standardized contracts for the future delivery of GNMA securities are traded.

GNMA mortgage-backed securities Securities, guaranteed by GNMA, that are issued by mortgage bankers, commercial banks, savings and loan associations, savings banks, and other institutions. The GNMA security holder is protected by the "full faith and credit of the U.S." GNMA securities are backed by FHA, VA or Farmers Home Administration mortgages.

Grace A period of time, usually fixed by state insurance statute during which period a past due premium may be paid without a penalty.

Grace period A period of time, usually thirty-one days following the premium due date, during which a premium may be paid. The policy remains in force throughout this period.

Graded commission Remuneration paid to an agent that varies with the type and volume of risks written.

Graded death benefits Generally found in juvenile life insurance policies. Death benefits in the early years of the contract are less than the face amount of the policy. These benefits increase with the age of the policy.

Graded premium life insurance A type of modified life insurance in which the premiums increase each year for the first several years and then level off. Frequently sold to young adults whose earnings will increase.

Graded Vesting That form of immediate or deferred vesting under which an increasing proportion of the accrued benefits of a participant becomes a vested benefit in accordance with a specific formula and requirements (usually in terms of attained age, years of service and/or plan membership). CIT

Grading schedule of cities & towns Schedule used to find the complete range of exposures within a particular community. Prepared by the National Board of Fire Underwriters.

Graduated lease A lease which provides for a certain rent for the first period, followed by either an increase or decrease in rents over the period of the lease.

Graduated life table An actuarial table derived from a mortality experience curve.

Graduated-payment mortgage A mortgage agreement in which initial payments are low compared to the traditional fixed-rate mortgage. Subsequent payments are increased by a gradation rate, which may be fixed or variable, based upon future income potential of the borrower.

Grant A term applied to all transfers of real estate.

Grantee A person to whom real estate is conveyed; the buyer.

Grantor One who transfers real estate. A person who conveys real estate by deed, the seller.

Gratuitous indemnity Feature of the Servicemen's Gratuity system established by the United States Government in 1951.

Green belt Forests, woods, parks, or fields surrounding or enclosing urban areas. *See* **Common areas.**

Grievance day A time set by taxing authorities and their agents for hearing protests on assessed valuations.

Gripsack general agent Individual representing one or several companies on a commission basis on sales in his area. He must pay his own expenses for travel and office, which is frequently his gripsack.

Gross area The total floor area of a building, except that of unenclosed areas, measured from the outside of the exterior walls.

Gross earnings Revenue from operating sources, before deduction of the expenses incurred in gaining such revenue.

Gross earnings form *See* **Business interruption insurance, gross earnings form.**

Gross income The actual or estimated total receipts for a given period.

Gross lease A lease of property under which the lessor agrees to meet all charges which would normally be incurred by the owner of that property.

Gross leasable area   The total floor area designated for tenant occupancy and on which tenants pay rent. Usually used in describing property used for retail sale establishments. *See* **Net rentable area.**

Gross line   The amount of insurance a company has on a risk without reinsurance. *See* **Net line.**

Gross Negligence   See Negligence.

Gross net premiums   Computed by deducting return premiums from gross premiums, but not less reinsurance premiums.

Gross premium   The raw premium before substracting costs for reinsurance or at times before any return premium. The total premium charged for the insurance coverage, which includes anticipated expenses such as losses and overhead.

Gross profits   Profits computed before the deduction of general expenses.

Gross rate   *See* **Flat rate.**

Gross rent multiplier   A figure used to compare rental properties. It gives the relationship between the gross rental income and the sales price. Synonyms: gross multiplier and gross income multiplier.

Gross revenue   Total revenue from all sources before deduction of expenses incurred in gaining such revenue.

Gross sale   The total of the sale before subtraction of such things as returns, allowances, taxes.

Ground coverage   Coverage applicable to an airplane when it is not flying.

Ground lease   A long-term lease covering land on which the tenant will construct buildings.

Ground rent   The rent paid for the right to use a parcel of unimproved land or that proportion or percentage of the total rent paid that represents the return for the use of only the land.

Group accident and health insurance   *See* **Group insurance.**

Group annuity   A pension plan providing annuities at retirement to a group of persons under a master contract. It is usually issued to an employer for the benefit of employees. The individual members of the group hold certificates as evidence of their coverage. The most common type of group annuity provides for the purchase each year of a paid-up deferred annuity for each member, the total amount received by the member at retirement being the sum of these deferred annuities. Another type is the deposit administration plan.

Group certificate   The policy issued each party to a group plan; stating the terms of the contract.

Group creditor insurance   Contract issued to the creditor on the lives of his debtors to pay the amount of the indebtedness in the event of death. Legitimately used by banks to reduce problem of collection from a deceased estate. It has been improperly used by some finance-loan companies to avoid the usury laws of some states.

Group disability insurance   Provides benefits for a group of individuals, usually employees of the covered company, to compensate for losses such as time lost because of accident, or sickness, hospitalization cost, medical or surgical expense.

Group insurance   Any insurance plan by which a number of employees (and their dependents) or other homogeneous group, are insured under a single policy, issued to their employer or leader with individual certificates given to each insured individual or family unit. The most commonly written lines are life, accidental death and dismemberment, weekly benefits, hospital, surgical and medical expense, and poliomyelitis expense.

Group Life Insurance   (a) That type of life insurance provided to members of a group of persons, such as employees of one or more employers, members of associations or labor unions, or individuals to whom credit has been extended; (b) the term usually used to distinguish this type of life insurance from individual life insurance.   CIT tentative.

Group of companies   Insurance companies affiliated with others under the same management.

Group permanent insurance   Contract providing permanent life insurance on a basis of level premiums payment. Cash equities accumulated necessitate higher premiums than for term group policies.

Guarantee bonds   Type of business insurance. Title is self-explanatory.

Guaranteed cost   *See* **Nonparticipating.**

Guaranteed Dividend Policies   Coupon policies issued by some nonparticipating companies. The coupons represent fixed and guaranteed "dividends" which may be applied on the payment of premiums. The so-called dividends are a series of pure endowments maturing each year.

Guaranteed insurability An option, which permits the holder of a standard policy, at stated intervals, to purchase specified amounts of additional insurance without evidence of insurability.

Guaranteed Interest Rate The minimum rate of interest by which the insured's values in the policy are increased each year.

Guaranteed investment policy *See* **Coupon policy.**

Guaranteed loan A loan guaranteed by the VA, the Farmers Home Administration, or any other interested party.

Guaranteed mortgage A mortgage on which there is a guarantee of payment of principal or interest or both. In years prior to 1930 this was frequently done by a mortgage guarantee corporation. Today most such mortgages are of the FHA or GI variety.

Guaranteed mortgage certificate A participation used when the total mortgage, generally of large amounts, is sold in smaller amounts to several buyers.

Guaranteed title policy *See* **Title guarantee policy.**

Guaranteed renewable A policy which is renewable at the option of the insured for a specified period of years, or more commonly to a stated age such as 60 or 65. A guaranteed renewable policy which is also noncancellable is usually referred to as a noncancellable or noncan., and sometimes simply as n.c.

Guaranteed-Renewable Hospital-Surgical Insurance This type of policy provides for payment of hospital and surgical expenses up to a specified amount and is non-cancellable by the company as long as premiums are paid.

Guarantor One who promises to answer for another e.g. an insurance company may guaranty a contractor in the performance of his contracts. The insurance company is a guarantor.

Guaranty A promise by one party to pay a debt or perform an obligation contracted by another in the event that the original obligor fails to pay or perform as contracted.

Guardian In relation to an infant, child or young person, appointed by Law to be a Guardian by deed or by the order of a Court.

Guardian ad Litem A Guardian ad Litem is a person appointed in particular proceedings, to represent the interests of an infant or other person who is under a disability, and who is therefore unable, so long as the disability continues, to act in person or to be directly represented as a party to the proceedings.

Guertin laws   Standard valuation and nonforfeiture laws in effect in all states since 1947.

Guest/host statute   Those state laws which in effect reduce the standard of care owed by the driver to guests riding in his or her car as passengers.

Guest law   Specific state legislation restricting a guest that is injured from collecting on grounds of ordinary negligence but requiring proof of willful and wanton negligence.

Guiding principles   It sometimes happens that the coverage afforded by one type of policy overlaps that coverage afforded by another, producing disputes as to which policy covers a given loss. Various underwriting organizations, such as the National Board of Fire Underwriters, the Inland Marine Underwriters Association, and the National Bureau of Casualty Underwriters have drawn up recommended guiding principles covering such situations to minimize disputes so that the insuring public will get the best adjustment possible. These principles are binding only on those companies signing the agreements.

H.C.   Honor contracts. *See* **P.P.I.** and **F.I.A.**

H.C.B.   Hollow Concrete Block

H.D.   Heavy Duty

H.H.F.   Household furniture.

H.H.G.   Household goods.

H.O.   Homeowners Policy

H.O.A.   Homeowner's A policy.

H.O.B.   Homeowner's B policy.

H.O.C.   Homeowner's C policy.

H.O.L.U.A.   Home Office Life Underwriters Association.

HUD   Department of Housing and Urban Development.

Habeas Corpus ad Subjiciendum   A most important prerogative Writ in English Law. It is used as a remedy against illegal confinement, and is addressed or forwarded to any person who has another in custody, commanding him to produce the body.

Hague Rules   Those 1936 internationally agreed upon rules concerning the carriage of goods.

Hail insurance   Contract of insurance covering property against damage caused by hail and hailstorms.

Hangar-keeper's liability insurance policy   Type of business insurance coverage specially designed to protect hangar-keeper's from the liabilities peculiar to that activity.

Hard dollars   Cash money given in exchange for an equity position in a transaction for real property.

Harter Act   Congressional Act limiting responsibility of an owner of a ship for damage or loss due to navigation error if he had a properly equipped and manned seaworthy vessel.

Hazard   A specific situation that introduces, or increases, the probability of occurrence of a loss arising from a peril, or that may influence the extent of a loss.
Comment: Accident, sickness, fire, flood, liability, burglary, explosion or perils. Slippery floors, unsanitary conditions, shingle roofs, congested traffic, unguarded premises, uninspected boilers are hazards.   CIT

Hazard, moral   Hazard arising from personal as distinguished from physical characteristics, e.g., habits, methods of management, financial standing, mental condition, and integrity are some of the moral hazards.

Hazard, peril or risk   The words are used as synonyms, to describe the damage against which the policy indemnifies the insured. Actually, in an insurance sense, they have a distinction.

Hazard, physical   Hazard arising from physical characteristics of animate or inanimate objects.

Head office   The principal office of an insurer, where its chief executives and supervisory departments are located and from which its operations are directed.

Head start fund   An argument used to stress the advantages of buying life insurance for young people. It gives them a head start financially by having a policy that will establish an increasingly larger cash value and will permit him to obtain coverage at a lower rate than if he waited until a more advanced age.

Health certificate   A statement filed with a request for reinstatement of a lapsed policy. It declares that the health of the insured is not impaired as of the date of the statement.

Health Insurance   Insurance against loss by sickness or accidental bodily injury.   CIT

Health insurance benefits   Those benefits in a policy which are payable as a result of disability from covered sicknesses. Health coverage is rarely written separately unless the insured also carries an equal amount of accident insurance with the same company.

Health maintenance organization (HMO)   A facility that offers group health care to individuals on a prearranged basis for services.

Hearsay Evidence   A witness in court is expected to give evidence only as to what the witness himself knows to be a fact because of what he himself witnessed. Generally he is not permitted to give evidence as to what somebody else tells him happened. The objection to the use of hearsay evidence is both because of the fact the person listening to the story may not follow it exactly as the person telling the story intended should be the case but more particularly on the fact that there would be no opportunity to examine under oath the party who originally related the story. There are exceptions e.g. see Res Gestae

Hearth   The floor of a fireplace.

Hedging   A method of shifting risk generally associated with the grain futures market, but the concept is tied to the area of insurance since by the purchase of a hedging futures contract the risk is transferred.

Held in trust   This term covers, and includes within the liability of the policy, property held by a bailee for another (Ex. goods held by a warehouseman for storage). The words should be always followed by the qualification "for which he (or they) is (or are) legally responsible."

Herd insurance   Special type of insurance on animals. Title is self-explanatory.

Hereditaments   Any type of property which may be inheritable, including such things as real and personal property, as well as corporal and incorporal property.

Hiatus   (1) A gap in the chain of title. (2) A gap or space inadvertently left between adjacent parcels of land when attempting to describe land; a faulty description.

Hidden defect   Any encumbrance on a title that is not apparent in the public records; for example, unknown heirs, secret marriages, forged instruments, mental incompetency, or infancy of a grantor.

High-pressure selling   The action of encouraging the buyer to purchase insurance without full consideration of needs for insurance and his ability to continue payments for the insurance.

Highest and best use   The utilization of a property which will produce the highest or maximum net return over the life of the property. The term does not necessarily refer to an intensive development of the site but considers the site in terms of the maximum net return.

Highly protected risk (HPR) A risk so protected with fire extinguishers, sprinkler systems, fences, and the like, that the insurer may write lower-cost policies.

Highrise A multistory building, usually an apartment, necessitating an elevator.

Hired car An automobile whose exclusive use and control has been temporarily given to another for a consideration. This should be distinguished from contract hauling, since in the latter case the owner retains control of the movements of the vehicle and simply agrees to furnish transportation.

Holdback (1) That portion of a loan commitment not funded until some additional requirement such as rental or completion is attained (*see* **Floor loan**). (2) In construction or interim lending, a percentage of the contractor's draw held back to provide additional protection for the interim lender, often an amount equal to the contractor's profit given over when the interim loan is closed (*see* **Retainage**).

Holder In Due Course Where one obtains a check, company debenture or bond or other bill of exchange in a bonafide way and value, that person is said to be Holder In Due Course. He takes such a bill of exchangee free of previous defects in title.

Hold-harmless agreement Liability of one party is assumed by a second party; frequently the second party is an insurance company.

Holdover tenant A tenant who remains in possession of leased property after the expiration of the lease term.

Hold up Robbery.

Holographic will Will written entirely in the handwriting of the person under whose name it appears.

Home loan A mortgage loan secured by a residence for one, two, three or four families.

Home office The place where an insurance company maintains its chief executive and general supervisory departments. The legal headquarters of an insurer in the jurisdiction in which it is domiciled, usually also its head office.

Home service ordinary Insurance policy that has premiums periodically collected according to the **debit** system.

Homeowners association An organization of homeowners residing within a particular development who have banded together to maintain and provide community facilities and services for the common enjoyment of the residents.

Homeowner's policy A form of package policy including fire and allied lines, theft insurance, and comprehensive personal liability. The premium is stated as one amount without specific enumeration for each hazard.

Homestead An artificial estate in land devised by the sovereign federal or state government to protect the possession and enjoyment of the owner against the claims of his creditors by withholding the property from the execution and forced sale so long as the land and building are occupied as a home. From one state to another the protection of the possessions that are considered as part of the homestead vary.

Honesty clause Trade appellation for full reporting clause. It provides a penalty on the insured if he revealed and reported less than required on his policy application. *See* **Full reporting clause.**

Honor contracts Policy proof of interest. Full interest admitted. Known as P.P.I. and F.I.A. *See* **both terms.**

Honorable undertaking Part of a phrase used in reinsurance contracts; the effect of which is to avoid a narrow interpretation of the wording of the contract.

Hoopeston Canning So et. al. vs. Thomas J. Cullen Regulation of foreign reciprocal insurance companies validated.

Hospital benefits Additional benefits in case a disability requires hospital confinement. *See also* **Hospitalization policy.**

Hospital liability insurance Indemnification against claims for damages that may have resulted from bodily injury, shock, mental anguish, or death of a patient resulting from malpractice mistakes or error on the part of the hospital staff.

Hospitalization insurance Various plans of coverage providing indemnity for hospital, nurse, surgical and miscellaneous medical expenses due to bodily injuries or illness. *See* **Blue Cross** and **Blue Shield.**

Hospitalization policy A limited accident and sickness policy. Provides payment in event of hospital expenses only unless plan provides additional coverage.

Hostile fire *See* **Fire.**

House confinement Accident and sickness insurance clause requiring house confinement to be eligible for benefits. House is expanded to include a hospital sanatorium, visit to a hospital or office of a physician, or certain activities made at the direction of his doctor for therapeutic purposes.

Household   A home or residence, a habitation, the place where a person ordinarily sleeps.

Household goods   Clothing, furniture, and other customary contents of a home.

Housekeeping.   The general care, cleanliness, and maintenance of an insured property. Good housekeeping is a primary consideration from the underwriter's and inspectors' points of view, for poor housekeeping is a major cause of fires and accidents.

Housing and Urban Development, Department of (HUD)   Established by the Housing and Urban Development Act of 1965 to supersede the Housing and Home Finance Agency. It is responsible for the implementation and administration of government housing and urban development programs. The broad range of programs includes community planning and development, housing production and mortgage credit (HFA), equal opportunity in housing, research and technology.

Housing authority   An agency set up by either the federal, state, or local government to construct or manage public housing generally for lower income group tenants.

Housing code   Local standards to ensure that maintenance and improvements of housing meet accepted standards for occupancy.

Hull coverage: Aircraft insurance policy   Type of business insurance coverage against loss to an aircraft or its machinery or equipment.

Hull coverage: Marine insurance policy   Type of business insurance coverage against loss to a vessel or its machinery or equipment.

Hull policy   An ocean or river marine or aviation insurance contract covering the ship or plane itself.

Hull syndicates   A combination of ocean marine insurance underwriters who share expenses and insurance on vessels.

Hundred percent location   The location or site in a city which is best adapted to carrying on a given type of business.

Hunter disability tables   Tables that give the rate of disability or the probability of total and permanent disability, the rate of mortality among disabled lives. The table was based upon the experience of several fraternal orders.

Hurricane   A large cyclone with rain, lightning, thunder, and violent windstorm especially common in the tropics and generally originating at sea.

Hypothecate The pledging of real or personal property as security. Thus an action of pledging property such as accounts receivable.

I/A Insurance Auditor

I.A.A. Insurance Accountants Association

I.A.A.H.U. International Association of Accident and Health Underwriters.

I.A.S.A. Insurance Accounting and Statistical Association

I.A.S.S. Insurance Accounting and Statistical Society.

I. & B. Improvements and betterments.

I.B.C. Insurance Bureau of Canada

I.B.N.R. Incurred But Not Reported

I.C.A. International Claim Association.

I.C.C. Interstate Commerce Commission.

I.E.C. Inherent Explosion Clause

I.H.O.U. Institute of Home Office Underwriters.

I.I.A. Insurance Institute of America

I.I.A.G. Interbureau Insurance Advisory Group.

I.I.C. Independent Insurance Conference; Insurance Institute of Canada

I.I.H.S. Insurance Institute for Highway Safety

I.I.I. Insurance Information Institute

I.M. Inland marine.

I.M.I.B. Inland Marine Insurance Bureau.

I.M.U.A. Inland Marine Underwriters Association.

I.P.G. Immediate Participation Guarantee Plan.

I.P.P.P. Industrial Property Policy Program

I.R.B. Insurance Rating Board

I.R.I.C. Inter-Regional Insurance Conference.

I.R.P.M. Individual Risk Premium Modification

Idem (Ad Idem) Both are the same thought.

Identification benefits A rather obsolete term describing a benefit which provided for the payment of specified sums by the insurer so that an insured, disabled while away from his residency (vacation, etc.) could be returned to his friends and/or relatives.

Illegal occupations or trades All insurances are issued subject to the provision that the property covered shall be used for legal purposes — trades or occupations of a legal character. A policy issued on a subject which is illegal is void, and cannot be enforced.

Immediate Annuity An annuity contract which provides for the first payment of the annuity at the end of the first interval of payment after purchase. The interval may be monthly, quarterly, semi-annual or annual.

Immediate life annuity *See* **Annuity, immediate life.**

Immediate participation guarantee plan Also called the pension administration plan or the direct rated deposit administration plan. A pension plan written on large groups with the employer's contribution, establishing a fund which is credited with interest earned by the insurance company and charged with expense of operation. There is no contingency fund or guarantee, and the fund must be adjusted annually to keep it in balance.

Immediate Vesting That form of vesting under which rights to vested benefits are acquired by a participant commencing immediately upon his entry into the plan.   CIT

Immunity is the exception from certain obligations which the law generally requires others to perform.

Impaired capital When liabilities and claims consume an insurance company's surplus the capital is impaired. Suspension of the right to do business normally follows.

Impaired risk A risk that is substandard or under average.

Implication Where certain circumstances suggest that a certain state of affairs exist, then in the absence of any evidence to the contrary and in certain cases, a Court will imply the state of affairs as existing e.g. Implied warranty of fitness.

Implied covenant One which infers by the context of a deed, or related instrument.

Implied warranty Representation, not in writing, that insurable conditions exist.

Import To bring goods from another country into one's own country.

Impound *See* **Escrow payment.**

Improper improvement Improvements which do not conform to the best utilization of the site.

Improvements and betterments Additions or changes made by a lessee at his own expense which enhance the value of a building he occupies. These become part of the realty (and not legally subject to removal) and require special insurance consideration.

Improvements and betterments insurance Protects a renter against suffering loss on the improvements and betterments he has made on his leased property. For example, if one rents a building and installs partitions or makes other improvements to the property, it is desirable to take out a fire insurance policy that protects the interest in those improvements, should fire destroy the building.

Improvements on land Structures, of whatever nature, usually privately rather than publicly owned, erected on a site to enable its utilization; e.g., buildings, fences, driveways, retaining walls, etc.

Improvements to land Usually publicly owned structures such as curbs, sidewalks, street lighting systems, and sewers constructed so as to enable the development of privately owned land for utilization.

Imputation of Negligence Where the law makes a person responsible for the negligence of another although not directly negligent himself but who was at privity with one who was negligent. A parent, for example may at times be held negligent for the acts of his child. A master may be held responsible for the negligence or negligent acts of his servant. A principal may be held responsible for the negligent acts of his agent.

Inadmitted asset Any asset prohibited from being included in regulated assets as reported by the insurance company to the state insurance examiners. These inadmitted assets are presumed to have little value to meet claims in case of liquidation of the insurance company.

In-and-out rates Rates for use in fire insurance on property that is sometimes in and sometimes out of a building. This property is subject to the hazards of a given building only part of the time, so that the rate for the contents of that building would not accurately measure the hazard involved.

In camera The hearing of a Court Case in private, usually in the Judge's chambers, not in open Court. Suits for annulity of marriage are sometimes held in camera, and in certain cases a Judge has power to direct that all persons not being parties to the case, shall be excluded from the Court during taking of evidence of a witness.

Incendiarism The willful and malicious burning of property, sometimes with the intent of defrauding the insurance companies.

Incendiary The malicious burning of property or the individual who starts such a fire. *See* **Arson.**

Inchmaree Clause in ocean marine insurance policies covering perils other than the perils of the sea.

Inchoate Not yet completed. Contracts are inchoate until executed by all the parties who should join in their execution, and a widow's right to dower is inchoate so long as her husband lives.

Incidents of ownership The rights to exercise any of the privileges in the policy; to change beneficiaries, withdraw cash values, make loans on the policy, assign it, etc. These may belong to the cestui que vie or, by assignment or original purchase, to the beneficiary or an assignee who is not the beneficiary. In whom they are vested is important in the application of various tax laws.

Income A stream of benefits generally measured in terms of money as of a certain time; a flow of services. It is the source of value. Loosely, the money a person or company has coming in from any source. Exactly, income is made up of the amount received from both earnings and investments.

Income approach to value The appraisal technique used to estimate real property value by capitalizing net income. *See* **Capitalization.**

Income bonds Promises to pay, usually secured, whose interest is payable only if earned.

Income Policy A life or endowment policy which provides definitely for specified monthly amounts in the payment of proceeds in place of the lump sum.

Income property A property in which the income is derived from commercial rentals or in which the returns attributable to the real estate can be so segregated as to permit direct estimation. The income production may be in several forms; e.g., commercial rents, business profits attributable to real estate other than rents, etc.

Incompetent One who is incapable of managing his affairs because of mental deficiency or undeveloped mentality. Children and idiots are incompetents in the eyes of the law.

Incontestable clause A clause in some accident and sickness and life insurance policies, making the contract incontestable as to any statement made in the application after a period of time such as two years. The application may require a statement of illnesses requiring hospitalization. If this information is not given, the policy may be voided by the company during the contestable period; after that period the insurance company cannot cancel on that ground. *See* **Contestable clause.**

Increase in hazard   Enlargement of a risk by the insured beyond the intent of the insurance company when the original policy was issued. Suspension of liability of the company will result from such material increase in hazard. A manufacturer producing a low risk noninflammable product would increase the hazard if he converted to making paint or explosives.

Increased cost of construction insurance   Property insurance used to cover additional costs resulting from compliance with city ordinances. Covers the cost of more expensive materials, etc. required by these ordinances.

Increment   An increase. Most frequently used to refer to the increase in the value of land that accompanies population growth and increasing wealth in the community. The term unearned increment is used in this connection since values are supposed to increase without effort on the part of the owner.

Incumbrance   Any right to or interest in property which diminishes its value to the owner and yet does not deprive him of the title thereto or use thereof, nor of the power to convey or transfer the same.

Incur   To become liable for a loss or expense.

Incurred-loss ratio   Ratio of losses incurred to earned premiums, expressed as a percentage.

In Curia   In open Court.

Incurred losses   Losses occurring within a fixed period whether adjusted and paid or not.

Indemnify   (1) To restore the victim of a loss, in whole or in part, by payment, repair, or replacement; (2) to afford indemnity. CIT

Indemnity   Restoration of the victim of a loss, in whole or in part, by payment, repair, or replacement.
Comment: To the extent that the obligation of the insurer is to do other than make good losses, the insurance contract is not one of indemnity. The term indemnity or indemnify should not be used to apply to an obligation other than to make good a loss.   CIT

Indemnity bond   A bond which indemnifies the obligee against loss which arises as a result of failure on the part of a principal to perform. Warehouse, lost instrument, freight charge, lien, are examples of indemnity bonds.

Indemnity company   A casualty insurance company.

Indenture A deed to which two or more persons are parties and under which they enter into obligations toward each other. It is an agreement in writing.

Independent adjuster *See* **Adjuster, independent.**

Independent Agency System A distribution system within which independent contractors known as agents sell and service property and liability insurance solely on a commission or fee basis and have agreements with one or more insurers which recognize the agents' ownership, use, and control of policy records and expiration data. The essence of independence is the ownership, use, and control of contract records.

Independent Appraisal Plan Technique adopted to prevent collusion resulting in inflated repair estimates and bills. Appraisers are not employees of repair shops, but are independent experts.

Independent contractor One who agrees to perform certain actions for another and is responsible only for the results but not subject to direction of the party hiring him. One who undertakes to perform certain results for another by his own methods and in his own manner, being responsible only for results and not being subject to the direction of the other party with respect to details of the work. An individual hired to erect a building is typically known as an independent contractor.

Indictment A formal accusation: the legal process in which this is proffered to and presented by the Grand Jury. The document containing the charge. A Bill of indictment is the written accusation as proffered to the Grand Jury.

Indirect damage Loss resulting from a peril, but not caused directly and immediately thereby. Indirect damage may be covered by insurance, as for example; business interruption, leasehold, interest, profits and commissions, rent or rental value, and consequential coverage.

Indirect loss *See* **Consequential loss.**

Individual fidelity bond Fidelity bond on an individual rather than on a group.

Individual Life Insurance (a) That type of life insurance which covers in one contract usually only one insured, but which sometimes covers several insureds, such as the members of a family; (b) the term usually used to distinguish this type of life insurance from group life insurance. CIT tentative

Individual policy pension trust A type of pension plan, frequently used for small groups, administered by trustees who are authorized to purchase individual level premium policies or annuity contracts for each member of the plan. The policies usually provide both life insurance and retirement benefits. A trust created to buy individual life insurance or annuity contracts.

Indorse Used with reference to the transfer of negotiable paper by writing the proper name on the back thereof.

Industrial accident *See* **Accident, industrial.**

Industrial group A group formed for group insurance among the employees of one employer as contrasted to association group.

Industrial insurance Insurance designed primarily for hourly wage workers exposed to some degree of occupational hazard and having difficulty in accumulating an amount of money to pay an annual or semiannual premium. It may be, however sold to any type of individual. It is distinguished by the fact that it is primarily intended to be paid on a weekly basis, although less frequent intervals of payment may be arranged, and the payments collected by an agent who calls at the home or place of work of the insured.

Industrial life insurance Life insurance issued in small amounts, usually not over $1,000. Premiums are payable on a weekly or monthly basis and are generally collected at the home by an agent of the company.

Industrial Park A controlled development designed for specific types of businesses. These developments provide required appurtenances, including public utilities, streets, railroad sidings, auto parking, and water and sewage facilities.

Industrial property In a broad sense, all the tangible and intangible assets pertinent to the conducting of an enterprise for the manufacturing, processing, and assembling of finished products from raw or fabricated materials. Also, in a limited sense, the land, fixed improvements, machinery, and all equipment, fixed or movable, comprising the facilities devoted to such enterprise.

Industrial property form A package policy insuring manufacturers against various losses to personal property and buildings at more than one location.

Inevitable accident An accident which cannot be foreseen and prevented from happening. *See* **Fortuitous event.**

Infant A person under age of twenty-one years or in some states a female under the age of eighteen years. Contracts of insurance made by infants are not enforceable against them, and policy may be repudiated later by the insured. Special state statutes alter the above generalization and provide that certain infants may contract for life insurance. For example, in New York infants not less than fifteen years of age may contract for insurance.

In force Insurance written but not expired or original premiums paid on policies that have not expired.

In Futuro In the future.

Infringement The interference with the right of another.

Inflation factor An adjustment of premiums to allow for increased costs due to inflation.

Inforce business *See* **In force.**

Ingress The act of going in; entrance. Used with **egress** to describe the right of access to land.

Inherent The results of a hazard which is commonly arising from the occupancy of a structure such as the water heater of a residence blowing up or exploding.

Inherent explosion A violent and noisy bursting caused by the normal processing such as to be found in operation of certain type of pressing operations. For example, explosion of a hot water heater in a residence would be an inherent explosion and is covered by the terms of a fire insurance policy.

Inherent hazards insurance policy Type of business insurance coverage protecting against inherent hazards. *See* **Inherent.**

Inherent vice A condition in property which causes deterioration or damage; for example, the painting of damp wood. This clause may be found in such policies as property floater policy. For example, an article of clothing might have some defects because of inferior material or workmanship which might cause it to go to pieces before it is worn out. Such a condition is caused by inherent vice and would not be covered under the terms of a personal property floater policy.

Initial premium Amount charged at the beginning of coverage but subject to change after additional experience or information has been obtained.

Injunction An order of a court of equity prohibiting an act or requiring that an act be carried out.

Injunction Bond Bond that guarantees defendants' ability to pay.

Injuria A legal wrong.

In kind Generally refers to payment of a loss through replacing the damage to a destroyed property with the same type of property, the option generally being with the insuring company. For example, under some policies such as a plate glass policy, the insurance company does not pay the loss in cash but replaces the glass.

Inland marine insurance   Covers property against various risks or losses while it is being transported from place to place or wherever the property may be located. It is not limited to water transportation. It now includes any goods in transit, except transocean, and numerous floaters, as personal effects, personal property, jewelry, furs, etc., the essential condition being that the insured property be movable. Bridges, tunnels, and similar instrumentalities of transportation are also considered to be inland marine.

Inland transit insurance policy   Type of inland marine coverage. *See* **Inland marine.**

In loc cit   In place cited.

In loco parentis   In place of a parent.

Innkeepers' legal liability policy   Insurance contract protecting innkeepers against liability for property of guests.

In-patient   A patient admitted to a hospital as a resident case.

In personum   A right or proceeding directed against a specific person (as in a damage law suit where one person is sued), as distinct from In rem (see below).

Inquest   An inquiry into "when, where and by what means a person died" — conducted by a coroner who is usually a doctor — evidence is sworn, but not usable in civil or criminal court.

In re   This is a brief expression used as the equivalent of "In the matter of."

In rem   An act or right against all other persons as distinct from an action "In personum" e.g. a right of ownership of real property is a right against every other person in the world and is accordingly a right "In rem."

Inside and outside holdup insurance   *See* **Messenger and interior robbery insurance.**

In Situ   In its original situation.

Insolvency clause   The reinsurer is liable under this clause for his share of the loss even though the ceding company (primary insurer) becomes insolvent.

Insolvency Funds   Funds required by state law to insure the payment of claims against insolvent insurers.

Insolvent debtor   An insolvent debtor has an insurable interest in his property until affairs have been wound up by the assignee, and his interest therein ceases.

Inspection   Examination of a risk to be insured to decide on acceptance, rejection, or rate.

Inspection bureau   Organization that investigates risks or establishes rates of risks.

Inspection Report   Filed by an investigator employed by the insurance company or credit agency, giving general information on the health, habits, finances, and reputation of the applicant.

Inspection slip   Written form of reporting on the examination of a risk.

Inspector   Sometimes called a surveyor. Individual who performs examination of risks for purpose of deciding whether to insure it or not.

Installation risk   Policy protecting machinery owner during process of installing his equipment on others property.

Installment payments   Periodic payments to discharge an indebtedness. Sometimes used synonymously with amortization payments.

Installment premium   Premium that is paid in several installments, as distinguished from a single payment.

Installment refund annuity   *See* **Annuity, installment refund.**

Installment sales floater   *See* **Conditional sales floater.**

Installment settlement   A clause in a policy permitting the beneficiary to elect to receive death proceeds in installments over a period of time.

Institutional lender   A financial institution that invests in mortgages and securities and carries them in its own portfolio. Mutual savings banks, life insurance companies, commercial banks, pension and trust funds, and savings and loan associations are examples.

Insulation   A heat-retarding material applied in outside walls, top floor ceiling, or in roof to prevent passage of heat or cold in or out of building.

Insurable interest   Relationship such that loss or destruction of life or property would cause a pecuniary loss. An interest in the life of an individual or in property by which there will be a financial loss if the insured dies or in the case of property if it is lost, damaged, or destroyed. For example, if you sell an automobile to another and are being repaid in instalments you have an insurable interest in the automobile in proportion to the amount of money still unpaid. The purchaser also has an insurable interest.

Insurable Risk   The requisites of an insurable risk are these:
  (1) There must be a large group of homogeneous exposure units;

(2) The loss produced by the risk must be definite;

(3) The occurrence of the loss in the individual cases must be accidental or fortuitous;

(4) The potential loss must be large enough to cause hardship;

(5) The cost of insuring must be economically feasible;

(6) The chance of loss must be calculable;

(7) The risk must be unlikely to produce loss to a great many insured units at the same time.

Insurable Title   A title on which a title insuring company is willing to issue its policy of insurance.

Insurable value   *See* **Actual cash value.**

Insurance   The contractual relationship which exists when one party, for a consideration, agrees to reimburse another for loss caused by designated contingencies. The first party is called the insurer; the second, the insured; the contract, the insurance policy; the consideration, the premium; the property in question, the risk; the contingency in question, the hazard or peril. The term assurance common in England, is ordinarily considered identical to and synonymous with insurance.

Insurance carrier   The insurance company, since it assumes the financial responsibility for the risks of the policyholders.

Insurance charge   That amount, related to retrospective rated risks, that reflects the possibility that losses will exceed the amount estimated by a rating bureau or underwriter but which is now the loss below the limits of the policy.

Insurance commissioner or commissioners   Individual or in some states individuals who enforce their own states' insurance codes. Some states refer to the individual as Superintendent of Insurance. For correct designation see your own state herein.

Insurance company   An organization chartered under state or provincial laws to act as an insurer. In the United States, insurance companies are usually classified as fire and marine, life, casualty, and surety companies and may write only those kinds of insurance policies which are specifically authorized in their charters. Many company charters have now been broadened to include several of these types.

Insurance coverage   The total amount of insurance carried.

Insurance department   The state department which has responsibility for the enforcement of the state insurance code. It is charged with the supervision and licensing of insurance companies and agents and the general administration of insurance laws of the state.

Insurance examiner   A public employee in several of the states whose duty is to make periodical examinations into the conditions of foreign and domestic companies operating there.

Insurance federation   A trade association that lobbies in each state in the field of insurance.

Insurance in force   The total face amount of insurance under contracts in force.

Insurance policy   Broadly, the entire written contract of insurance. More narrowly, the basic written or printed document as distinguished from the form and endorsements added thereto.

Insurance premium   Charge by the insurance company to individual or company for the insurance contract. The premium reimburses the insurance company for the risk they have assumed.

Insurance rate   The ratio of the insurance premium to the total amount of insurance carried thereby. Usually expressed in dollars per $100 or per $1,000; sometimes in percent.

Insurance register   Record of important data about insurance carried such as dates of purchase, amounts of premiums, expiration, and companies.

Insurance risk   A general or relative term denoting the hazard involved in the insuring of property. The premium or cost of insurance is predicated upon the relative risk or hazard considered to be involved.

Insurance Services Office (ISO)   A national rate-making organization in the property and liability area. It promulgates rates for its members.

Insurance superintendent   *See* **Insurance commissioner** or own state.

Insurance to value   The amount of insurance written on other property in question is approximately equal to its value. *See* **Actual cash value.**

Insured   An individual or business organization protected in case of loss of property or life under the terms of the insurance policy. Also called assured, obligee in connection with surety bonds, and called the Employer in some fidelity bonds. When used as a noun, designates the policyholder. It should be noted that when the beneficiary has all the incidents of ownership, he or she is the insured rather than the person on whose life the policy is written. The latter is, technically in all cases, the cestui que vie.

Insured additional A person other than the original named insured, who is protected under an insurance contract.

Insured closing letter A document issued by a title insurance company in connection with a to-be-issued title insurance policy. It protects a mortgagee who is forwarding funds to a title insurance company's agent or approved attorney against an embezzlement of funds or a failure to follow specific closing instructions.

Insured loan A loan insured by FHA or a private mortgage insurance company.

Insured mail The United States Post Office Department will insure third and fourth class mail with an indemnity maximum of $200. The insurance fee depends on the stated value of the product being sent. Should the value be higher than $200, it may be sent registered mail and may be insured up to $1,000. If the value is higher than $1,000, it may be insured with insurance companies that provide that service.

Insured named The insured with whom the insurance contract is made and who is specifically named as such.

Insurer The party to the insurance contract who promises to pay losses or render service.

Insuring agreement That part of an insurance policy or bond which recites the agreement of the insurance company to protect the insured against loss or damage. This agreement is the basis of the insurance contract. *See* **Insuring clause.**

Insuring clause That part of an insurance policy or bond which recites the agreement of the insurer to protect the insured against some form of loss or damage. This is the heart of the contract of insurance.

Insuror A member of the National Association of Insurance Agents.

Insurrection insurance policy Specialized type of insurance protection against loss caused by insurrection or revolution.

Intangible property The elements of property in an enterprise that are represented in the establishment doing business, good will, and other rights incident to the enterprise. Distinguished from the physical items comprising the plant facilities and working capital.

Intangible tax A tax levied on certain intangibles such as mortgages, stocks, and bonds.

Intentional injury An injury resulting from an act, the doer of which intended to inflict injury. Self-inflicted injuries are not covered by an accident policy because they are not an accident. In general, intentional injuries inflicted upon the insured by someone else are covered unless expressly excluded.

Inter alia   Among other things.

Inter vivos   During life — between living persons.

Inter-vivos trust   A trust between people who are living, as compared with a testamentary trust. See for comparison testamentary trust.

Interest   The sum paid for the use of money; a participation. Also, a property in land or chattels used in conjunction with the terms, right estate, and title.

Interest accrued   Interest on Bonds, Debentures, Mortages, etc. which is earned but is not yet payable.

Interest adjusted cost   A particular means of determining the cost of life insurance. This method takes into account the interest that might have been earned on premium payments if these funds had been invested rather than put into premiums.

Interest-adjusted method   The technique of expressing the cost of insurance by utilizing the time value of the money paid for premiums.

Interest and dividends due   Interest on Bonds, Debentures, Mortgages, etc. and Dividends on Stocks due and payable but for which payment has not been received.

Interest factor   The decimal equivalent for an interest rate on a unit amount for a period of time. Computed by interest rate divided by basic year, multiplied by days accrued.

Interest policy   Policy that permits a person who is not an absolute owner of property but has an insurable interest to become insured.

Interest rate   The percentage of the principal sum charged for its use.

Interim binder   *See* **Binder.**

Interim financing   Financing during the time from project commencement to closing of a permanent loan, usually in the form of a construction loan and/or development loan.

Interim receipt   An interim receipt — or as it is sometimes called a "cover note" is a preliminary contract of insurance which is furnished to a proposer or applicant pending the approval and issue of the contract. It is generally good for thirty days and cannot be renewed. If the preliminary period is to be extended a new interim receipt should be prepared. It has been held that an interim receipt extended over the period for which is was issued is demonstrative of the company's acceptance to the risk, and remains in force for the full term of the insurance applied for.

Interinsurance   *See* **Reciprocal insurance.**

Interinsurance exchange   A voluntary unincorporated association organized to write insurance for its members. All policyholders are both insurers and policyholders, and may be assessed for additional sums if needed to pay losses. *See* **Reciprocal exchange.**

Intermediary   A broker of reinsurance.

Intermediate   When used as an adjective, in reference to a policy or line of policies, it designates those combining some features of ordinary policies and some of industrial; usually policies written for amounts from $500 to $1,000 and collected monthly by the agent. The definition varies somewhat from company to company.

Intermediate disability   *See* **Partial disability.**

Intermediate notice   A report required by many policies to be furnished after preliminary notice of loss and before final proof to inform the company regarding the progress of a continuing of disability. Sometimes also called second preliminary notice.

Intermediate Policy   Usually means a contract combining certain characteristics of the weekly premium policy and the ordinary contract. It is usually written for $500 or for additional amounts in multiples of $100. Premiums are collected at the homes of the policyholders. The rates are slightly lower than on weekly premium policies, the latter usually being written for smaller amounts. Usually sold by industrial agents.

Interpleader   This is a process of law whereby a person in possession of property claimed by two other persons can protect himself by handing over the property to the court and allowing the court to decide the rightful owner of it, e.g. "A" has some property in his possession but both "B" and "C" are making claim for that property. "A" can start action of interpleader making "B" and "C" as parties defendant. "A" then pays the money or delivers the property into court and withdraws from the case letting "B" and "C" dispute the action and determine the rightful owner of the property.

Internal Revenue bonds   Bonds required by the United States Government, which guarantees payment of federal taxes and compliance with government regulations.

International carrier   A company that carries goods and/or individuals between countries for fees.

Interstate carrier   A common carrier doing business across state boundaries.

Interstate commerce   Commerce between two or more states. Insurance is legally considered to be interstate commerce.

Intestate   One who dies leaving no will.

Intimidation   A contract procured by intimidation or force is void. , The use of undue pressure or force to obtain what may appear to be consent.

Intoxicants   Beverages and other substances that cause drunkenness and intoxication. Accident and sickness insurance denies liability for claims resulting from their use unless administered upon the advice of a medical doctor.

Intrastate carrier   A common carrier whose business is confined entirely within the boundaries of a state. An insurance company whose business is confined entirely within the boundaries of one state. The context should be clear as to which is referred to.

Intrastate commerce   Commerce conducted solely within a state's geographic borders.

Intra vires   Within the power of.

In Tuto   In the whole.

Invalidity   *See* **Sickness.**

Inventory   A listing or tabulation of the separate items comprising an assembled property.

Investment   The productive employment of capital under conditions that provide reasonable assurance of both income and the repayment of the principal.

Investment income   The amount earned by the investment portfolio of the insurance company.

Investment property   The property which is within itself a business enterprise consisting of all tangible and intangible assets considered as integral with the property, assembled and developed as a single unit of utility for lease or rental, in whole or in part to others for profit.

Investment reserve   A special sector of capital funds set aside to act as a buffer account as respects fluctuations in the market value of securities in the company's portfolio.

Invitee   In law this is a person who is expressly or impliedly invited on to the premises for some purpose involving economic or potential economic benefit to the occupier of the premises e.g. a customer entering a store for the purpose of making a purchase.

An invitee, using reasonable care on his own part for his own safety, is entitled to expect that the occupier shall on his part use reasonable care to prevent damage from any unusual danger which he knows or ought to know exists. It is the duty of an occupier to see the premises are reasonably safe for an invitee.

See also Licensee and Trespasser.

Involuntary lien   A lien imposed against property without consent of its owner. Examples include taxes, special assessments, federal income tax liens, judgment liens, mechanics liens, and materials liens.

I.O.U.   A memo acknowledging a debt: consisting of the name of a creditor the three letters "I.O.U.", the amount of the debt, the date, and the signature of the debtor. It is simply an acknowledgment of a debt, and does not require to be stamped; but if the words "which I promise to pay" be added, it becomes a Promissory Note and stamping is required.

Ipso facto   By the mere fact.

Iron safe clause   Part of some fire insurance policies requiring the policyholder to keep his major records and books in an iron safe when not in business use.

Irregular Premium   The fractional or proportionate premium paid to change the regular premium due date from one month or season of the year to another.

Irrevocable beneficiary   The stated beneficiary of a policy that cannot be changed without the permission of the beneficiary or by his death.

Irrevocable trust   A trust that cannot be altered by the person that created the trust.

Irrigation district   Quasi-political districts created under special state laws to provide water services to property owners in a district. Districts have the power to tax, borrow, and condemn.

Issue department   The department of the secretary, registrar, or the manager of selection or other title. This department prepares policies and keeps records of them.

Issued business   Those applications that have as a result of being signed by the applicant, the applicant having been medically examined, and the premium having been paid, have had policies made out by the insurance company but the policies have not been delivered to the applicant as yet. See distinction between delivered, examined, paid, placed, issued, and written business.

Jeopardy Peril, danger.

Jeopardy assessment bond Bond to stay jeopardy assessment pending appeal; Form 1129. A bond required to guarantee payment of federal income taxes which are due or are claimed to be due. Form 1129 is the Treasury Department form.

Jettison The throwing overboard of part of the cargo of a ship to save it. The loss sustained by the owner of the cargo thrown overboard is generally averaged, that is, the owner of the ship and the owners of the rest of the cargo proportionately reimburse the loss.

Jeweler's block insurance Inland marine insurance coverage on most losses to jeweler's merchandise. Subject to certain exceptions, insurance of a jeweler's stock against all risks of loss; also covers to some extent property of others entrusted to the insured.

Jewelry floater Insurance on specific listed jewelry where ever it is.

Joint and several note A note signed by two or more persons, each of whom is liable for the full amount of the debt.

Joint-and-survivor annuity An annuity that provides income to be paid periodically during the lifetime of the two individuals; upon the death of one, the typical amount payable decreases.

Joint and survivorship option Policy option that permits having the cash proceeds of an insurance contract being distributed only after the death of the final survivor of those listed in the policy. Frequently used as a retirement income in cases of man and wife.

Joint annuity Incorrect designation for joint and survivor annuity. *See* that definition.

Joint Committee of Interpretation and Complaint Group of interested individuals and state and insurance department representatives formed to interpret the standard definition of marine insurance.

Joint control bond A bond required before the assets of an estate are transferred to the custody of the principal.

Joint liability   Liability for which more than one person or company share responsibility.

Joint Life and Survivorship Annuity   An annuity contract covering two or more lives and continuing in force as long as any one of them survives.

Joint Life Annuity   An annuity contract covering the lives of two or more persons and terminating at the first death among the lives covered.

Joint life insurance   Insurance on two or more persons, the benefits of which are payable on the first death.

Joint ownership   Ownership in which two or more individuals are coowners. The property passes to the survivor if one of them dies. The property in this form of ownership does not enter into a decedent's estate for probate purposes.

Joint schedule policies   Automobile liability insurance used by insureds with many employees. It insures the employee and the employer. The schedule refers to a list of names of those insured.

Joint tenancy   An estate shared equally by two or more parties with the survivor obtaining complete possession.

Joint Tortfeasor   A tortfeasor is Norman-French for a wrong doer. If one has acted with another in committing a wrong he is known as a joint tortfeasor.

Joint venture   An association between two or more parties to own and/or develop real estate. It may take a variety of legal forms such as partnership, tenancy in common, or a corporation. It is formed for a specific purpose and duration.

Judgment   The conclusion of the law, delivered by a court of justice or other competent tribunal. Also means an adjudication for the payment of money.

Judgment creditor   The person in whose favor a judgment was given.

Judgment debtor   A party who has been ordered by a Court of Law to pay a sum of money to another person.

Judgment lien   A lien upon the property of a debtor resulting from a court decree.

Judgment rates   Rates established by the judgment of the underwriter without application of a formal set of rules or schedule.

Judicial bonds   *See* **Court bond.**

Judicial foreclosure   A type of foreclosure proceeding used in some states, handled as a civil lawsuit and conducted entirely under auspices of a court.

Jumbo line   A much larger risk than normally accepted by the underwriter. May be reinsured.

Jumbo risk   An exceptionally large policy or risk.

Jumping juvenile   Popular trade designation for a junior estate builder or other similar type of policy. *See* **Junior estate builder.**

Junior accumulator   One of several trade designations for jumping juvenile, junior estate builder, and like policies.

Junior estate builder   One of several trade designations for a juvenile policy that is sold in units of $1,000 protection to juveniles. When the child reaches a mature age, frequently 21, the insurance automatically is increased and does not require either additional premium or new medical examination.

Junior interest   A mortgage participation junior to another participation. A legal right that is subordinate to another interest.

Junior lien   A lien placed upon a property that has a senior lien made and recorded. The rights are enforceable only after the previous liens have been satisfied.

Junior mortgage   A lien that is subsequent to the claims of the holders of a prior (senior) mortgage. *See* **Subordinate**.

Jurat   That part of an affidavit in which the officer certifies that the same was sworn to before him.

Jurisdiction   The power to hear and determine causes.

Jurisprudence   Common law being based partly on decisions made in previous cases and quotations from these earlier cases support the decision that should be reached in any particular case presently before the Court. These previous cases which are all cases previously decided, are known as Jurisprudence.

Jury   A body of persons impanelled in a Court or put under oath and are charged with the responsibility of making decisions of facts relating to the case. They have no responsibility with respect to the law of the case. That aspect of the case is decided by the presiding Judge.

Justice of the peace bond   Bond issued to judicial officers of inferior rank who hold courts not of record and are limited in civil and criminal jurisdiction. The bond covers the faithful performance of the ministerial functions and not his judicial functions.

Juvenile insurance   Policies on lives of children below the regular adult minimum as indicated by each state's insurance code. It is insurance on the life of a child, applied for by and issued to a person liable for the child's support.

K.O.   Keep off—do not insure this.

Kenny Ratio   According to this rule of thumb proposed by Roger Kenny, property-liability insurers should not write premiums equal to more than twice the capital and surplus of the firm.

Keogh Act Plan   Established under the Self-Employed Individuals Tax Retirement Act which allows a self-employed person to establish and develop a formal retirement plan for himself. Certain tax advantages are obtained as a result. The provisions are similar to those found in qualified corporate pension plans.

Keyman insurance   Protection of a business firm against the financial loss caused by the death of or disablement of a vital member of a firm. A means of protecting a business from the adverse results of the loss of individuals possessing special managerial skill or experience.

Kicker   A term describing any benefit to a lender above ordinary interest payments. It may be an equity in a property or a participation in the income stream.

Kidnaping coverage   Insurance against the hazard of a person being seized outside the insured premises and forced to return and open the premises or a safe therein, or to give information which will enable the criminals to do so.

Kin or Kindred   Relationship by blood.

King's evidence   Evidence for the Crown, given by an accomplice in crime, who accuses another or others of the same offence, and is properly known as giving king's evidence.

Kinne rule   A formula for adjusters' use in nonconcurrent policy loss apportioning.

Kit   A portfolio or traveling case that has been equipped with manuals, forms, applications, and various other sales aids such as advertising, charts, diagrams, estate plans, and other related material so that an insurance agent may make a more efficient sales presentation.

Kiting   Technique of drawing checks against deposits that have to clear through the banking system. Kiting takes advantage of the time needed for checks to clear and permits the kiter to use funds that are not his.

Kurtosis   Actuarial term to indicate the degree of concentration about the central value of a distribution.

L   Life.

L.C.L.   Less-than-Carload Lot

L.E.A.   Loss Executives Association

L.I.A.A.   Life Insurance Association of America.

L.I.F.O.   Last In, First Out

L. & M.   Labor and material bond.

Li   Liability.

L.I.A.M.A.   Life Insurance Agency Management Association.

L.I.M.R.F.   Life Insurance Medical Research Fund.

L.O.M.A.   Life Office Management Association.

L.T.D.   Long Term Disability

L.U.T.C.   Life Underwriter Training Council.

Label   *See* **Underwriter's Laboratories.**

Laches   A defendant in a law suit may plead laches as his defense if he can prove that he has suffered from the fact that the plaintiff delayed in bringing suit.

Land   In a legal sense, the solid part of the surface of the earth as distinguished from water; any ground, soil, or earth whatsoever, regarded as the subject of ownership, and everything annexed to it, whether by nature; e.g., trees, and everything in or on the earth, such as minerals and running water, or annexed to it by man, as buildings, fences, etc. In an economic sense, land consists of all those elements in the wealth of a nation which are supposed to be furnished by nature, as distinguished from those improvements which owe their value to the labor and organizing power of man.

Land acquisition loan   A loan that provides the mortgagor with funds to acquire land.

Land contract   A legal instrument to deliver a deed to the property given to the purchaser of the real estate, who customarily pays a small portion of the purchase price when the contract is signed and agrees to pay additional sums at specified intervals and in specified amounts until the total purchase price is paid. Since the possession of the land, that is, the ownership, does not become final until the whole payments have been made; this serves as a means of financing some properties in certain states.

Land improvements   Physical changes in or construction of, a more or less permanent nature attached to or appurtenant to land, of such character as to increase its utility and/or value.

Land planner   A person or firm that seeks to determine appropriate land use.

Land speculation   The purchase of unimproved land for investment purposes with expectations of rapid value increases.

Land trust certificate An instrument which grants participation in benefits of the ownership of real estate, while the title remains in a trustee.

Landlord Owner or lessor of real property.

Landlord's liability insurance policy Type of business insurance coverage. Self-explanatory.

Landlord's protective liability Contract of insurance covering liability for accidents on owned property leased to others.

Landmark In land surveys, any conspicuous object that helps establish land boundaries.

Lapping Theft from one customer being covered by theft from another, generally by means of false entries in books of accounts.

Lapse The expiration or forfeiture of an insurance policy by nonpayment of the due premium. Default in premiums before a policy has a nonforfeiture value. Loosely used to indicate any termination because of premium default.

Lapse ratio The ratio for a company or agent of the number of insurance policies lapsed without value or surrendered for cash during a year to those in force at the beginning of the year.

Lapsed policy A policy terminated because of nonpayment of premiums. For accounting purposes, the term is sometimes limited to a termination occurring before the policy has a cash or other value. Technically, discontinuance of a contract by the insured by nonpayment of premium before the policy has a cash value or other nonforfeiture value; popularly, loss or reduction of rights by nonpayment of premium at any time.

Larceny Generally, the unlawful taking of the personal property of another without his consent or against his will and with intent to deprive him of ownership or use thereof. This offense is defined by statute in practically all states and provinces and these statutory definitions differ somewhat.

Larceny insurance policy Type of business insurance coverage. Self-explanatory.

Last Clear Chance In the law of negligence an accident frequently is the result of the negligence of someone who has started a chain of events resulting ultimateley in the injury or damage. If the chain of events are unbroken then a person who started the events would probably be responsible for the ultimate result. However where there is a clear break, usually in a matter of time thus giving someone in the chain of events an opportunity by the use of reasonable care to have avoided the loss then that person may be held liable by the "Last clear chance" rule. (He did not use that last clear chance to avoid the result).

Last Survivor   An annuity payable as long as any one of the two or more individuals remain alive. Also called "Joint and Survivor Annuity."

Last survivor annuity   *See* **Annuity, joint and survivor.**

Last survivor insurance   Life insurance on two or more persons, the benefits of which are payable on the death of the last survivor.

Late charge   An additional charge a borrower is required to pay as penalty for late payment of a regular installment.

Latent defect   Blemishes not immediately discernible.

Laundry insurance policy   Type of business insurance coverage. Self-explanatory.

Law of large numbers   Theory of probability that is the basis of insurance. The larger number of risks or exposure, the more closely will the actual results obtained approach the probable results expected from an infinite number of exposures.

Lay days   The stated period of time a charted vessel without any penalty may stay in a port for purposes of loading and unloading.

Lay underwriter   Home office representative that evaluates a risk or risks based upon known probability and statistics as well as evaluation of the human element. He is not a medical doctor but will generally have a thorough knowledge of medical risks.

Lay-up refund   Return of part of premium because a ship is laid up and thus not subject to ocean perils.

Lay-up warranty   Guarantee by policyholder that the insured ship will be laid up and not used for certain periods. Since the vessel is not subject to ocean perils for these periods the premiums charged can be lower.

Leading Questions   Questions which suggest to a witness as to the answers he should give e.g. "You did stop at the Stop Street didn't you?" Such questions are not generally allowed in examination in chief (examination by the person's own lawyer) although there are a few exceptions. Such questions are however permissible in cross-examination by the lawyer for the other side.

Leakage insurance policy   Type of business insurance coverage. Self-explanatory.

Lease A contract between an owner of real estate and the tenant which states the considerations and conditions upon which the tenant may occupy and use the property, as well as the responsibilities of both owner and tenant. If for a period of over a year, to be legally enforceable, the lease must be in writing.

Leased fee A property held in fee with the right of use and occupancy conveyed under lease to others. A property consisting of the right to receive ground rentals over a period of time, and the further right of ultimate repossession.

Leasehold A property held under tenure of lease. A property consisting of the right of use and occupancy of real property by virtue of lease agreement.

Leasehold insurance Protects against the loss sustained through the termination of a lease by hazards specifically insured against such as, for example, fire. For example, you might lease a building for ten years for an annual rental of $1,000 a year and re-rent it to another for $2,000 a year. If a fire destroys the property at the end of the third year, leasehold insurance would repay you the $7,000 (seven years at $1,000 a year) which you would otherwise lose as a result of the fire.

Leasehold interest The interest that is developed when a lease is either higher or lower than the prevailing rentals for coverable property.

Leasehold mortgage A loan to a lessee secured by a leasehold interest in a property.

Ledger Cost The true net cost of a life insurance policy over a period of years. The dividends, if any, are subtracted from the gross premiums; from this figure, the cash surrender value is subtracted; the remainder is the ledger cost for the given period.

Legacy A legacy may be either general, residuary, or specific. A general legacy is paid from the general funds and property of the testator. A residuary legacy is the amount left after the general and specific legacies have been paid. A specific legacy is gift by will of specified property or money.

Legal description A statement containing a designation by which land is identified according to a system set up by law or approved by law.

Legal liability An obligation enforceable by law most often considered in a monetary sense. Broadly, any legally enforceable obligation. The term is most commonly used in a pecuniary sense. For example, if you own an automobile you may have a legal liability, or liability under the law, to reimburse anyone who may be injured through your negligence in the operation of that automobile.

Legal liability insurance policy Type of business insurance coverage which protects the insured against injury or damage claims from other parties.

Legal lists A term describing investments that life insurance companies, mutual savings banks, or other regulated investors may make under a state charter or court order.

Legal reserve The minimum reserve which a company must keep to meet future claims and obligations as they are calculated under the state insurance code. When used as an adjective, as in "legal-reserve company" it denotes a company whose reserves are calculated on this basis, in contrast to an assessment company or one writing a policy contract permitting the assessment of an additional amount of premiums. The legal reserves are a bookkeeping liability calculated by actuaries, but are offset by admitted assets.

Legal reserve life insurance company A life insurance company operating under insurance laws specifying the minimum basis for the reserves the company must maintain on its policies.

Lenders' bond *See* **Bond, completion.**

Lessee One who possesses the right to use or occupy a property under a lease; the tenant.

Lessee's interest A leasehold estate.

Lessor One who holds title to and conveys the right to use and occupy a property under lease agreement.

Let To lease, demise or convey; thus a sign "to let."

Letter of credit A letter authorizing a person or company to draw on a bank or stating that the bank will honor their credit up to a stated amount.

Level payment mortgage A mortgage that provides for a constant, fixed payment at periodic intervals during its term. Part of each payment is credited to interest, with the balance of the payment used to reduce the principal.

Level premium insurance Insurance for which the cost is distributed evenly over the period during which premiums are paid. The premium remains the same from year to year, and is more than the actual cost of protection in the earlier years of the policy and less than the actual cost in the later years. The excess paid in the early years builds up the reserve.

Level Term Insurance Term insurance on which the face value remains the same from the date the policy comes into force to the date the policy expires.

Leverage The use of borrowed money to increase one's return on cash investment. For leverage to be profitable, the rate of return on the investment must be higher than the cost of the money borrowed (interest plus amortization).

Levy A levy is a seizure of property by an officer of the law for debt. Levies apply to personal property only.

Lex fori The law of the Court in which the case is tried.

Liability The condition of being bound in law and justice to do something which may be enforced in the courts. An obligation, usually financial. The probable cost of meeting an obligation.

Liability, assumed *See* **Liability, contractual.**

Liability, contingent Liability for damages arising out of the acts or ommissions of others, not employees nor agents.

Liability, contractual An obligation assumed by contract to pay damages for which another is legally liable. *See also* **Hold harmless agreement.**

Liability, legal An obligation enforceable at law.

Liability insurance Refers to the form of coverage whereby the insured is protected against injury or damage claims from other parties. Any form of coverage whereby the insured is protected against claims of other parties from specified causes. Most liability insurance is written by casualty companies, but some forms, especially those referring to property in the care of the insured, are underwritten in connection with fire or marine business. The insured's liability for damages under such claims may arise from his negligence or through the operation of law or a contract. Credit insurance refers to the effort of the debtor to assure the payment of his loan from risks of death and accident and in this way to insure his liabilities. *See* for contrast **Assets insurance.**

Liability insurance, bodily injury Insurance against loss due to claims for damages because of bodily injury (including death) to persons not employees.

Liability insurance, comprehensive general Insurance against loss due to all claims against the insured for damages arising from his business premises or operations (except those arising from motor vehicles away from the premises, and other stated exclusions).

Liability insurance, comprehensive personal Insurance against loss due to all claims for damages arising from personal, nonbusiness premises or conduct (except those arising from automobiles away from premises, and other stated exclusions).

Liability insurance, contractual   Insurance against loss under a contractual liability agreement.

Liability insurance, elevator   Insurance against loss due to claims for damages arising out of the ownership, maintenance, or use of elevators or other hoisting devices.

Liability insurance, employers'   Insurance against loss to claims for damages by employees for bodily injuries (including death); excludes liability under workmen's compensation laws.

Liability insurance, owners', landlords' and tenants'   Insurance against loss due to claims for damages against owners, landlords, or tenants arising out of ownership, maintenance, or use of specified premises.

Liability insurance, physicians' and surgeons'   Insurance against loss due to claims for damages alleging malpractice by physicians or surgeons in the exercise of their professions.

Liability insurance, products   Insurance against loss due to claims against the insured for damages arising from handling, use of, or any condition in products manufactured, sold, handled, or distributed by the insured, the accident or occurence on which claims are based taking place away from the premises of the insured.

Liability insurance, property damage   Insurance against loss due to claims for damages because of injury to others' property.

Liability insurance, protective   Insurance against loss due to claims for damages because of injury to others' property.

Liability insurance, public   *See* **Liability insurance, bodily injury.**

Liability limits   The sum or sums beyond which a liability insurance company does not protect the insured on a particular policy. The majority of policies covering liability for bodily injury have two limits, a limit of liability to any one person, and, subject to ths personal limit, another and usually higher limit for any single accident, where more than one person is involved. Coverage for property damage is written with a limit per accident, but certain forms, such as malpractice, product and manufacturer's and contractor's liability, there is also an aggregate limit of liability, for the total amount of all claims during the policy period. Basic limits of liability are the lowest limits which are ordinarily written and are the limits contemplated by manual rates and minimum premiums.

Liability Other Than Automobile A form of coverage that pertains, for the most part, to claims arising out of the insured's liability for injuries caused by ownership of property, manufacturing operations, contracting operations, sale or distribution of products, and the operation of elevators and the like, as well as professional services.

Libel A legal action directed against a vessel as well as publication of defamatory information.

Libel insurance Insurance coverage for publishers and other disseminators of information against claims of alleged defamation, slander, and libel.

Licence Permission to do something which would otherwise be improper or wrongful, e.g. A person may grant a licence to use certain parts of land or the Crown may grant a licence to drive a car or operate a business where to do so without such licence would be prohibited. British usage. In U. S. A. "license" is preferred.

License, Agents Certification, issued by state department of insurance, that an individual is qualified to solicit insurance applications for the period covered. Usually issued for period of one year, renewable on application without necessity of the individual's periodic repetition of the original qualifying requirements. Each agent should study carefully the licensing laws and regulations of his own state.

License and permit bonds Bonds required by various municipalities or public authorities to indemnify them against loss in the event of violation of regulations or ordinance under which the permit is required.

Licensee One who is allowed to go on premises of another for his own interest, e.g. a man taking a short cut across a corner service station to shorten his trip home. An occupier's liability to a licensee is that the occupier is required to use ordinary care but the licensee takes the property as he finds it.

Lien A hold or claim which one person has upon the property of another as a security for some debt or charge.

Lien plan Used for substandard risk life insurance policies as a marketing aid. A regular policy was issued at standard rates with a lien against it to compensate for the higher risk. Its use in the U.S. today is minimal and it is illegal in some states.

However, it is extensively used in Great Britain and Canada.

Life annuity A contract that provides an income for life, payable annually or more frequently.

Life annuity with ten years certain An annuity clause that provides payments throughout the life of the annuitant but for no less than ten years.

Life conservation The medical research and programs which have as their objective the preserving of human life. Health legislation, pure food and drug laws, and medical examinations are aids in life conservation.

Life estate A freehold interest in land, the duration of which is confined to the life of one or more persons or contingent upon certain happenings.

Life expectancy The average number of years of life remaining for persons at any given age, according to the particular mortality table in use.

Life Expectancy Term Insurance A special policy type, issued at each individual age for that age's "expectation of life" at the required premium. As an example, with a standard life expectancy at age 24 of 43 additional years, this would simply be "Term to Age 67," with the insurance expiring if the insured lives beyond age 67.

Life insurance Insurance providing for payment of a specified amount on the insured's death either to his estate or to a designated beneficiary.

Life insurance, industrial *See* **Industrial insurance.**

Life insurance, legal reserve Life insurance for which the law requires certain minimum reserves.

Life insurance, limited payment Whole-life insurance for which premiums are payable for a stated number of years or until the prior death of the insured.

Life insurance, ordinary Whole-life insurance written under a a contract providing for periodic payment of premiums as long as the insured lives. Life insurance (other than group) usually in amounts of $1,000 or more with premiums paid monthly or at longer intervals.

Life insurance policy reserve The financial liability for future benefits payable under the policy that approximates the cash value of the policy.

Life insurance programming The integration of the proceeds of a life insurance program with other assets of an estate so that certain financial objectives are achieved.

Life insurance, straight *See* **Life insurance, ordinary.**

Life insurance, term Life insurance providing for payment of benefits if the insured dies within a specified period, usually of one or more years.

Life Insurance Trust Life insurance companies usually cannot act as trustees or guardians, nor exercise discretion in making payments to beneficiaries. In some cases it is advisable to have the policy proceeds paid to a trust company and distributed under the terms of a trust agreement, thereby permitting greater flexibility in the distribution of the proceeds. The trustee is given not only control over the policy and proceeds but also securities or other property to provide funds out of which to pay the premiums.

Life insurance, whole-life Life insurance providing for payments of benefits whenever the insured dies.

Life Paid-Up At Age A form of limited-payment whole life insurance that requires that all the premiums for the policy be paid by the time the insured reaches a certain age. See Whole Life Insurance.

Life table A tabulated statement presenting mortality and survivor characteristics of a given population.

Life Underwriter The title frequently given to the agent who acts in behalf of a life insurance company and to the broker who is appointed by a life insurance company to represent it on behalf of the insured. A life underwriter should be not only a salesman but also a properly qualified life insurance adviser.

Lifetime policy (a) A policy which pays disability benefits for life or (b) A policy which is guaranteed to be renewable or noncancellable to age 65 or above.

Lightning The policy conditions make the company liable for all losses caused by lightning, even when no fire occurs. Most policies, however, carry the electrical apparatus clause, which excludes loss caused by lightning to electrical equipment.

Lightning clause A clause covering direct damage caused by lightning.

Limit, aggregate The maximum amount of damages that the insurer will pay under a contract or section of insurance policy during the contract period.

Limitation of Action See Prescription.

Limit, basic The limit of liability for which the basic rate on a liability insurance contract is quoted. Generally, in bodily injury liability insurance, $5,000 in respect of one person, and $10,000 in respect of one accident or occurrence, in property damage liability insurance, $1,000 (in automobile insurance $5,000) in respect of one accident or occurrence.

Limit, excess   A limit higher than the basic limit.

Limit, standard   *See* **Limit, basic.**

Limit of liability   The maximum amount which an insurance company agrees to pay in the case of loss. (*See* **Liability limits**).

Limitations   Exceptions or reductions to the general coverage.

Limited common area   **Common area** assigned to a specific owner for personal private use.

Limited partnership   A partnership that consists of one or more general partners who are fully liable and one or more limited partners who are liable only for the amount of their investment.

Limited payment life insurance   A plan of insurance for the whole of life on which the premiums are payable for a specified number of years, or until death if death occurs before the end of the specified period.

Limited policy   A policy providing insurance against specified types of accidents or restricted in indemnity payments as contrasted with full coverage policies.

Limits   The sum or sums beyond which a liability insurance company does not protect the insured on a particular policy.

The majority of policies covering liability for bodily injury have two limits, a limit of liability to any one person, and, subject to the personal limit, another and usually higher limit for any single accident, where more than one person is involved.

Coverage for protection against damages is written with a limit per accident, but in certain forms such as malpractice, product and manufacturer's, and contractor's liability, there is also an aggregate limit of liability, for the total amount of all claims during the policy period.

Basic limits of liablity are the lowest limits which are ordinarily written and are the limits contemplated by manual rates and minimum premiums.

Lincoln National Life vs. Commissioner of Insurance—Oklahoma
U. S. Supreme Court decision of tax of foreign insurance company at a differential rate from domestic insurance companies.

Line   Has several colloquial meanings. Type of insurance such as *fidelity line.* Company writing the policy. Amount of insurance. The meaning must be obtained by the contexts.

Line card   A record of insurance sold to one client.

Line fence   A common expression for a fence placed on a boundary line.

Line of business   The general classification of business as utilized in the insurance industry, i.e., fire, allied lines, homeowners, etc.

Line of credit   An agreement by a commercial bank or other financial institution to extend credit up to a certain amount for a certain time to a specific borrower.

Line sheet   A guide prepared by an insurance company for its underwriters, setting forth the amount of liability it is willing to assume on the various classes of risks.

Liquidity   The ability of an individual or business to quickly convert assets into cash without incurring a considerable loss.

Liquor license bond   Insurance required by a regulatory body for those having liquor licenses.

Lis pendens   Literally, a suit pending.

Listing   The record of a property for sale or lease by a broker who has been authorized in writing by the owner to act as his agent.

Litigation   The act of carrying on a lawsuit.

Littoral   The zone comprised between high and low water marks. Sometimes also referring to a coastal region or the seashore.

Livery insurance   An automobile insurance that covers drivers and/or owners who carry hired passengers.

Livestock cattle insurance   Indemnification against the accidental death of covered cattle.

Livestock insurance policy   Type of insurance coverage protecting against loss due to death of live stock.

Livestock transit insurance   Coverage on accidents from movement by rail or truck for livestock.

Lloyd's Association   A group of individual underwriters who make contributions to a common fund. The individual contributors are liable for the amount of the risk placed after their respective names in the policy in proportion to their contribution. Any individual underwriter is not liable for the others' assumed risk or loss.

Lloyds Broker   A broker that can deal with Lloyd's of London underwriters.

Lloyd's of London   A corporation that maintains facilities for the insurance business of underwriting and broker members, regulates membership and collects and disseminates information. Located in London.

Lloyd's Register   A list of ships and their descriptions maintained by Lloyd's of London.

Lloyd's Register of American Yachts   A list of American yachts and their descriptions maintained by Lloyd's of London.

Lloyd's Syndicate   Combination of underwriters at Lloyd's of London that operates as a unit.

Lloyd's underwriter   A member of Lloyd's of London who underwrites insurance at Lloyd's.

Loading   An amount added to the basic rate or premium to cover the expense to the insurance company in securing and maintaining the business. This term is also used in   connection with inland marine insurance, as the amount added to the fire rate to cover additional perils. The amounts or percentages added to the pure (or in life insurance, net) premium to provide for expenses, contingencies, or profits, or to adjust the premium rate for special situations. An amount added to the fire insurance rate in determining the inland-marine insurance rate.

Loan   A loan made to a life-insurance policyholder on the security of the cash value of his policy contract. *See also* **Automatic premium loan** and **Loan value.**

Loan guaranty certificate   A certificate issued to a lending institution by the Veterans Administration indicating the percentage of the loan that is guaranteed.

Loan submission   A package of pertinent papers and documents regarding specific property or properties. It is delivered to a prospective lender for review and consideration in anticipation of a mortgage loan.

Loan-to-value ratio   The relationship between the amount of the mortgage loan and the appraised value of the security, expressed as a percentage of the appraised value.

Loan value   The largest amount that can be borrowed by the insured on the security of the cash value of his life insurance. Generally the loan is from the life insurance company but at times may be made by other lenders.

Local agent   *See* **Agent.**

Local board   Society of agents in a locality that promotes the interest of its members.

Local housing authority   A city agency that monitors and implements community housing development needs. Local agencies do not necessarily possess renewal or redevelopment authority.

Locality card   A system of recording liability on cards, instead of posting it on fire (Sanborn) maps.

Location card   A record of insurance placed on a location.

Location plat   A plan or map of a certain piece or pieces of land.

Locked-In Vesting   That form of vesting in a contributory plan under which the participant has no right to withdraw his contribution after benefits attributable to employer contributions have vested (except, possibly, upon disability or with tax penalty).   CIT

Locus standi   The right to be heard in Court or other proceedings.

Lodge system of insurance   *See* **Fraternal insurance.**

Long term disability   A disability lasting longer than a short term disability. The qualifying duration varies from policy to poilcy but is generally longer than 90 days. Benefits may be paid for as long as five years or more depending upon the policy.

Long term insurance   A term used to describe insurance which is written for a longer term than one year. In this country long term insurances are confined to a three year period. (See also Short Term Insurance).

Loss   The basis for a claim for indemnity or damages under the terms of an insurance policy. Any diminution of quantity, quality, or value of property. With reference to policies of indemnity, this term means a valid claim for recovery thereunder. In its application to liability policies, the term refers to payments made in behalf of the insured. *See* **Claim.**

Loss adjustment expenses   Expenses involved in the adjusting of losses — Adjuster's fees — Court costs — Lawyers' fees, etc. For government purpose adjustment expenses incurred under a condition of third party liability must be included with losses.

Loss and damage   Loss is technically distinguished from damage in fire insurance, when all or any portion of the property insured is consumed. "Loss" designates that portion which is entirely consumed, while "damages" designates that part of the property which is not consumed, but remains after the fire in a more or less damaged condition.

Loss constant   A flat sum or amount included in the premium of a risk too small for experienced ratings to be applied. It is generally associated with workmen's compensation insurance.

Loss conversion factor   An amount added to the actual losses to provide for the expenses incurred in the insurance handling of the claims. It is normally associated with a retrospective rating plan of Workmen's Compensation Insurance.

Loss department   Sometimes called claim department. That part of an insurance company that pays and handles claims or losses.

Loss draft   Insurance payments in settlement of a claim for damage to mortgaged property.

Loss expectancy   The underwriter's estimate of damage that would result from the peril insured against. An underwriter must consider (1) "probable maximum loss expectancy," which is an estimate of damage if there had been the normally expected control and protection against the peril, and (2) "above-normal loss expectancy"—the estimate of damage occuring if the peril were not controlled by the protection to be reasonably expected.

Loss information service   A card service provided to an insurance company by the National Board of Fire Underwriters, giving the names of individuals involved in arson or fires of suspicious nature.

Loss loading or "multiplier"   A factor applied to pure loss cost or losses to produce a reinsurance rate or premium.

Loss of income benefits   Benefits paid because the insured is disabled and unable to work.

Loss of time benefits   Benefits paid because the insured is disabled and unable to work.

Loss of use insurance   Compensation through insurance for loss caused because the policyholder has not the use of his property. An automobile hired to replace one stolen would be an example of the need and use of such coverage.

Loss outstanding   Tabulation of losses that an insurance company has in the form of claims but which it has not settled.

Loss payable clause   A clause in an insurance contract providing for payment of a loss, for which the insurer is liable to the insured, to someone other than the insured.

Loss payable to   It is customary to insert a "loss payable" clause in insurance policies. If there is no other interest in the property insured, the clause is completed by inserting the word "insured". When there are other interests, mortgagees, etc. — the clause is completed by inserting the name of such interested parties. Thus "Loss payable to the insured" or "Loss payable to the insured" or "Loss payable to the Canadian Loan Company" (generally followed by) "as their interest may appear". It is better to state what the interest of the other party is, and not leave any loophole for trouble. The words "as mortagagee" or "trustee" etc. definitely fixes the character of the interest. (See "As interest may appear")

Loss pocket Container holding documents concerning a specific loss.

Loss prevention service Engineering and inspection work done by insurance companies or independent organizations for the purpose of changing or removing conditions which would be likely to cause loss.

Loss ratio The percentage of losses to premiums. The proportion which losses incurred bear to the earned premiums.

Loss report Agent's written account of a claim or loss suffered by his client.

Loss reserve That portion of the assets of an insurance company kept in a readily available form to meet probable claims. A fund provided for the payment of losses which have been incurred but not yet due.

Losses incurred The total losses sustained by a company under a policy or policies whether paid or unpaid. For example, a workman breaks his leg, and the total claim under workmen's compensation for lost time and medical amounts to $1,000. Of the $1,000 an amount of $500 has been paid. The incurred loss is $1,000.

Losses outstanding The amount of loss for which the insurer is liable and which it expects to pay in the future.

Losses paid Tabulation of claims that have been paid. The amount of loss for which money has been disbursed by the insurer.

Lost instrument bond A bond available to owners of securities that have been lost, stolen, destroyed, or have mysteriously disappeared, which covers not only the reissuance of a duplicate instrument, but the risk that the original missing security may be negotiated.

Lost or not lost clause Portion of ocean marine insurance policy providing for coverage even if loss had occurred before the insurance was placed. Before radio and wireless a ship might be lost and the owners unaware of it.

Lost policy release A statement signed by the insured releasing the insurance company from all liability under a lost or mislaid contract of insurance.

Lot   A measured parcel of land having fixed boundaries as shown on the recorded plat.

Lotteries   Schemes for distributing prizes by chance.

Lousiana state insurance official
　　Title: Commissioner of Insurance.
　　Location: Baton Rouge, La.

Lump sum   The method of settlement provided by most policies unless an alternate settlement is elected by the policyholder before death or the beneficiary before receiving the payment. Specifically the whole amount due or still owing under the policy contract.

M.   Marine.

MAI   Member, Appraisal Institute.

M.A.P.   Multi-Coverage Account Program

M. & C.   Manufacturers and contractors.

M.D.O.   Monthly debit ordinary.

M.I.B.   Medical Impairment Bureau.

M.I.C.   Multiperil Insurance Conference.

M.I.P.   Master Insurance Program

MIP   Mortgage insurance premium.

M.L.   Multi-Line; Multiple Location

M.L.E.   .Maximum loss expectancy.

M.L.R.   Multiple location risk.

M.O.   Mark off or Manufacturer's output.

M.L.I.R.B.   Multi-Line Insurance Rating Bureau

M.P.   Minimum Premium; Multi-Peril

M.P.G.   Miles per Gallon

M.P.H.   Miles per Hour

M.P.I.R.O.   Multiple Peril Insurance Rating Organization. Has been succeeded by Multi-peril Insurance Conference.

M.S.T.   Mountain Standard Time

Machine issuance   Policies prepared and issued by electronic equipment. This system is best utilized for a large volume of policies having common information.

Machinery   Strictly, the word machinery implies any combination or modification, moveable or permanent, of mechanical principles when given expression in the form of apparatus, and which posses the requisites of force, motion or weight, separately or combined.

Fixed machinery includes engines, shafting, together with its hangings, that are fixed to the realty and would remain with the realty.

Movable Machinery as opposed to fixed machinery includes all machines attached to the floor which can be readily removed.

Machinery breakdown insurance Contract of indemnification against loss due to breakdown or failure of machinery.

Machinery clause A clause in an insurance contract providing that, in case of loss to a machine consisting of several parts, the insurer will not be liable for more than the insured value of the part to which loss occurs.

Machinery insurance policy Type of business insurance coverage. *See* **Boiler and machinery insurance.**

Maintenance The act of keeping, or the expenditures required to keep a property in condition to perform adequately and efficiently the service for which it is used.

Maintenance bond *See* **Bond, maintenance.**

Maintenance reserve An amount reserved to cover costs of maintenance.

Major hospitalization policy Same as major medical insurance except this policy pays benefits.

Major medical expense insurance Contractual protection for large surgical, hospital, or medical expenses. A high deductible is established and insurance protection above that amount is payable upon claim. *See* **Catastrophe policy.**

Major Medical Insurance A type of health insurance that provides benefits for most types of medical expenses incurred up to a high limit, subject to a large deductible. Such contracts may contain internal limits and a percentage participation clause (sometimes called a coinsurance clause).

Major tenants A term used in shopping-center, office building, and commercial property dealings to describe nationally recognized lessees with high credit standing, who occupy the major amount of space and pay the major percentage of the development's gross rent.

Majority See Full Age.

Malfeasance The doing of an unlawful act, e.g. Trespass.

Malice Commonly this means ill-will against a person. In the legal sense, it means a wrongful act — done intentionally, without proper cause or excuse.

Malicious mischief Injury to the rights or property of another with a wicked or perverse intent.

Malicious mischief insurance policy   Type of business insurance coverage. Self-explanatory.

Malingering   A period of deliberate protraction of feigning disability.

Mall   A promenade or walk, as between stores in a shopping center.

Malpractice   Alleged professional misconduct or lack of ordinary skill in the performance of a professional act. A practitioner is liable for damage or injuries caused by malpractice. Such liability, for some professions, can be covered by insurance.

Malpractice liability insurance   Insures against loss for damages because of injury or death resulting from malpractice or error by the insured.

Manager   An insurance company employee in charge of one of the company's branch offices. The branch manager supervises all activities of the branch offices and is responsible for hiring and training agents.

Mandamus   A prerogative writ, directed to some person or inferior court within the jurisdiction, requiring or demanding that some particular thing, therein specified be done.

Mandatory   Requiring strict conformity or obedience.

Mandatory valuation reserve   A reserve designed to protect against adverse fluctuations in the values of bonds and stocks held by insurance companies as admitted assets.

Manslaughter   The unlawful killing of a person without malice or forethought, either involuntary or by negligence.

Manual   A book published by an agency, company, or rating bureau for the guidance of its users. In it are found rates, classifications, specifications, and rules governing the subject covered.

Manual rates   Refers to the cost of a unit of insurance protection as quoted in the rating manual. It may also refer to those rates developed by the application of a recognized rating plan.

Manufactured, unmanufactured, and in process of manufacture   This phrase is often used to describe raw materials, materials in process or partly manufactured, and finished manufactured articles. Alternative expressions are "raw, wrought, and in process" and "finished, unfinished and in process of finishing". These expressions are commonly found in policies on manufacturing risks, and are intended to cover all needful and useful materials used in the ordinary operation of the premises.

"Manufactured", "Wrought" and "Finished" includes all finished goods whether in bales, packages or loose.

"Unmanufactured", "Raw" or "Unfinished" includes all the materials or substances used in the manufacture of the completed article, whether loose or in containers.

"In process" or "while being finished" will include not only the goods themselves, but the cost of manufacturing up to the point arrived at

Manufacturer's and contractor's liability insurance Contractual coverage of liability as a result of ownership or operation of a business such as installation, construction, or manufacturing.

Manufacturer's liability insurance policy Type of business insurance coverage. Self-explanatory.

Manufacturer's output policy Broad form of all risks coverage of personal property of insured manufacturer. It covers property of manufacturer except on the premises of the manufacturer.

Manuscripts Despite the fact the word "book" includes bound and unbound documents ranging from a single sheet to many sheets, manuscripts are not generally covered by a fire policy unless specifically stated, and under an agreement as to their value. In such a case where the value is stated, the policy becomes insofar as the item on manuscripts is concerned, a valued policy. As a matter of practice where agreed upon, manuscripts are included under a proviso that in case of loss no single manuscript shall exceed a stated sum in value. This avoids the valued feature, as the value of the manuscript is left for appraisement when the loss occurs.

Manuscripts insurance policy Type of business insurance coverage. Self-explanatory.

Map clerk A junior underwriter who enters on the maps essential data (policy number, amount, property covered, and expiration date) regarding certain types of policies.

Maps In fire insurance, maps are used by underwriters to locate and indicate the character of the risk, especially in large cities. Notations on the maps indicate the amount of liability carried on a particular risk in a certain area.

Marginal land That which barely pays the cost of working or using. Land whereon the costs of operating approximately equal the gross income.

Marine insurance That form of coverage which is primarily concerned with the protection of goods in transit and the means of transportation. This term is applied in common usage to risks involving ocean transit. *See* **Inland marine.**

Marine perils Risks covered by marine insurance policy. Perils "ejusdem generis" with the perils noted in the policy. Each word that is used in the marine policy has been defined by admiralty decisions.

Marine syndicates Associations of insurance companies acting in common to inspect, survey, establish standards, and to insure ocean marine risks.

Marital deduction That value which a deceased leaves his spouse outright, up to one-half of the net estate, subject to specific interpretation, for the applicable legislation in effect by the Internal Revenue Division.

Maritime law Rules of conduct or action set forth by specific court (Admiralty) having jurisdiction on maritime questions and offenses.

Market approach to value In appraising, the market value estimate is predicated upon actual prices paid in market transactions. It is a correlation and analysis of similar recently sold properties. The reliability of this technique is dependent upon the degree of comparability of each property with the subject property, the time of sale, the verification of the sale dates, the absence of unusual conditions affecting the sale, and the terms of the sale.

Market price The price actually paid or the price considered to be obtainable in the open market under the conditions currently existing.

Market Rent The price a tenant pays a landlord for the use and occupancy of real property, based upon current prices for comparable property.

Market value The value of assets (stocks, bonds, debentures, real estate etc.) based on a current market valuation.

Market value clause In a policy provides that the insurance company will pay, in the event of loss, the selling price of the finished merchandise, rather than the cost of replacement or its actual value.

Marketable title A title that may not be completely clear, but has only minor objections that a well-informed and prudent buyer of real estate would accept. *See* **Clear title.**

Martial law In the ordinary sense of the term, it means the suspension of civil law and government of the country, or parts of it, by military tribunal.

Marx plan System of placing automobile accidents on a compensation basis, on the assumption that any automobile using public highways is absolutely liable for injuries to the public. No defense could be raised to relieve the driver from a scheduled compensation of the injured parties.

Mass merchandising The sale of insurance through such techniques as payroll deduction.

Master The person having the exercising control.

Master and Servant A relationship between two persons in which a master not only prescribes to the servant or workman the end result of the work but also directs, or may at any moment direct or retains the power of directing, the means by which this end should be achieved.

Master mortgage A standard-form mortgage recorded in the public record to help reduce recording fees as mortgage documents become more elaborate. Succeeding individual mortgages refer to the record and the master mortgage for the printed language to be incorporated into the individual mortgages.

Master policy An insurance policy which covers a group of persons or establishments to whom certificates of insurance are issued as their evidence of coverage under the policy. Such a policy is frequently associated in group health and in accident insurance. The employer maintains the master policy which designates all the coverages of the policy, while certificate of insurance are given to the individuals covered, the certificate being a brief statement or highlight of the master policy.

Master's deed A deed issued by a master in chancery in satisfaction of a judgment and under a court order.

Material bond Insurance to the beneficiary (contractor) that the person posting the bond (supplier) will provide the materials necessary for the completion of contracted work.

Material fact Statement of something that is done or exists of such importance that disclosure of it would alter an underwriting decision or loss settlement.

Material release *See* **Waiver of lien.**

Materiality "The law imposes upon the insured as a preliminary duty, in the nature of condition precedent, the disclosure of all material facts known to him in connection with the risk. The test of materiality is in the enhancement of the premium had the true facts of the case been given. When the nature of the substance of the insurance, if known, might influence the insurer to decline the risk or to write it only at an advanced rate of premium, it would be deemed material to the risk. Whatever the form of expression used by the insured, if it has the effect of misleading the insurer, or imposing upon him, it will be held to be material, and upon due proof void the policy. If a fact, usually immaterial, be enquired about specifically, it will be considered material. A disclosure waived is an admission of immateriality" (Griswold). All changes which substantially affect and increase the risk involved are material.

Matured Value   The proceeds payable on an endowment contract at the end of the specified endowment period, or payable on an ordinary life contract at the last age of the mortality table if the insured is still living at that age.

Maturity   The date at which the face value becomes payable either by death or endowment.

Maturity Date   The date upon which an endowment policy becomes payable if the insured is still living.

Maximum disability policy   Noncancellable disability income insurance with a limit on the insurers liability for each claim but containing no limit on the aggregate amount of all claims.

Maximum loss expectancy   *See* **Loss expectancy**.

Maximum possible loss   The largest loss possible for a given risk. Preferred over maximum probable loss.

Maximum probable loss   The largest loss expected for a given risk assuming normal circumstances.

Maximum rent   That rent established by a legally impowered authority such as a rent stabilization agency, of the Office of Rent Stabilization, Economic Stabilization Agency.

Maximum retrospective premium   The highest premium which would be required for workmen's compensation insurance under a retrospective rating plan.

McCarran-Ferguson Act (Public Law 15, 1945)   A federal law that exempts insurers from federal antitrust constraints.

McCarran-Wiler Bill (S. 1508)   Extended moratorium on insurance granted by Public Law 15.

McClintock Tables   First widely used American mortality tables prepared in 1896 by McClintock from experience of fifteen American companies and influenced by foreign underwriting experience.

Mechanic's lien   A lien given by law upon building or other improvement upon land, and upon the land itself, to secure the price of labor done upon, and materials furnished for the improvement.

Mechanic's permit Endorsement or clause allowing the insured to use and employ workmen near the insured risk.

MEDICAID State programs of public assistance designed to help persons whose income and other assets are inadequate to pay for their health care.

Medical attendance Attendance on the insured by a physician, surgeon, and sometimes an osteopath, other than himself.

Medical care plans A form of group insurance. Self-explanatory.

Medical examination An examination by a physician, required as a part of the policy application. Medical examinations are usually required with noncancellable applications and may not be required with other kinds of applications unless the underwriting department so requests. Examination of a claimant by a physician to determine extent, validity, or duration of a disabiilty.

Medical Examiners Doctors approved by the company to make medical examinations of persons applying for insurance.

Medical Expense Insurance A form of health insurance that provides benefits for medical care. CIT

Medical Impairment Bureau A clearinghouse of information on people who have applied for life insurance in the past. Any adverse findings on previous examinations are recorded in code and sent to companies subscribing to the service.

Medical payments insurance An agreement by an insurer to pay, subject to a limit, medical, surgical, hospital, and funeral expenses, regardless of liability of the insured. Usually included in the automobile and other public liability policies, whereby the insurance company agrees to pay medical, hospital, and funeral expenses resulting from an accident covered by the policy to certain limits whether the insured is liable therefore or not.

Medicare Government insurance plan attached to the Social Security Act in 1965 which provides a health insurance program for the aged.

MEDIGAP insurance Those policies which pay all or part of the expenses for health care not covered by Medicare.

Member, Appraisal Institute (MAI) The highest professional designation awarded by the American Institute of Real Estate Appraisers.

Mendola vs. Superintendent of Insurance   New York State, N. Y. Supreme Court upheld licensing provisions of state law.

Mens Rae   "The guilty mind". This is an essential ingredient in many, but not all crimes in order to obtain a criminal conviction.

Mercantile open-stock burglary insurance   Indemnification against loss of merchandise due to burglary caused by felonious entry using force and/or violence when the premises are closed for business. The force and violence may be indicated by entry using tools, chemicals, electricity, or explosives. The coverage also includes damage caused to furniture and fixtures.

Mercantile report   *See* **Credit Report.**

Mercantile risk   Hazard of peril of a merchant in selling his stock of goods.

Mercantile Robbery Coverage   Coverage against robbery of money, securities and other property.

Mercantile safe burglary insurance   Indemnification against loss caused by burglary in which the opening of a safe with force and violence through the use of tools, explosives, chemicals, or electricity leaves marks on the safe. The coverage not only covers damage to safe, but the property in the safe, furniture, fixtures, and the premises.

Merchandise   Stock of goods.

Merchandise installment floater   A contract insuring the vendor, or the vendor and vendee, against loss to merchandise sold on the installment plan as long as the vendor has an interest in the merchandise.

Merchantable   Salable in the ordinary way; fit for ordinary uses to which it is put.

Merchantable title   A title that a court of equity considers so clear that it will force acceptance of it by a purchaser.

Merchants' protective bond   Insurance for a limited amount for loss or damage due to embezzlement, robbery of messengers, interior robbery, safe burglary, forgery, counterfeit money, plate door damage, stock and fixture damage, and other specified coverage.

Merit rating   A system used in measuring the differences of a specific risk from some moral, or other standard, in order to correct the manual rate for that risk.

Messenger   A messenger may be the insured, a partner, an officer or an employee of the firm who is in the regular service of and duly authorized by the insured to have the care and custody of the insured property *outside* the premises.

Messenger and interior robbery insurance. At times called inside and outside holdup insurance. Contract of insurance against loss of property, securities, or money either inside an insured premises or while the valuables are being delivered by a messenger.

Messenger robbery insurance policy Type of business insurance coverage. Self-explanatory.

Metayage Also known as share cropping. A system of farm leasing under which the owner provides the tools, seed, fertilizer, land, etc., and the tenant provides his labor. The agricultural products of the farm, are shared in some agreed proportion.

Metes and bounds A method of describing land through the use of boundaries and measurements of a parcel of real estate. It is used mostly in states not having the U.S. Rectangular Survey System of locating and describing real estate. These states are mostly in the East.

Metropolitan districts Include, in addition to the central city or cities, all adjacent and contiguous civil divisions having a density of not less than 150 inhabitants per square mile, and also, as a rule, those civil divisions of less density that are directly contiguous to the central cities, or are entirely or nearly surrounded by minor civil divisions that have the required density.

Military indulgence The protection enacted and provided by the Soldiers and Sailors Civil Relief Act to a mortgagor who is about to enter or is in military service and whose ability to keep a loan current has been materially affected by military service.

Military service in the armed forces Military service in time of war may void certain policy benefits. Disability as a result of war or any act of war is uninsurable.

Mill One-tenth of 1 percent, the measure used to state the property tax rate.

Mill construction Also called "slow burning." A building with thick brick walls, floors of three- or four-inch planks, on eight- or twelve-inch wood posts and girders, no concealed spaces behind interior finish.

Miller Dual Bond Act Federal act requiring that two bonds be posted by any one awarded a contract for $2,000 or more construction, repair or alteration of any United States Government project, building, or device. The two bonds are: (1) to protect the government that performance will be made and (2) a payment bond to protect all individuals and companies that supply material or labor for the contractor.

Minimum amount policy   Generally, a life insurance contract which is sold only with a minimum face amount.

Minimum deposit policy   A life insurance contract whose cash value provides a first year loan value which is made available immediately for borrowing upon payment of the first year's premium.

Minimum premium   The lowest consideration for which an insurance company will accept a risk for a specified period. *See* **Premium, minimum.**

Minimum Property Standards   FHA regulations that set forth minimum acceptable technical standards for insurable loans.

Minimum rate   A general class for risks of low hazard, with many units in the class. Opposed to "schedule rate" and "specific rate." *See* **Class rate.**

Minimum retrospective premium   Refers to the lowest premium which would be charged in any event under a retrospective rating plan for workmen's compensation insurance.

Minor   A person below the age of legal capacity. A minor is incapable of making a contract. A parent or guardian must sign any application for insurance for a minor unless state law permits an earlier age limit.

Miscellaneous expenses   Hospital charges other than board, room, and floor nursing.

Misfeasance   The improper performance of a lawful act e.g. where there is negligence. The performance of something in an improper manner.

Misnomer   A wrong name.

Misplaced improvements   Building improvements of a use type not conforming to that making for best utilization of the site.

Misrepresentation   Written or verbal misstatement or falsehood of a material fact concerning an insurance application or loss claim.

Misstatement of age   Most state laws require that life insurance policies include a provision that if the age of the insured is misstated, the amount of insurance will be that which the premium would have purchased at the correct age based upon the company's published rate at the date of policy issuance.

Mixed agency Company selling policies of stock and mutual insurance companies.

Mobile home park A tract of land providing roads, utility connections, and concrete slabs for mobile homes.

Modernization loan Loans for repair and modernization purposes made by private institutional investors, frequently guaranteed and insured by the Federal Housing Administration. The monthly payments include interest, part of principal, and insurance.

Modified Life Ordinary insurance with a premium payable during the first few years, only slightly larger than the rate for term insurance. Afterwards the premium is larger for the remainder of life than the premium for ordinary life at the original age of issue but less than the rate at the attained age at the time of change.

Modular house A factory-assembled residence built in units or sections, transported to a permanent site, and erected on a foundation. The term excludes mobile homes.

Modus Operandi A system or manner of working.

Monetary indemnity A specified amount benefit as contrasted to expense reimbursement.

Money and securities broad form policy Insurance contract for protection of a business against most losses of securities and money except from forgery and dishonesty of employees. The loss may occur either outside or inside the employers place of business.

Money and securities insurance policy Type of business insurance coverage. Self-explanatory.

Money-purchase plan An arrangement for applying periodically an amount of money (usually a percentage of wages) to the purchase of an annuity as part of a pension.

Monopolistic state fund A state or provincial workmen's compensation insurance plan which prohibits the writing of this coverage by private carriers.

Monthly debit ordinary A hybrid policy having the small face value of industrial policies and being handled as ordinary insurance.

Monument A permanent object such as a stone, concrete, or metal marker used to establish certain real estate boundaries.

Monument of survey   Visible marks or indications left on natural or other objects indicating the lines and boundaries of a survey.

Moral hazard   Refers to the risk resulting from the personal habits of the insured which may increase the possibility of loss due to carelessness or dishonesty. This is frequently associated where an individual has had a series of losses such as fires. The possibility of loss being caused or aggravated by dishonesty or carelessness of the insured, his agents, or employees. It arises from the character and circumstances of the insured, apart from the nature of the interest or property covered, or its location. The latter is called the physical hazard.

Moratorium   A period during which a borrower is granted the right to delay fulfillment of an obligation.

Morbidity   Sickness. A morbidity table shows the incidence of sickness as a mortality table shows the incidence of death.

More or less   Those words, when used in a contract, are intended to cover only a reasonable excess or deficit.

Mortality Savings   The difference between the actual mortality losses and the amount expected according to the mortality table in use.

Mortality table   A statistical table showing the death rate at each age, usually expressed as so many per thousand.

Mortgage   A conveyance of property upon condition, as security for the payment of a debt or the performance of a duty and to become void upon payment or performance. Also, the instrument by which a mortgage conveyance is made. The state of the property so conveyed or the interest of the mortgage therein.

Mortgage-backed securities   Bond-type investment securities representing an undivided interest in a pool of mortgages or trust deeds. Income from the underlying mortgage is used to pay off the securities. *See* **GNMA mortgage-backed securities.**

Mortgage banker   A firm or individual active in the field of mortgage banking. Mortgage bankers, as local representatives of regional or national institutional lenders, act as correspondents between lenders and borrowers.

Mortgage banking   The packaging of mortgage loans secured by real property to be sold to a permanent investor with servicing retained for the life of the loan for a fee. The origination, sale, and servicing of mortgage loans by a firm or individual.

The investor-correspondent system is the foundation of the mortgage banking industry.

Mortgage broker   A firm or individual who brings the borrower and lender together, receiving a commission. A mortgage broker does not retain servicing.

Mortgage certificate   An interest in a mortgage evidenced by the instrument, generally a fractional portion of the mortgage, which certifies as to the agreement between the mortgagees who hold the certificates and the mortgagor as to such terms as principal, amount, date of payment, place of payment. Such certificates are not obligations to pay money, as in a bond or note, but are merely a certification by the holder of the mortgage, generally a corporate depository, that he holds such mortgage for the beneficial and undivided interest of all the certificate holders. The certificate itself generally sets forth a full agreement between the holder and the depository, although in some cases a more lengthy document, known as a depository agreement is executed.

Mortgage clause   Clause in an insurance policy which makes the proceeds payable to the holder of a mortgage on the insured property to the extent of his interest in that property.

Mortgage discount   The difference between the principal amount of a mortgage and the amount it actually sells for. Sometimes called points, loan brokerage fee, or new loan fee. The discount is computed on the amount of the loan, not the sales price.

Mortgage guarantee policy   A policy issued on a guaranteed mortgage.

Mortgage insurance   A type of term life insurance available to mortgagors. The amount of coverage decreases as the mortgage balance declines. In the event that the borrower dies while the policy is in force, the debt is automatically satisfied by insurance proceeds.

Mortgage Insurance Premium (MIP)   The consideration paid by a mortgagor for mortgage insurance either to FHA or to a private mortgage insurance (PMI) company. On an FHA loan, the payment is one-half of 1 percent annually on the declining balance of the mortgage. It is part of the regular monthly payment used by FHA to meet operating expenses and provide loss reserves.

Mortgage note   A written promise to pay a sum of money at a stated interest rate during a specified term. It is secured by a mortgage.

Mortgage portfolio   The aggregate of mortgage loans held by an investor, or services by a mortgage banker.

Mortgagee   The source of the funds for a mortgage loan and in whose favor the property serving as security is mortgaged. A person or company to whom property is conveyed as security for a loan made by such person or company. The creditor.

Mortgagee clause   A clause in an insurance contract making the proceeds payable to a named mortgagee, as his interest may appear, and stating the terms of the contract between the insurer and the mortgagee. Preferable usage but same as mortgage clause.

Mortgagee in possession   A mortgagee creditor who takes over the income from the mortgaged property upon default of the mortgage by the debtor.

Mortgagor   An owner who conveys his property as security for a loan. The debtor.

Motel policy   Various insurance coverages applicable to motels.

Motion   An application to a court for a rule or order affecting a case. Some of the motions are:
>   for a summary judgement
>   for a judgement on the pleadings
>   for a directed verdict
>   for a new trial

Motion picture negative floater insurance   An all-risk indemnification against damage or loss to negative motion picture films caused by physical risks.

Motor Truck Cargo Insurance (Owner's Form)   Insures the owner of the truck and cargo against loss to his property while it is being transported.

Motor truck carrier's insurance form   Type of business insurance coverage especially designed to protect operators of motor trucks.

Motor Truck Contents floater insurance   Indemnification against loss or damaged goods carried by motor trucks due to specific perils. Under one type, the Owner's Form, merchants and manufacturers insure goods on trucks either owned or operated by them. The Truckmen's Form is used by furniture movers and public truckmen to insure goods carried by them.

Mud sill   The lowest sill of a house.

Multiperil   Refers to the rather recent trend to package a spectrum of previously specified-peril policies into one form. This may or may not include multiple lines of insurance. To the general public, however, multiperil probably has little meaning other than a vague recognition of protection which extends to some point beyond a single peril. CIT tentative

Multi-peril policy In the insurance business, contrary to what the name might imply, the term "multi-peril policy" does not mean a policy insuring against two or more perils. It is, instead, a policy which is a combination of fire and casualty (or fire, casualty and marine coverages) in a single contract such as the Homeowners policy.

Multiple indemnity A provision under which the principal sum (and sometimes other indemnities) will be 100%, 200%, or more in case of death from certain types of accidents.

Multiple Line has special meaning to persons within the industry. It refers to the opportunity to write fire-allied lines covers in the same contract with what were classified by law as casualty lines, which included some property covers as well as liability covers. This was a privilege forbidden prior to passage of multiple lines legislation in the 1950s. To the general public, however, no clear distinction between multiperil and multiple line likely exists. The similarity of these terms only serves to confound and confuse the buying public, especially when a distinction between these terms is desired or intended. CIT tentative

Multiple-line carrier An insurer that writes more than one kind of insurance, usually used to mean an insurer writing a considerable number of lines of insurance.

Multiple Line Law Until recent years most states have divided companies into two different classes: "Fire" companies (which could write certain lines other than fire) and "Casualty" companies which could write still different lines. "Multiple Line" laws have combined the two classes.

Multiple-line underwriting The issuance of several kinds of insurance by a single company by authority granted under multiple line underwriting laws.

Multiple-line underwriting laws Statutes granting underwriting powers which enable one company to write both fire and casualty insurance.

Multiple listing A listing, usually an exclusive right to sell, taken by an organization, such as a multiple listing bureau, composed of real estate brokers. Non-members of the bureau cannot sell the property.

Multiple-location insurance An insurance contract covering goods at various locations, at each of which the amount of the insurance varies with the fluctuations of value of the goods. *See* **General-cover Contract** and **Reporting contract.**

Multiple location risks insurance Protection of property owned or controlled by one person or corporation in a number of different locations. *See* **Master policy.**

Multiple protection insurance These contracts promise to pay a multiple of the face amount if the insured should die within a specified period and only the face value if the person dies after the end of the period.

Muniments Those elements which improve, strengthen, or fortify the rights in property.

Musical instrument floater insurance Protection against loss or damage to the covered musical instruments.

Mutatis Mutandis In the same general form but with the necessary points of detail changed.

Mutual Atomic Energy Reinsurance Pool A reinsurance pool of mutual insurance companies for policies written on private nuclear energy reactor installations.

Mutual benefit associations Fraternal, social, organizations or corporations for the relief of members of the group operating on a corporate or assessment plan. The features of which provide that the payment of losses is not met by fixed premiums payable in advance but by assessments intended to liquidate specific losses.

Mutual insurance companies Companies with no capital stock, owned by policyholders. Trustees of the company are chosen by the policyholders. The earnings of the company over and above the payments of the losses and operating expenses and reserves are the property of the policyholders. There are two types of mutual insurance companies, the nonassessable and the assessable premium mutual. The nonassessable charges a fixed premium and the policyholders cannot be assessed. Legal reserves and surpluses are maintained to provide payment of all claims. Assessable mutuals are those companies that charge an initial fixed premium, and if that is not sufficient may assess the policyholders to meet losses in excess of the premiums that have been charged. as well as provide statistical services.

Mutual life insurance company A life insurance company owned and controlled by policyholders. The company issues, in general, participating policies which entitle the policyholder to share in the surplus earnings through dividends reflecting the difference between the premium charged and the actual experience.

Mutual Mortgage Insurance Fund One of four FHA insurance funds into which all mortgage insurance premiums and other specified revenue of the FHA are paid and from which losses are met.

Mysterious disappearance The vanishing of covered property that cannot be explained.

N.A.I.A. National Association of Insurance Agents.
N.A.I.B. National Association of Insurance Brokers.
N.A.I.C. National Association of Insurance Commissioners.
N.A.I.I. National Association of Independent Insurers
N.A.I.W. National Association of Insurance Women
N.A.L.U. National Association of Life Underwriters.
N.A.M.C.C. National Association of Mutual Casualty Companies.
N.A.M.I.A. National Association of Mutual Insurance Agents
N.A.T.B. National Automobile Theft Bureau
N.A.U.A. National Auto Underwriters Association.
N.B.C.U. National Bureau of Casualty Underwriters.
N.B.F.U. National Board of Fire Underwriters.
N.C. No Charge
N.C.I. No common interest.
N.E.L.I.A. Nuclear Energy Liability Insurance Association.
N.E.P.I.A. Nuclear Energy Property Insurance Association.
N.F.C. National Fraternal Congress of America.
N.F.P.A. National Fire Protection Association.
N.F.W.C. National Fire Waste Council.
N.I.A.C. Nuclear Insurance Association of Canada
N.I.A.S.A. National Insurance Actuarial and Statistical Association
N.I.B.A. National Insurance Buyers Association.
N.L.t. Night Letter
N.O.C. Not otherwise classified.
N.P. Note Payable
N.P.D. No payroll division.
N.Q.(or NQA) Net Quick Assets
N.R. Note Receivable
N.S.B.I.U. Nova Scotia Board of Insurance Underwriters

N.S.C.   National Safety Council
N.S.L.I.   National Service Life Insurance.
N.T.O.   Not Taken Out or Not Taken
N.W.   Net Worth
Non-can   Noncancellable.
Non-par   Nonparticipating.
Named insured   Refers to the person or business organization with whom an insurance contract is made and who is specifically designated by name as being protected against loss under the various terms of the policy. In case of automobile liability policies an individual driving the car with the consent of the insured, though unnamed, would also be protected from liability under the terms of certain policies.
Named perils   Named perils or hazards policies specify what specific perils or hazards are covered or insured against. All risk policies do not name the perils specifically.
Narcotics   Certain drugs legally defined as narcotics. Accident and sickness insurance denies liability for claim resulting from their use unless administered upon the advice of a medical doctor.
National Service Life Insurance   Insurance created by Act of Congress in 1940 for provision of policies for individuals on active service with naval and military forces.
Nationwide marine definition   A statement of the types of insurance that may properly be written under marine or inland marine policies. This statement, on recommendation by the National Association of Insurance Commissioners, has been adopted in most states, with exceptions in some. There is a committee on interpretation (of this definition) composed of representatives of fire, casualty, and marine and inland marine departments of the industry.
Natural death   Any death that is not accidental.
Natural premium   The cost of life insurance based upon pure mortality for one year at any specific age.
Natural Resource Property   A property involving primarily recoverable or adaptable resources of nature which may be or are susceptible to being commercially exploited.
Necessities of Life   Goods, food, clothing, etc. Generally an infant being a person under the legal age to contract, cannot enter into a valid binding contract with certain exceptions. One of these exceptions is for the necessities of life such as food, clothing, shelter, etc.

Negative cash flow Cash expenditures of an income-producing property in excess of the cash receipts.

Negative film syndicate An organization of insurance companies that write floater insurance on professional motion picture negatives.

Negligence Failure to do what a reasonably prudent individual would ordinarily do under the circumstances of a particular case, or doing what a prudent person would not have done. Negligence may be caused by acts of omission, commission, or both.

Negligence Concurrent Where two or more persons acting independently cause injury to a third party in the same accident (see joint feasors).

Negligence Contributory A situation wherein the person complaining that he was injured or damaged by another person's negligence may have himself been guilty of want of due care for his own safety. In some jurisdictions this would be a bar to recovery and in others would reduce the amount of recovery.

Negligence Gross The reckless, wanton and wilful misconduct — where the standard of due care of a reasonable prudent person has been ignored by such a shockingly wide margin that it reflects an indifference to the natural and probable consequences as to almost amount to an intentional act.

Negligence liability insurance policy Type of business insurance coverage. Self-explanatory.

Negligence Per Se Self-evident negligence e. g. violation of certain criminal statutes or motor vehicle laws may in itself indicate negligence. Care must be taken however not to confuse this with liability. The negligence so incurred may be the sole factor involved in the accident in which case there would be liability but alternatively there may be contributory negligence or it may be that negligence itself was not a factor in causing the accident.

Negotiable Certificate of Deposit (CD) Certificates issued by commercial banks under Federal Reserve Regulation Q with a stated return (discounted) or interest rate with a maturity usually of one year. The bank pays the holder in due course at maturity.

Negotiable instrument A written paper that may be transferred to another in the course of business. The negotiable instrument must meet certain legal tests and is subject to the Uniform Negotiable Instruments Law.

Nemo tenetur seitsum accusare No one is compelled to accuse himself.

Net amount at risk The difference between the face amount of the insurance contract and the reserve.

Net cost The total premiums paid on a policy, minus any dividends and the surrender value as of the date of the determination of the so-called net cost.

Net earnings Revenue from operating sources, after deduction of the operating expenses, maintenance, uncollectible revenues, and taxes applicable to operating properties or revenues, but before deduction of financial charges and generally before deduction of provision for depreciation and retirements.

Net income In general, synonymous with net earnings, but considered a broader and better term, the balance remaining, after deducting from the gross income all operating expense, maintenance, taxes, and losses pertaining to operating properties, excepting interest or other financial charges on borrowed or other capital.

Net lease A lease where, in addition to the rental stipulated, the lessee assumes payment of all property charges such as taxes, insurance, and maintenance.

Net level premium The cost of life insurance based upon pure mortality from the inception of the contract until its maturity date.

Net line The amount of liability the company is prepared to expose to loss for its own account. *See* **Amount subject.**

Net loss The amount of loss sustained by an insurer after giving effect to all applicable reinsurance, salvage, and subrogation recoveries.

Net option A written instrument which grants the right to purchase property at a specified price to the owner.

Net payments cost index One of the measures of the cost of a life insurance policy, that includes interest foregone if a policy is kept in force until the insured dies.

Net premium Several meanings depending on context. The billed premium less the agent's commission. The original premium less granted return premiums. The original gross premium less return premiums and premiums for reinsurance.

Net profits Used without qualifying expression, to describe only the profits remaining after including all earnings, and other income or profit, and after deducting all expenses and charges of every character, including interest, depreciation, and taxes.

Net rate   The amount of the premiums before loading for expense. The actual amount paid after subtracting any dividends. In the case of a nonpar policy, this is identical with the rate book figure. The context will determine which is intended.

Net rentable area   The actual square footage of a building that can be rented. Halls, lobbies, stairways, elevator shafts, maintenance areas, and the like are not included.

Net retention (Also **Net Retained Liability**)   The amount of insurance which a ceding company keeps for its own account and does not reinsure in any way.

Net single premium   The premium that will cover the present value of future claims under the policy.

Net spendable   The amount of cash that remains from the gross income after deducting operating expenses, principal and interest payments, and income taxes.

Net worth   The value of all assets, including cash, less total liabilities. Often used as an underwriting guideline to indicate credit worthiness and financial strength.

Net yield   That part of gross yield that remains after the deductions of all costs, such as servicing, and any reserves for losses.

New for old   Marine insurance term that applies discount based upon depreciation of the new or repaired part that is installed in settlement of a claim. The discount approaches the wearing out or depreciation of the item indemnified.

Next friend   Infants sue by a Next Friend. It makes no difference that the infant happens to be a married person, the next friend may be any person willing to act in that capacity.

Next of kin   Those related in the nearest degree to another person.

N.F.C. Mortality Table   National Fraternal Congress Table of Mortality prepared in 1898 to permit fraternal insurance to establish better mortality and lapse experience. A crude table but a successful one.

Nineteen Hundred and Thirty-Seven Standard Annuity Table   Published in 1938, used a five-year set back for men. Men on the average were assumed to die five years before women.

Nisi   Generally used after the word decree, order, or such, and denotes that it shall take effect at a given time, unless before that time it is modified.

No-amount policy   Also called actual cash value policy. Shows no fixed amount of insurance on the face of contract but pay the actual cash value of the claim or loss on the property. Physical damage automobile policies are examples of this type of coverage and insurance.

No fault insurance Many states have laws permitting auto accident victims to collect directly from their own insurance companies for medical and hospital expenses and loss of income regardless of who was at fault. Massachusetts includes property damage. Some states limit right to sue third parties.

No-fault threshold The financial amount below which one may not bring tort liability actions against those responsible for the accident.

Nominator's Clause See Payor Insurance.

Non-Admitted Assets Assets such as accrued interest on bonds in default, the excess of ledger values over market values of investments, furniture and supplies, which are not allowed to be listed for the purpose of a balance sheet by the state insurance departments.

Nonadmitted carrier An insurer that has not been licensed to write insurance in a given jurisdiction.

Nonadmitted company Insurance company that has not been licensed to do business in a particular state. In that state it is nonadmitted.

Non-admitted reinsurance No credit is given in the ceding company's anual report for this reinsurance because the reinsurer is not licensed to do business in the ceding company's jurisdiction.

Nonassessable insurance Insurance under which the insured may not be called upon to pay an assessment in addition to his premium.

Nonassessable policies Limits the liability of the policyholder to the amount of premium which is paid and no additional levy can be made against the policyholder.

Nonassignable Incapable of being assigned; policy benefits or rights that cannot be assigned to a third party.

Nonboard company An insurance company that does not subscribe to the rates and rules of the respective rating bureaus.

Noncancellable disability insurance Usually disability insurance which may be continued at the option of the insured to a specified age, such as 60 years. Sometimes disability insurance which may not be canceled by the carrier during the period for which the policy is written, e.g., one year.

Noncancellable policy An insurance contract that may not be terminated. Most insurance policies permit cancellation by either the insured or the insurance company, but a noncancellable policy may limit one or both parties to the contract. Where many claims have been made such as involving automobile damage or hospitalization the company may wish to cancel.

Non compos mentis   Not sound in mind.

Nonconcurrency   The situation which exists where a number of insurance policies, intended to cover the same property, for the same interests and against the same perils or hazards, are not identical as to the extent of coverage. Nonconcurrency which seems most frequent and troublesome involves policies insuring partly the same and partly different subjects, or using different coinsurance percentages.

Non-concurrent   The term is applied to policies which are not in agreement as to range, condition and wording, with other policies on the same owner, or other. (See concurrent)

Nonconcurrent insurance   Insurance under two or more contracts, on all or part of the same risk, varying in their description of the risk or in particulars other than amounts of insurance or policy dates.

Nonconfining sickness   Sickness which prevents the insured from working but does not confine him to his home.

Noncontributory   A group or pension plan in which the employer pays all the premium. Opposed to contributory.

Nondisabling   An injury which does not cause loss of time.

Non-disturbace agreement   An agreement that permits a tenant under a lease to remain in possession despite any foreclosure.

Non-duplication of payments   Provision, found in some health insurance contracts, whereby the insurer is not liable for benefits provided by other insurers.

Nonfeasance   The neglect or failure to do some act which ought to be done e. g., failure to effect repairs where such repairs creat a hazard for others.

Nonforfeiture option   The value, if any, either in cash or in another form of insurance available upon failure to continue the required premium payments. The other forms of insurance available are extended term insurance, which provides the original amount for a limited period of time; and reduced paid-up insurance, which continues the original insurance plan, but for a reduced amount.

Nonforfeiture values   Values such as loans, cash, paid-up insurance, and extended term which are not lost by nonpayment of premiums.

Non-hazardous A risk not involving the ordinary or average hazard of its class of property is termed "non hazardous in class".

Non-insurable risk A risk for which no insurance can be written. The chance of loss is very high or cannot be accurately measured.

Nonledger assets Assets due and payable in the current year but not received by the company.

Nonmedical Life insurance issued on the regular basis but without the requirement of an examination by a physician. However, a statement of health and physical condition is taken from the applicant and becomes a part of the policy.

Nonoccupational policy A policy which does not cover disability resulting from injury or sickness covered by workmen's compensation. Group accident and sickness policies, for instance, are almost always nonoccupational.

Nonownership automobile liability Coverage against liability for damage or loss caused while driving an automobile not owned or leased to the insured.

Nonownership automobile liability insurance Protects the policyholder against the claims for property damage or public liability which may be caused by automobiles not owned or hired by him but which may be used by his employees or agents in the conduct of the policyholder's business activity.

Nonparticipating A policy which guarantees the final cost in advance. It is called nonparticipating because it does not have dividends. Nonparticipating policies are written by stock insurance companies, participating policies are written by mutual insurance companies. Stock companies, however, may permit their policies to participate.

Nonparticipating insurance Insurance on which no dividends are payable. Insurance written for a fixed premium, without provision for dividends to, or assessment of, insureds.

Nonpolicywriting agent A fire insurance agent who does not prepare his own policies, but rather submits business to the company by means of applications; also called a "survey agent."

Nonprofit insurers Insurance associations organized under nonprofit laws (exempting them from certain types of taxation). The various Blue Cross and Blue Shield groups are often so organized.

Non-proportional insurance Life reinsurance whereby the re-insurer makes payments to the ceding company only after the ceding company's claims exceed a preset aggregate loss limit.

Non-recording chattel mortgage policy Insurance protection for the lender on chattels from loss due to failure to record a chattel mortgage.

Non-recourse note A debt instrument giving the lender no recourse to the borrower. The lender must rely solely on the property for repayment.

Nonresident Persons who do not reside within the state.

Nonresident agents An agent who does not reside in a state in which he is licensed.

Nonstock corporation A corporation such as a mutual life insurance company that has no issued shares.

Nonsuit A plaintiff in a suit has to prove his case. His evidence at trial is given first and if at the end of his evidence either the plaintiff decides to abandon the action because he has been unable to prove his case or if the defendant moves for a nonsuit and the court rules that he has not made out his case, the verdict is handed down accordingly. This is known as nonsuit.

Nonvalued policy A contract of insurance in terms of which the insurance company agrees to pay the actual cash value of property destroyed within the limits of the policy.

Nonwaiver agreement Assent by the insured that investigation and determination of the value of the claim by the insurance company does not constitute an admission that the insurance company has assumed liability.

Noon Policy terms are often designated as from noon of one date to noon of another. Noon is 12 M standard time of the place where the insured resides.

Noon clause Portion of insurance contract that states at what time insurance coverage starts. Since loss may occur at a period that may be stated as daylight saving time, Central standard time, or Eastern daylight saving time, there is need to make certain at which time the coverage starts and ends.

Normal loss expectancy *See* **Loss expectancy.**

North Little Rock Transportation Company Inc. vs. Casualty Reciprocal Exchange et. al. Contention that rating activities of insurance companies violated Sherman Anti-Trust Act was dismissed.

Notary One authorized by the state to take acknowledgments and give oaths.

Note An instrument of credit given to attest a debt.

Notice of commencement A document used in some states and recorded after a construction loan mortgage has been recorded. All mechanic's liens relate back to the date of recording of the notice, thereby enabling the mortgage to remain a first lien, not subordinated to any labor, supplier, or other claim for non-payment of bills.

Notice of completion Notice recorded after completion of construction. Mechanic's liens must be filed within a specific period thereafter.

Notice of default (1) A notice recorded after the occurrence of a default under a deed of trust or mortgage. (2) A notice required by an interested third party who has insured or guaranteed a loan (FHA, VA, OR PMI).

Notice of loss The conditions of the insurance policy, require that any person sustaining a loss against the property insured by the policy shall forthwith (immediately) give notice to the company of such loss. This notice is a condition precedent to recovery, unless waived by the insurer. Failure to give notice as required, has been held to be a bar against recovery. The notice is required to be in writing, and verbal notice to the agent will not be sufficient to comply with the condition.

Notice to company *See* **Notice of loss.**

Notice to quit A notice given by a landlord to his tenant, requiring him to quit and surrender the leased premises by a time therein named. An eviction notice.

Novation The substitution of a new contract or obligation between the same parties or different parties. The substitution, by mutual agreement, of one debtor for another or one creditor for another whereby the existing debt is extinguished.

Nuisance In law this refers to a class of wrong that arises out of unreasonable, unwarranted or unlawful use by a person of his own propetry whether that property by real or personal or from his own improper, indecent or unlawful personal contact, and producing an annoyance, inconvience, discomfort or hurt that the law would presume a consequential damage; e.g. *public nuisance* — the blocking of streets or highways or the air or a water pollution e.g. *private nuisance* — unwarranted noise from a loud playing musical instrument, records etc. or the keeping of animals on a property so as to incommode the neighbours.

In insurance claims, it is most frequently met as a cause of action, arising from the escape of some obnoxious substance, such as waters, smoke, gas, noise, etc. It may also apply to the wrongful disturbance of an easement. The remedy (1) an injunction requiring cessation of the nuisance; (2) mandamus, or an action in tort, for damages.

Nuisance value   This is not a true value but is the amount that someone, other than the owner of a property will pay for it, not for its own sake but because in its present hands it is an annoyance or is actually damaging to the prospective buyer.

Null and void   Of no legal or binding force.

Nulla bona   The return of a writ made by a sheriff, in which he indicates he has been unable to find any goods to seize.

Numc pro tunc   "Now and then" — as when a Court directs a proceeding to be dated as of an earlier date than that on which it was actually taken.

Numerical rating system   This system is based upon the principle that a large number of factors are involved in determining the composition of a risk. Statistical studies of each factor are used to determine the degree of risk involved. Rates are based upon the studies.

Nurses fees   A health insurance benefit occasionally included in policies. There is generally a maximum limit per day as well as an overall time limit. This benefit generally applies only to hospital care, however, in some cases it may be extended to cover the home.

O.A.S.I.   Old Age and Survivers Insurance, which is also known as Social Security.

O.C.S.F.   Office Contents Special Form

O.I.A.   Oil Insurance Association.

O.L.T.   Owners, landlords, and tenants (liability insurance).

O.P.   Original premium (also order policy).

O/S   Out of Stock

O.T.   Occupational Therapy

Oath   Appealing to the Almighty to witness the truth of the statement.

Obiter Dictum   The general comment of a Judge on certain legal questions on which a direct legal decision has not been given.

Such statements are not binding as precedents although are sometimes used for persuasive purposes.

Objective risk The relative variation of the actual from the probable loss.

Obligatory Treaty *See* **Reinsurance Treaty, automatic.**

Obligee A firm or person protected by a bond similar to the insured under a policy of insurance.

Obligor Commonly called principal; one bound by an obligation. Under a bond, strictly speaking, both the principal and the surety are obligors. The surety.

Obsolescence Impairment of desirability and usefulness brought about by changes in public preference or by forces in addition to those which cause deterioration. Functional obsolescence refers to impairment of functional capacity or efficiency. Economic obsolescence refers to impairment of desirability or utility arising from economic forces such as changes in highest and best land use, legislative enactments which restrict or impair property rights, and changes in supply-demand relationships.

Occupancy The type and character of the use of property. It plays a very important part in computing rates and in determining the acceptance or rejection of risks.

Occupancy permit An endorsement on an insurance policy permitting occupancy which might otherwise suspend the contract or make it invalid.

Occupational accident An accident occurring in the course of one's employment and caused by inherent or related hazards.

Occupational classification Classification of occupations according to the degree of risk inherently involved in the practice of that occupation.

Occupational disease Impairment of health caused by continued exposure to conditions inherent in a person's occupation.

Occupational hazard A danger inherent in the insured's line of work.

Occurrence A continuance or repeated exposure to conditions which results in injury. A clause frequently found under a personal liability policy; e.g., all damages which arise out of the same general conditions are considered as arising from one occurrence. A leaky gas heater in a home might cause illness over a period of days without the person exposed to it being completely overcome at any one time. Such illness would be described as due to one occurrence under terms of a personal liability policy.

Occurence basis The liability insurance clause under which covered acts must satisfy stated conditions. For example, the results must be accidental and unintended although the occurrence may be a deliberate act of an insured.

Ocean marine insurance Insurance associated with insurance of vessels and their cargoes as well as the related areas.

Odds The probable number of incidents that will occur within a statistical universe. For example, the odds are one in two that a head will come up on any given toss of a coin. Insurance actuaries compute their tables on the basis of past experience and other factors including the odds of probability.

Off premises A clause used to provide insurance protection on personal property covered while it is away from the premises named in the policy.

Offer A proposal to perform something, or to pay certain consideration for something, which when accepted, constitutes a contract. It may be withdrawn or revoked at any time prior to acceptance, or will cease to exist if not accepted within a reasonable time.

Offer and Acceptance As applied to life insurance, the "offer" may be made by the applicant through signing of application, submitting to physical examination and pre-payment of first premium. Policy issuance, as applied for, constitutes "acceptance" by the company. Or the "offer" may be made by the company where no premium payment has been submitted with application and medical. Premium payment on the offered policy then constitutes "acceptance" by the applicant.

Office burglary and robbery policy An insurance contract of broad coverage covering loss of insured either inside or outside his office. The areas covered are money, securities, office fixtures, and equipment as well as burglary.

Office contents special form All-risk coverage of furniture, fixtures, office supplies, and equipment of an office.

Office policy A part of a Special Multi-Peril Policy combining the various coverages applicable to ownership and operation of an office building.

Officer's and director's liability insurance policy Type of business insurance coverage. Self-explanatory.

Off-site improvements Improvements, such as sidewalks, streets, curbs, and gutters, outside the boundaries of a property, that enhance its value.

O'Gorman and Young Inc. vs. Hartford Fire Insurance Company and vs. Phoenix Assurance Company Ltd. State legislative regulation of agents commissions upheld as well as all administrative expenses of insurance companies.

Old Age and Survivors Insurance *See* **Social Security.**

Old line Phrase used by reserve system companies to differentiate their type of operation from the fraternal insurance system. However a fraternal which adopts a legal reserve would not be old line until it discontinues its lodge system.

Old line legal reserve Legal reserve companies not engaged in fraternal insurance sales.

Omnibus blocks Omnibus blocks are blocks of buildings consisting of two or more structures under one continuous roof. The term is also applied to blocks of property which are occupied by many tenants, for divers purposes. They are considered to be more hazardous risks.

Omnibus clause Found in a standard automobile liability policy which extends the coverage to others who are using the car within the limits of the policy.

Omnibus risk A building containing a number of tenants engaged in various businesses.

On-site improvements Any construction of buildings or other improvements within the boundaries of a property that increases its value.

Onus (onus propondi) The burden of proof.

Open certificate An insurance policy under which the rates and policy provisions may be changed. Fraternal insurance companies are required by law to issue this type of certificate.

Open cover A facility commonly used in reinsurance whereby risks in a particular category became known and are insured.

Open-end mortgage A loan reduced by amortization which can be increased to the original amount and secured by the original mortgage. A mortgage that by mutual agreement may have the balance or maturity extended to provide for modernization or improvement of the property.

Open-end policy *See* **Open certificate.**

Open mortgage A mortgage of which the date of maturity has passed but the unamortized balance has not been called.

Open policy An insurance contract covering all described types of cargo shipped by, or to the insured, within a specified geographical area, the amounts being reported as shipments are made by or notified to, the insured. An insurance contract on a specified risk or group of risks, in which the amount and terms are not specified, and under which reports of individual amounts insured and periods of coverage are made to the insurer by the insured. More properly called open certificate. *See* **Open certificate.**

Open stock Goods in show windows, on display, or on shelves.

Open stock burglary policy Contractual insurance coverage against loss caused by burglary of merchandise on shelves, on display, or in show windows.

Operating budget A detailed projection of all income and expenses for a given period.

Operating expenses In general, all expenses of a property with the exception of real estate taxes, depreciation, interest, and amortization.

Operating ratio The percentage relationship between budgeted or actual operating expenses, plus taxes, and effective gross income.

Operations The activities of the insured and his employees in the conduct of a business. For example, in a garage the operations include all the work done in and out of the garage by the owner and his employees. A garage public liability policy protects the owner against claims which may arise out of the operations of his own business whether they occur in his own place of business, in adjoining public ways, or wherever the performance of his business requires him or his employees to work.

Option An agreement granting the exclusive rights during a stated period of time, without creating any obligation, to purchase, sell, or otherwise direct or contract the use of a property. The privilege for a consideration of buying or leasing property for a specified price within a specified time. Also, choice of one of several alternatives as payment options of a policy.

Optional benefits Lump sum indemnities for specified injuries (usually dislocations, sprains, and fractures). In some policies, the insured may elect to receive these benefits in lieu of loss-of-time benefits.

Optional modes of settlement Many life insurance policies permit the insured or his beneficiary or beneficiaries to choose one of several options or methods of being paid. The typical options permit a single lump sum payment, payment of interest on the principal, or some instalment or annuity payments.

Optional Settlement clause A clause in an insurance policy permitting the insured under certain circumstances to have a choice of benefits.

In Accident and Health policies the insured may have a choice of payment of various bills for the provided amount of time or a lump sum settlement of a predetermined amount set out in the policy.

In a fire policy, a dwelling owner who carries insurance to 80% of the value may have repairs made to damage resulting from a peril insured, without charge for depreciation and providing the repairs do not exceed the actual value of the property.

Optionally Renewable A contract of health insurance in which the insurer reserves the unrestricted right to terminate the coverage at any anniversary or, in some cases, at any premium-due date, but does not have the right to terminate coverage between such dates.

Ordinary annuity *See* **Annuity.**

Ordinary construction A building in which the supporting walls are brick and the floors are wood joists; the interior finish usually conceals space in which fire can spread, and with little protection of stair shafts. *See* **Mill construction** for contrast.

Ordinary life insurance Life insurance usually issued in amounts of $1,000 or more with the premiums payable on an annual, semiannual, quarterly, or monthly basis. The term is also used to mean straight life insurance, a plan of insurance for the whole of life with premiums payable until death. All policies not classified as industrial or group. Designates the continuous premium. The context will determine which definition is appropriate.

Ordinary Life—Whole Life—Straight Life These three terms are synonymous and are applied to the type of policy which continues during the whole of the insured's life and provides for the payment of amount insured at his death, or at age 96 (on basis of American Experience Table of Mortality or at age 100 on the C.S.O. Tables) if he still is living at that age.

Original cost The actual payment for a property by its present owner or the actual cost at the time the building was first constructed and placed into service.

Origination fee A fee or charge for the work involved in the evaluation, preparation, and submission of a proposed mortgage loan.

Osborne et. al., vs. Ozlin et. al. U. S. Supreme Court interpretation of Resident Agents Laws.

Other insurance clause Clause in an insurance policy, states the matter of apportioning the insurance where two or more policies cover the same clause. The customary practice is on a pro rata or excess basis. For example, if you have two $5,000 fire insurance policies on a building and suffer a $3,000 loss, the "other insurance clause" in your policies provides that the loss would be divided between the two policies on a pro rata basis. In this case each policy would pay $1,500. However, if an employer carries a $10,000 nonownership automobile liability policy on an automobile used by an employee, also insured for $10,000, in the case of an accident involving a $12,000 loss, the employer's policy would be settled on an "excess basis." The employee's policy would pay the first $10,000 and the $2,000 excess would be paid by the nonownership policy should the employer be liable.

Outage insurance Insurance against loss due to failure of machinery to operate.

Outboard motor boat and outdoor motor policy A policy covering boats, motors, and equipment for named perils such as fire, collision, and theft or, at a higher premium, for all risks.

Out-patient A patient who does not reside in a hospital in which he has received treatment.

Outservant An employee whose principal work is outside a dwelling.

Outside employee A person who works for wages away from the main place of business.

Outside holdup insurance Insures the owner of property, securities, or money against loss caused by robbery away from the insured's place of business.

Over line The amount of insurance or reinsurance which exceeds the insurers or reinsurers normal capacity. Also applies to a commitment to write insurance exceeding this capacity.

Over the counter selling A nonagency system of selling insurance in which the insured obtains his insurance by going to the insurance company and purchasing it. Savings bank life insurance departments and certain direct writers engage in over the counter selling.

Over-age insurance   Accident and sickness insurance written at ages beyond which ordinary policies do not go. Usually the benefits are hospitalization and medical care.

Overall capitalization rate   The relationship between net operating income and the total project cost.

Over-all property tax limitation   A constitutional or statutory limitation on the total amount of taxes which may be levied for all purposes against any parcel of real estate within one year, such over-all limit to be fixed percentage of the true value of such parcel of real estate. It is so called to distinguish it from the limitations on separate portions of the real estate tax now in effect in nearly all states.

Overcharging   An abuse where the insured is charged an amount in excess of his actual premiums. The National Association of Insurance Commissioners in their report of 1954 listed overcharging as an abuse by certain undesirable elements in credit life insurance.

Overhead   Charges of a fairly fixed nature which do not vary with the volume of activity. Light, water, rent, and some taxes are overhead items.

Overhead writing   Insurance companies acceptance of business from a broker or agent other than an agent that has an exclusive territorial agreement.

Overimprovement   An addition or alteration which is not in the highest and best use for the site on which it is placed, thus a very expensive building on a very poor or cheap site.

Overinsurance   The situation which exists where a risk is insured for more than its fair or reasonable value.

Overlapping insurance   Insurance coverage from two or more policies or companies which in part duplicate the insurance of certain risks. Since the insured's premium includes the duplicated coverage he is paying a needless amount of premium.

Overriding commission   Sometimes called overwriting commission. The fee paid to an agent or special agent who by contract is entitled to a fee on business written in his territory.

Overt Act   A clear open, unhidden, observable act.

Overwriting commission   *See* **Overriding commission.**

Owner's and contractor's protective liability   Contract of insurance protecting the owner and contractor against the negligent actions of subcontractors they have hired.

Owners, Landlords and Tenants Liability Coverage (OL&T) Legal liability coverage with respect to the ownership, maintenance, and use of the premises, and all operations necessary or incidental thereto.

Owner's liability insurance policy Type of business insurance coverage. Self-explanatory.

Ownership form A particular policy where ownership is vested in someone other than the insured.

Ownership of expirations Agreement by the insurance company that certain information regarding details of a policy such as expiration will not be revealed to any other agent or broker except the originating agent. This agreement permits the original agent to contact the client for renewal or extension of a policy.

P.A. Particular Average; Public Accountant

P/A Power of attorney.

P.A.P. Pension administration plan.

P.C. Petty Cash

P.C.B.B. Primary commercial blanket bond.

P.D. Property damage.

P.D.C. Premium & Dispersion Credits

P.E.B.B. Public Employees Blanket Bond

P.E.F. Personal effects floater.

P. & I. Protection and indemnity.

P.I.P. Public and Institutional Property

P.I.V. Post indicator valve: valve which projects above the ground, indicating whether it is open or closed.

P&L Profit and Loss

P.L. Public liability.

P.L.E. Primary Loss Expectancy

P.L.R. Primary loss retention.

P.M.I. Private mortgage insurance.

P.M.L. Probable Maximum Loss

P.N. Promissory Note

P.O. Public official.

P.P.F. Personal property floater.

P.P.I. Policy proof of interest.

P.R. Pro rata.

P.R.A. Payroll Auditor

P.R.D. Pro rata distribution (clause).

P.S.C. Public service commission.

P.S.S.B.B. Public School System Blanket Bond

P.T. · Pacific Time

P.U.C. Public utilities commission.

PUD *See* **Planned Unit Development.**

Package insurance A combination of coverage in a single policy. The ownership, maintenance, and use of property exposes the owner to a wide variety of risks. All these risks are covered in a package insurance policy.

Package loan Interim and take-out loans made by the same investor, as in construction lending.

Package mortgage A loan by which not only the real property is financed but also certain personal property such as washing machine, dishwasher, etc.

Package policies Combination policies wherein several coverages are included in one contract; e.g., storekeepers' burglary and robbery policy, residence all-in one policy, homeowner's policy, comprehensive dwelling policy, and DDD policy.

Pad A term used to describe graded land for residential use or the concrete slab with utility connections on which a mobile home is placed.

Paid business Applications have been signed by the applicant, and the applicant has received a medical examination and has paid the first premium. *See* distinction between delivered, examined, paid, placed, issued, and written business.

Paid-for life insurance Insurance on which there has been settlement for the first premium regardless of whether the application has yet been accepted by the company or the policy yet issued.

Paid losses Total payments made to discharge obligations under policies issued.

Paid-up additions Units of single premium insurance purchased with participating policy dividends under one of the customary dividend options.

Paid-up insurance Insurance on which all required premiums have been paid. The term is frequently used to mean the nonforfeiture option, reduced paid-up insurance.

Par The principal amount of a security or mortgage with no premium or discount.

Paramedic A person with professional training in health care other than an M.D. and D.O.

Parapet   The structure above a roof serving as a fire wall.

Parcel post insurance   Indemnity for damage or loss to package while being processed by the United States Post Office Department. This type of coverage may be purchased from either the Post Office Department or private insurance companies.

Parent company   Oldest or controlling company in a fleet of companies.

Parking index   A standard comparison indicating the number of parking spaces required for the gross leasable area or the number of leasable units.

Parol   Oral, as distinguished from written.

Parole Contract   Contracts made verbally are called "parole contracts". When entered into by a duly authorized person, a parole contract is, in the absence of any law to the contrary, binding, and if made by a duly appointed agent, would bind the company. "Insurance agreements of this character are generally contracts to issue a policy rather than insurance by contract. The policy when issued will be expected to show the conditions entered into verbally, and on the acceptance of the policy, any condition which has been omitted will be considered as waived unless error can be proved, in which case the policy will be subject to rectification for any error of fact". (Griswold).

Parole Evidence (oral evidence)   A written instrument is considered to be complete in itself and oral or "Parole Evidence" is not admissable to vary, alter or change the terms of such an instrument. The rule is based on a concept that all prior negotiations between the parties have been superseded by and merged into the instrument itself.

Partial disability   Reduction in ability to do things and work that one could when in full health. The degree of disability will vary with the severity of the injury or illness.

Partial limitation clause   Provides in an insurance policy for the payment of the total loss when a loss is more than a specified amount. A loss of $15.00 under a policy with a $25.00 partial limitation clause would not be reimbursed. However, a covered loss of $75.00 would be completely paid.

Partial loss   A loss under an insurance policy which does not either completely destroy or render worthless the insured property or exhaust the insurance applied to the property.

Partial payment   In loan collection, less than the full payment due, usually not credited until the balance is received.

Partial Vesting That form of immediate or deferred vesting under which a specified portion of the accrued benefits of a participant becomes a vested benefit.   CIT

Partially amortized mortgage A mortgage which is partly repaid by amortization during the life of the mortgage and partly repaid at the end of the term.

Participant An employee, or former employee, who may become eligible to receive, or is receiving, benefits under the plan as a result of his credited service.   CIT

Participating insurance Insurance on which the policyholder is entitled to share in the surplus earnings of the company through dividends which reflect the difference between the premium charged and actual experience. Also Insurance or reinsurance which contributes proportionately with other insurance on the same risk. Compare with excess insurance and also see reinsurance.

Participating policies Provide for returning to the insureds, in the form of dividends, part of the premium paid—this action is voted upon by the directors of the company. Stock, as well as mutual, companies issue this type of policy.

Participation clause A provision in an insurance policy that calls for the insured to pay a specified percentage of the cost of health care covered by the policy.

Participation loan (1) A mortgage made by one lender, known as the lead lender, in which one or more other lenders, known as participants, own a part interest. (2) A mortgage originated by two or more lenders.

Particular average Loss borne by one of a number of carriers in marine insurance, such as partial loss of cargo, hull, or freight, falling entirely on the interest concerned. This means, primarily, a loss suffered by the insured without benefit to or right of remuneration from others. It is also used synonymously with partial loss in marine insurance. *See* **General average.**

Partition The act of dividing property among the several owners thereof who may hold in either joint tenancy or as tenants in common.

Partition proceedings A legal procedure by which an estate held by tenants in common is divided and title in severalty to a designated portion passed to each of the previous tenants in common.

Partnership entity plan Provides a buy and sell agreement: upon the death of a partner, the partnership will purchase the share of the deceased partner for the account of the surviving partners. The premiums are payable by the partnership out of income and the cash value of the insurance is an asset of the firm.

Partnership insurance *See* **Buy-Sell agreement.**

Parts & Labor, Manual (The Chilton) (The National Standard) A pricing guide for repair or replacement of automobile parts based on manufacturers parts prices and time studies for necessary operations.

Party wall A dividing wall erected upon and over a line separating two adjoining properties and in which the owners of the respective parcels have common rights to its use.

Past-due loan A mortgage loan that is delinquent or has matured and not been paid in full.

Past Service Benefit That portion of a participant's retirement benefit that relates to his period of credited service before the effective date of the plan. CIT

Patent The title deed by which the United States or a state conveys its lands.

Patent insurance Insurance against loss due to infringement of the insured's patent, or due to claim of infringement of the other's patent by the insured.

Patient supervision clause Provision that patient must be continually under supervision of doctor or nurse.

Patterns insurance policy Type of business insurance coverage. Self-explanatory.

Paul vs. Virginia Legal decision in 1869 and upheld until 1944 that insurance was not commerce, and not being commerce could thus not be interstate commerce. Since insurance was not interstate commerce it was not subject to control by the United States Government.

Pay As in 20-pay, limited pay. An abbreviation for payment. It is written without a period.

Pay off To satisfy in full an existing indebtedness.

Paymaster robbery insurance Indemnification for loss or damage of property due to robbery of the insured's payroll. Also covered is loss or damage of property other than the payroll; this coverage typically is limited to 10 percent of the total sum insured.

Payee　The person to whom money is paid.

Payee clause　A clause in an insurance contract providing for payment of loss to a person or class of persons.

Payer　The party who pays the bill.

Payment into Court　The deposit of money with an official of the Court pending the outcome of litigation.

Payments, deferred　Deferred payments.

Payor benefit　A rider attached to juvenile policies and waiving future premiums if the payor (usually the parent) becomes disabled or dies before maturity of the policy or at the end of a certain period of years.

Payor clause　A clause in a policy issued on a juvenile's life under which all future premiums are waived if the parent dies before the child reaches a stated age or maturity.

Payor Insurance　The benefit available under certain juvenile policies, upon payment of an extra premium, which provides for the waiver of future premiums in event the person responsible for the payment of the premiums dies or is disabled before the child reaches a specified age.

Payroll audit　An examination of the insured's payroll records by a representative of the insurer to determine the premium due on a policy written on a payroll basis. *See* **Audit.**

Payroll deduction insurance　Employer is authorized to deduct from the earnings of employee amounts to cover the premium of individual life insurance policies.

Payroll robbery insurance　*See* **Paymaster robbery insurance.**

Payroll savings life insurance　*See* **Payroll deduction insurance.**

Penalty　The limit of an insurance company's liability on a bond.

Pend file　A diary, or suspense, file containing all correspondence and related material in one location. It is referred to the appropriate individuals, on an automatic basis, when the diary date is reached.

Pendent lite　While a suit is pending or after a suit has been commenced.

Pension administration plan　*See* **Immediate participation guarantee plan.**

Pension fund　An institution that holds assets invested in long-term mortgages and high-grade stocks and bonds having acceptable yields and security. The purpose of a pension fund is to accumulate funds to hold and invest in such a manner that it will provide retirement income to individuals on an agreed-upon plan.

Pension plan A system, frequently using insurance companies, for the payment of annuities or pensions to qualified individuals. Sections 165 and 23 of the Internal Revenue Code establish requirements for taxes based upon pension plans.

Pension trust A trust that has been created to administer a pension plan.

Percentage lease A lease in which a percentage of the tenant's gross business receipts constitutes the rent. Although a straight percentage lease is occasionally encountered, most percentage leases contain a provision for a minimum rent amount.

Percentage paid off The equity build-up of a loan, the accumulated payments to principal as a percent of the face amount of the loan.

Percentage Participation A provision in a health insurance contract that the insurer and the insured will share covered losses in agreed proportions. CIT

Percolation test A test performed on soil to determine its water seepage capacity when the use of a septic tank is being considered.

Per diem business interruption Coverage that provides a stated and fixed amount that will be paid for each day the business is not in operation due to insured peril.

Perfecting title The elimination of any claims against a title.

Performance bond *See* **Bid bond** also **Bond, contract.**

Peril Cause of a possible loss.
Comment: A broad generic term, under which specific situations giving rise to loss may be classified as hazards. CIT

Perils of the sea Collision, sinking, and heavy storm are examples of perils of the sea. Marine insurance is concerned with these perils.

Perjury False statement made under oath.

Permanent disability *See* **Disability, permanent.**

Permanent investor One who provides permanent financing.

Permanent life insurance policy Ordinary life and whole life are considered to be permanent life insurance policies and will stay in that status as long as premiums are paid.

Permanent loan A long-term loan or mortgage that is fully amortized and extended for a period of not less than two years.

Permanent partial disability benefits Periodic indemnities for a disability which impairs earning capacity but which does not involve total inability to work.

Permanent total disability benefits Periodic indemnities, generally weekly, for a disability of a kind that renders any employment impossible. Such compensation may be limited by maximum time or maximum amount, but if unlimited may run for life.

Permit bond *See* **Bond, permit.**

Perpetual easement A constantly maintained easement under which certain privileges or rights of the owner of the land are granted to another.

Perpetual insurance Uncommon form of fire insurance policy that has no expiration date.

Per risk excess insurance Reinsurance on a per risk basis as contrasted from a per accident or aggregate basis.

Per se By itself.

Persistency The maintenance of policies in full force until completion of the term for which the policy was written (in life insurance, includes death or maturity). May also refer to continuance and renewal of insurance contracts upon their expiration.

Personal accident insurance Contractual protection of an individual against damage caused by an accident.

Personal Articles Floater Sold as a separate policy or attached to an existing property policy. For the protection of either specific items such as a fur coat or jewelry or to cover virtually all personal property owned by you, regardless of where loss or damage occurs. Guests property is also covered while in your home.

Personal Auto Policy (PAP) A policy for personal automobile insurance. It has replaced the family auto policy (FAP).

Personal bond or security A guaranty executed by an individual as additional security for specific performance of an obligation.

Personal effects floater A contract affording insurance against loss to personal effects usually carried by travelers and located away from the domicile of the insured. *See* **Personal property floater.**

Personal fur insurance Contractual coverage against loss of fur garment individually owned.

Personal hazard *See* **Moral hazard.**

Personal holdup insurance Covers the insured for loss of property if held up.

Personal injury Bodily harm to a human.

Personal Injury Coverage An extension of liability coverage to provide for libel, slander, false arrest, invasion of privacy and the like.

Personal liability The sum owed by a natural person.

Personal liability insurance policy Type of insurance coverage. Self-explanatory.

Personal property This is defined to mean the right or interest which a person may have in things personal, movable, or separable from the realty. A building standing on leased ground is personal of the lessee. If land and building thereon under one owner, it is real property or realty.

Personal property floater An insurance policy with broad coverage for personal property either at home or away. Contractual coverage of insured's personal effects against loss or theft.

Personal surety Surety provided by an individual as compared to surety provided by an insurance company.

Personal suretyship The giving of a bond by an individual.

Personal theft insurance Contractual protection against loss caused by theft of household goods or other personal property either in or outside of a residence.

Personalty Property which is movable. All property is either personalty, realty, or mixed.

Per stirpes Succession by right of representation.

Per unit allocation The method of allocating costs over the total number of units affected.

Physical approach to value An appraisal method whereby property value is derived by estimating the replacement cost of improvements, less estimated depreciation plus estimated land value by use of market data. *See* **Market approach to value**.

Physical depreciation A term that is frequently used when physical deterioration is meant. In a broad concept it may relate to those elements that are inherent in the physical property itself, as distinguished from other and external circumstances that may influence its utilization. Not a• clear or proper term without qualification and explanation. Deterioration due to the adverse changes in the physical condition of property such as the loss of top soil, the rotting or wearing away of buildings, as well as damage caused by physical elements, rain, storm, sleet.

Physical hazard 'The material, structural, or operational features of the risk itself, apart from the persons owning or managing it.

Physical value A term erroneously used to designate an estimate of reproduction or replacement cost, or the estimated value of physical assets as distinct from nonphysical assets.

Physically Impaired Risk A person having a physical disability or disease which may affect his acceptability as a risk. Some impairments can be offset by mechanical aids or prosthetic devices; others improve or disappear with the passage of time or are controlled or compensated for by medication.

Physicians, Dentists, Druggists and hospital liability insurance Coverage against loss or damages because of bodily injuries or death as a result of error in preparation of materials or of malpractice.

Physicians' and Surgeons' Professional Liability Insurance Insurance against loss due to claims for damages alleging malpractice by physicians or surgeons in the exercise of their professions.

Physician's liability insurance policy Type of business insurance coverage. Self-explanatory. *See* **Liability insurance, physician's and surgeon's.**

P.I.E. card A card having a threefold use: (1) Payroll audit, (2) Indexing, and (3) Expiration. The initials are the first letters of each function.

Piece-of-the-action *See* **Kicker.**

Pilferage Any petty thievery or the theft of a portion of property such as theft of a tire from an automobile.

Pillage and looting Insurance protection for loss occurring by reason of theft of property during a riot or civil commotion.

Piracy Theft on the high seas.

Piscary The right or privilege of fishing in another man's waters.

PITI (Principal, Interest, Taxes, and Insurance) The Principal and Interest payment on most loans is fixed for the term of the loan; the Tax and Insurance portion may be adjusted to reflect changes in taxes or insurance costs.

Placed business Policies whose applications have been examined and the policies made out and delivered to the policyholder, who has paid for the first premium. *See* distinctions between **Delivered, Examined, Paid, Issued,** and **Written business.**

Placer Individual in a broker's office who places or obtains the acceptance of insurance risks.

Plaintiff Individual who brings a lawsuit against a defendant.

Planned Unit Development (PUD) (1) A comprehensive development plan for a large land area. It usually includes residences, roads, schools, recreational facilities, and service areas plus commercial, office, and industrial areas. (2) A subdivision having lots or areas owned in common and reserved for the use of some or all of the owners of the separately owned lots.

Planning commission A local or regional organization, normally a government agency, responsible for the preparation and adoption of comprehensive long-term general plans for the physical development of property within its jurisdiction.

Plans and specifications Architectural and engineering drawings and specifications for construction of a building or project. They include a description of materials to be used and the manner in which they are to be applied.

Plat A small plot of ground or a plan, map, or chart especially of a subdivision.

Plat book The record showing the size, the location, the name of the owner of each of the lots, parcels, or plots of land within the agency's stated area.

Plate glass insurance policy Type of business insurance coverage that indemnifies the insured against loss caused by breakage of glass.

Plates (inside studs) Horizontal wood members nailed at bottom and top of partition uprights.

Pledge The transference of property such as the cash value of a life insurance policy to a creditor as security for a debt.

Plot plan A layout of improvements on a site, including their location, dimensions, and landscapes. It is generally a part of the architectural plan.

Plottage increment The increase or appreciation of the unit value resulting from the joining together of smaller lots, parcels, or land units into one large single ownership, the resulting total value being larger than the individual unit values.

Point An amount equal to 1 percent of the principal amount of an investment or note. Loan discount points are a one-time charge assessed at closing by the lender to increase the yield on the mortgage loan to a competitive position with other types of investments.

Police power   That right by which the state or other governmental authority may take, condemn, destroy, impair the value of, limit the use of, or otherwise invade property rights. It must be affirmatively shown that the property was taken to protect the public health, public morals, public safety, or the general welfare.

Policies, kinds of   There are several kinds of policies. "Specific" policies are policies that cover one building, or the contents of one building at one location. They may be written either with, or without co-insurance. "Blanket" policies embrace buildings and/or the contents of several buildings in one sum, and at one premium rate without respect to the individual values in each. The sum insured "blankets" the whole of the risk. Such policies are only permitted under the Underwriters' rules when they contain a co-insurance clause, a precaution essential to the protection of the company against gross under insurance. (See partial Insurance to Value). "Floater" policies are policies covering at two or more locations and in one or more buildings at each location, under one sum, and at one rate of premium. They are generally subject to 100% co-insurance. (See Floater Policies).

Policy   The printed document issued to the insured by the company stating the terms of the insurance contract. A written contract of insurance between an insurance company and the policyholder.

Policy conditions   Under the law every policy must have the Statutory Conditions imposed by the Insurance Act printed on the back thereof, when the written (or typed) conditions of the policy are, in any degree, inconsistent with the printed conditions, the written conditions will apply, as they are held to be "superadded" and are entitled to have greater effect, as they constitute the language and terms of the parties to the contract. However, when any written condition waives, or modifies a Statutory Condition, it is essential that the policy be marked in clear type in a different coloured ink, and with a notice to the effect that such conditions of a Statutory character have been waived or modified. Such waivers or modifications are subject to decision by the Courts as to whether they are a "reasonable waiver or modification".

Policy contract   An insurance contract embodied in a policy.

Policy Dividend   The annual dividend represents the policyholder's share of the company's divisible surplus earnings.

Policy fee   Charge, illegal in most states, made by an agent in addition to the premium. Small policies were the main source of a policy fee. An amount sometimes charged in addition to the first annual premium as a fee for issuance of the policy. Usually it goes to the agent and is a method of paying the acquisition cost or part of it immediately rather than amortizing it over a period of several years of premiums.

Policy loan   A loan made by an insurance company to a policyholder on the security of the cash value of his policy.

Policy period   The period during which a policy contract affords insurance.

Policy proof of interest   A clause in an open contract of marine insurance covering peculiar conditions of risk concerning anticipated freight. For example, if a captain of a vessel has gone to pick up freight that is destroyed by some hazard he has suffered loss in terms of shipping fees. Protection by a P.P.I. or F.I.A. policy will indemnify him for his loss.

Policy register   A record maintained by the company for noting the issuance of, and thus accounting for, all of its policies.

Policy reserves   The funds that an insurance company holds specifically for the fulfillment of its policy obligations. Reserves are so calculated that, together with the future premiums and interest earnings, they will enable the company to pay all future claims.

Policy term   The term of policy, usually the period for which the premium is paid.

Policy writing agent   Individual having right to make out his own policy. Many agents can only prepare a survey or application from which the insurance company prepares the policy. The recording agent does not have to send in the survey or application to make a binding contract. *See* **Agent, policy writing; recording agent.**

Policy year   The 365 or 366 days between annual premium dates. The year commencing with the effective date of the policy or with an anniversary of that date.

Policy year experience   Experience on business during the twelve months period from the effective date of the policy which became effective during a given year irrespective of when the transactions (payment of premium or loss payment) may actually have taken place.

Policyholder   The individual or firm in whose name an insurance policy is written. Synonymous with insured.

Policyholders' surplus   The net worth of an insurance company adjusted for any overstatements of liabilities.

Policyowner   *See* **Policyholder**. A synonym.

Polish National Alliance of the U. S. of A. Petitioner vs. National Labor Relations Board   U. S. Supreme Court held that case involved Wagner Act unfair labor practices and that Congress had power to regulate practices affecting commerce between states.

Pool   Group of insurance companies that have joined together for the purpose of sharing certain risks on an agreed-upon basis.

Port   A place where vessels may receive or discharge cargo.

Portability   The right to transfer pension credits when an individual changes positions and companies.

Portfolio   The securities in which the assets of the company are invested; also applied to the reinsurance held by an insurer.

Portfolio reinsurance   A type of reinsurance whereby the reinsurer assumes all obligations of the ceding company in a particular class.

Position bond   *See* **Bond, position.**

Position schedule bond   An insurance contract that guarantees the honesty of individuals filling certain stated positions in a company as compared to a bond that covers individuals that are named.

Post Date   To use a date in the future as related to the time of use.

Posthumous child   A child born after death of its father.

Post mortem   After death.

Post Mortem Dividend   A dividend allotted after the death of the insured and constituting a pro rata portion of the dividend that would have been payable at a later date if the policyholder had lived.

Post Office life insurance   Proposal made in 1939 that U. S. Post Offices sell life insurance as found in Japan. Not adopted.

Potential value   A loose term signifying a value which would or will exist if and when future probabilities become actualities.

Power interruption insurance policy   Type of insurance coverage against loss due to interruption of power supply from a public utility caused by accidental breakdown of the utility's machinery.

Power of agency   *See* **Agent's authority.**

Power of attorney   The written instrument by which the authority of one person to act in the place and stead of another as his attorney in fact is set forth.

Power of sale   A clause in a will or trust agreement authorizing the sale or transfer of property in accordance with the terms of the clause.

Power plant insurance   Contract of insurance insuring electric generating plants and stations. Insurance against loss caused by accidental injury to objects used for generation control, storage, or distribution of energy. *See also* **Boiler and machinery insurance.**

Preaudit   Examination of invoices, claims accounts, and other pertinent records prior to payment.

Precedent   In the courts of law a judged case becomes "precedent" for future cases with facts and reasons that are analogous. Thus, in establishing a case one quotes "precedent" from previous similar cases in support of the present case.

Pre-existing condition   A condition, usually of health, which existed prior to the issuance of a specific policy.

Preferred risk   A cestui que vie who is considered to be less of a mortality risk than the standard risk.

Preliminary proofs of loss   When a fire occurs and a loss is sustained under an insurance policy, it is incumbent upon the policy-holder to make a statement of the particulars of the loss, as indicated in the Statutory Conditions of the policy. This statement is termed a "preliminary proof" which must be followed by supplementary details prepared under oath. Such proofs must be delivered in accordance with the law as laid down in the Statutory Conditions, and must be as explicit as to the particulars of the loss as the circumstances will admit.

Preliminary term   Insurance protection for a temporary period which precedes the effective date of a permanent policy form.

Preliminary Term Premium   In order that prospects who depend on certan seasons of the year for ready money may arrange to pay their premiums at such times, most companies will attach to a new policy a provision for term insurance for a preliminary period of one to eleven months. If the applicant's insurance age changes before the end of the preliminary period, the rate for the regular policy is based on the advanced age.

Preliminary title report   A title search by a title company prior to issuance of a title binder or commitment to insure.

Premises   Particular location or portion thereof as stated by the policy contract.

Premium The payment or one of the regular periodical payments a policyholder is required to make for an insurance policy. The amount of money which the policyholder agrees to pay to the insurance company for the policy of insurance.

Premium deposit Prepaid premiums. The insured pays a premium or premiums before the due date.

Premium discount plan A plan available in some rating jurisdictions providing for a percentage reduction on premium dependent upon the size of the premium. In workmen's compensation insurance it is recognized that the proportionate cost of issuing and servicing a policy is less as the premium increases. The premium discount plan gives the policyholder the benefit of this reduction.

Premium earned The amount of the premium which has been paid for in advance that has been "earned" by virtue of the fact that time has passed without claim. A three-year policy that has been paid in advance and is one year old would have only partly earned the premium.

Premium estimated A provisional premium subject to final adjustment on ascertainment of the necessary facts.

Premiums in force The initial premium on all policies not canceled or expired.

Premium loan A policy loan made for the purpose of paying premiums.

Premium, minimum The lowest consideration for which an insurer will insure a risk for a specified period.

Premium, net The portion of the premium calculated on the basis of a particular mortality table and interest rate, to enable the insurer to pay benefits as provided by the insurance contract, no account being taken of expenses, contingencies, or profit. Except in life insurance, the premiums earned or written by an insurer after deducting premiums returned to policyholders and premiums paid for reinsurance.

Premium notice Notice of a premium due, sent out by the company or one of its agencies to an insured.

Premium, pure The portion of the premium rate calculated to enable the insurer to pay losses and in some cases, allocated, claim expenses.

Premium rate The price per unit of insurance.

Premium Refund A special policy provision, effective for a specified period in event of death of the insured, calling for payment to the beneficiary of principal sum plus all premiums paid to date of death. Amount reverts to principal sum only if insured lives beyond specified period. Sometimes written as a special policy form; sometimes added by rider to standard policy.

Premium, restoration The premium charged to restore an insurance or surety contract to its original amount after payment of a loss.

Premium, return Premiums returned to policyholders principally on cancellation or partial cancellation of contracts, on rate adjustments, or on determination that an advance premium is in excess of the actual premium.

Premium, single The amount that constitutes payment in full for a contract at its inception.

Premium/surplus ratio The ratio of premiums written to policyholder's surplus.

Premium, unearned That part of the premium applicable to the unexpired part of the policy period. *See also* **Premium, earned.**

Premiums written The entire amount of premium on policy contracts written by an insurer.

Premiums written — gross Total premiums received from all sources including reinsurance assumed from other companies.

Premiums written — net Gross premiums written less reinsurance ceded to other companies.

Prepaid expense An expenditure, often recurrent, for benefits as yet not received. Unexpired insurance is a prepaid expense from the policyholder's point of view.

Prepaid group practice plan A system whereby participating doctors and dentists provide services to groups of individuals. The patients pay computed amounts in advance of the service being rendered.

Prepayment fee A consideration paid to the mortgagee for the prepayment privilege. Also known as a prepayment penalty or reinvestment fee.

Prepayment privilege The right given a borrower to pay all or part of a debt prior to its maturity. The mortgagee cannot be compelled to accept any payment other than those originally agreed to.

Prescription A time, after which a cause of action ceases. The Statutes set out a period of time in various circumstances, and any action to recover in such circumstances must be within that period of time, otherwise the cause of action fails because the action was not started within the prescribed time.

Present value or **present worth** The value or discounted worth, at the time of appraisal, of an amount or amounts receivable in the future.

Pressure vessel A container designed to hold steam, gas, or other vapor under pressure.

Presumption Is a rule of law that a particular inference is to be drawn from a particular fact or evidence which is assumed to be correct unless it is disproved. Some examples of presumption are: That human life continues for a reasonable time; that letters properly addressed and mailed have been received; that everyone is sane; that death was accidental and not suicidal; that marriage is legal; that all know the law. Some presumptions are conclusive. Others however are subject to rebuttal e. g. the lack of knowledge of the law is not acceptable as a breach of the law. Therefore, that all know the is conclusive. On the other hand that death was accidental and not suicidal is subject to rebuttal. It is presumed death was accidental but if it can be proven that it was suicide then such proof is acceptable.

Prevention Elimination of causes of loss. *See also* **protection**.

Price Quantity of one thing obtainable or paid in exchange for another.

Price level A relative position in the scale of prices as determined by a comparison of prices (of labor, materials, capital, etc.), as of one time with prices as of other times.

Prima facie At first view. Prima facie evidence is such as in law sufficient to establish a fact, unless rebutted.

Prima beneficiary *See* **Beneficiary, primary**.

Primary "Primary" means first in rank as importance, chief, principle, basic, or fundamental.

Primary earthquake *See* **Direct damage, earthquake**.

Primary financing A loan secured by a first mortgage or trust deed on real property. *See also* **Secondary financing**.

Primary insurance Provides coverage up to a specified amount or against specific perils.

Primary loss The stated amount of deductible in a credit insurance policy that is intended to reflect the normal credit losses of the insured company.

Primary rating factor The index number showing the added risks of various insured classes. It is used in rate-making plans.

Prime tenant A tenant, or related group of tenants, that is the largest single occupant of a building. Such occupancy is generally for 25 percent or more of the aggregate square footage.

Principal An individual or company whose performance of certain obligations is covered by a bond. The money due under the policy; the party to a transaction, as distinguished from the broker or agent. A sum lent or employed as a fund or investment, as distinguished from its income or profits. The original amount (as of a loan) of the total due and payable at a certain date. A party to a transaction as distinguished from an agent.

Principal amount The party, in suretyship, whose actions, honesty or responsibility are to be guaranteed. In the case of a fidelity bond, for example, the bonded employee is the principal. (*See* **Obligor**).

Principal balance The outstanding balance of a mortgage, exclusive of interest and any other charges.

Principal sum The amount specified in a policy to be paid in the event of certain losses, such as a designated amount of money to be paid in case of loss of limb.

Principle of indemnity The concept that an insured may collect up to the actual cash value of the property covered.

Principle of insurable interest The concept that the insured must have a demonstrated financial interest in the subject of the insurance before being paid by the insuring company in the event of a loss.

Priority As applied to claims against property, the status of being prior or having precedence over other claims. Priority is usually established by filing or recordation in point in time, but may be established by statute or agreement.

Prior insurance Insurance written prior to present policy on present risk.

Priority Legal preference.

Prior Service Benefit That portion of a participant's retirement benefit that relates to his period of credited service before a specified date. CIT

Private carrier A contract carrier as compared to a common or public carrier.

Private mortgage insurance (PMI) Insurance written by a private company protecting the mortgage lender against loss occasioned by a mortgage default.

Private passenger car An automobile operated for personal use by the owner.

Privately insured mortgage A conventional mortgage loan in which a private mortgage insurance company protects the lender against loss.

Privity Exists where heirs, executors, and certain others succeed to the rights of a contract. This permits them to have the same rights as the original party. Privity may be a factor in action of negligence.

Probability The likelihood that a future event will take place.

Probable life curve A statistical curve obtained from a frequency distribution and used to plot probable mortality.

Probable maximum loss (P.M.L.) The maximum amount of loss that can be expected under normal circumstances. Extraordinary circumstances, such as delayed alarm, insufficient water supply etc. can result in a loss exceeding the P.M.L. (*See* **Above-normal loss**).

Probate Proofs of a will before the proper Court; the official copy of the will with a certificate of it having been proved.

Probate court A court having jurisdiction of the proof of wills, the settlement of estates, and usually, of guardianships. In some states it is the district court.

Probation period The time after the beginning date of a policy during which sickness benefits will not be payable. The purpose of the period is to eliminate sickness actually contracted before the policy went into force. Not to be confused with waiting or elimination period.

Proceeds The face value of the policy plus any additions payable at maturity or death.

Processor One who changes the condition of products without changing their fundamental characteristics.

Processor's policy Contract of insurance that protects the policyholder when the insured property is in another's possession for processing, such as dyeing or pressing. Goods in the state of being delivered to or from the processor also are covered.

Producer Term commonly applied to an agent, solicitor, broker, or any other person who sells insurance; producing business for the company and for a commission (if so paid) for himself. He also creates the insurance product; namely, security and relief from risk for the insured.

Product liability Liability imposed for damages caused by accident and arising out of goods or products manufactured, sold, handled, or distributed by the insured or others trading under his name. The accident must have occurred after possession of goods has been relinquished to others, and away from premises owned, rented, or controlled by the insured. In the case of food products, accident does not have to occur away from premises (restaurants, etc.).

Production office An office having the necessary underwriting staff, and supporting clerical personnel, for the production of profitable business. Claims, payroll audit, and engineering personnel will be staffed as required. (*See* **Branch and regional offices**).

Products—Completed Operations Liability Coverage Liability protection against claims arising from products manufactured, sold, handled or distributed; liability protection against claims arising out of operations which have been completed or abandoned.

Products liability insurance Protection provided against claims arising from the utilization of the covered product manufactured, sold, handled, or distributed by the insured or others trading under his name if the accident occurs after possession has been relinquished to others and away from premises owned, rented, or controlled by the insured.

Professional liability *See* **Malpractice.**

Professional liability insurance policy Type of business insurance coverage. Self-explanatory.

Professional reinsurer An agent or agency whose only business is providing reinsurance and associated services.

Profit Commission *See* **Contingent Commission.**

Profits and commissions insurance Contractual coverage for salesmen who will not be able to earn commissions if the property they would normally sell is lost or destroyed.

Profits insurance Contract of insurance that pays the insured for the loss of profit he would have had if the damage or loss had not occurred.

Profit (loss) underwriting See underwriting profit (loss).

Pro forma statement A financial or accounting statement projecting income and performance of real estate within a period of time (usually one year), based upon estimates and assumptions.

Progressive impairment A physical condition in which the body deteriorates. Diabetes and cancer are two examples of progressive impairment. *See* for contrast, **Static impairment.**

Prohibited articles All fire policies now contain a clause against the keeping of certain classes of extra hazardous property upon the insured premises, unless special permission to do so is endorsed on the policy. Such clauses, when at issue, have generally been upheld by the Courts as conditions precedent to the issue of the contract. Hence, violation of their terms in the event of loss, may void the policy.

Prohibited list   A roster of risks that the insurance company has decided not to insure.

Prohibited risk   A line which an insurance company will not insure under any condition.

Projected dividend   An estimate of future policy dividends based upon certain assumptions. These dividends are not guaranteed but are believed to be reasonable as of the time the projection is made.

Promissory Note   An unconditional promise in writing to pay money to another person either on demand or at a set date in the future.

Proof of loss   A written statement complying with certain conditions made by the insured and given to the insurance company. The purpose of it is to place before the company sufficient information concerning the loss to enable it to determine its liability under the policy or bond.

Property   The exclusive right to control an economic good. The recognized attribute that human beings may have in their relation with wealth. A property refers to units capable of being used independently in single ownership. A property may consist of the rights to a single parcel of land, a house and lot, a complete manufacturing plant, or any one of the items assembled together to constitute such a plant. It may also consist of the rights developed and inherent in the attached business of an enterprise or any one of the elements reflected therein, such as the rights to patent, a trademark, a contract, or the proved good will of the public. The exclusive right to possess, enjoy, and dispose of a thing; ownership in a broad sense; any valuable right or interest considered primarily as a source of wealth; that to which a person has a legal title; a thing owned, an estate. It is incorrectly used as a synonym for the term real estate. Real property consists of land and, generally, whatever is erected or growing upon or affixed to it, including rights issuing out of, annexed to, and exercisable within or about the same. Personal property includes every kind of property which is not real.

Property, all types, insurance policy   Broad form of insurance coverage.

Property Damage   In Insurance this generally refers to damage to physical property of others as distinct from personal injuries to others. It is commonly written in conjunction with such public liability or personal injury insurance.

Property damage insurance Covers the insured against claims which arise out of destruction or damages of other's property.

Property Damage Liability Generally sold in combination with bodily injury liability coverage. It pays for damage to the property of others, caused by you.

Property, preservation of The policy requires that it shall be the duty of the insured to do whatever he reasonably can to save and protect the property insured at, during and after a fire. In case he does not do so, the company will not be liable for loss arising out of such failure. This means that the insured is, under the conditions of his policy, bound to do whatever he can to minimize the loss of the company.

Proposal *See* **Application.**

Pro rata In proportion.

Pro rata cancellation The termination of an insurance contract or bond, the premium charge being adjusted in proportion to the exact time the protection has been in force. Compare with short rate.

Pro rata clause A clause in an insurance contract providing that losses will be paid in the proportion that the amount of the contract bears to the entire amount of insurance covering the loss.

Pro rata distribution clause In a fire insurance policy it provides that the amount of insurance written shall apply to each building or location in that proportion which the value of each building or location bears to the total value of the described property.

Pro rata liability clause Provides that the insurance company is liable for not more than the proportion of loss which the amount insured under the policy bears to all insurance policies covering the loss.

Pro rata rate A premium rate charged for a short term at the same proportion of the rate for a longer term as the short term bears to the longer term. *See also* **Short rate.**

Pro rata treaty A reinsurance agreement under which the insuring companies share in an agreed-upon manner in both the premiums and the losses.

Pro-rate To allocate proportionate shares of income (such as rents) or of an obligation (such as taxes and insurance premiums), paid or due, between seller and buyer at closing.

Pro rate reinsurance *See* **Quota share reinsurance.**

Pro rate unearned premium reserve *See* **Unearned premium and reserve.**

Proration The adjustment of the benefits paid by reason of change of occupation or the existence of other insurance covering the same accident or disability.

Prospect A prospective customer, contestant, candidate, applicant for the purchase of a policy.

Prospective earnings *See* **Business interruption.**

Prospective Future Service Benefit That portion of a participant's retirement benefit that relates to his period of credited service to be rendered after a specified current date. CIT

Prospective rating (Also Self Rating or Experience Rating) A method used in arriving at the reinsurance rate and premium for a specified period, based in whole or in part, on the loss experience of a prior period. *See* **Experience rating.**

Prospective rating plan The formula in a reinsurance contract for determining reinsurance premium for a specified period on the basis, in whole or in part, of the loss experience of a prior period. *See* **Spread loss reinsurance.**

Prospective reserve A reserve based upon the present value of assumed future claims minus the present value of net premiums assuming a given rate of interest for both sums.

Prospectus A printed statement of a forthcoming enterprise.

Pro tanto For a certain amount.

Protected In fire insurance—a risk located in an area protected by a fire department. In burglary insurance—a risk equipped with a burglar alarm.

Protection The safeguarding against loss provided under the terms of the insurance policy, and is known also as coverage. In fire insurance, it may refer to the existence of facilities for fire fighting within the insured's property.

Protection and indemnity clause A clause in a marine insurance contract affording protection and indemnity insurance.

Protection and indemnity insurance Insurance against loss due to claims for damages against vessel owners or operators not covered by the basic marine insurance contract, often written by mutual associations called clubs.

Protective liability insurance Provides against claims which may arise out of secondary or indirect responsibilities; such as association with independent contractors. *See* **Liability insurance, protective.**

Protest A master's statement on the circumstances concerning an ocean marine loss.

Provisional premium *See* **Deposit premium.**

Proviso A provision or condition in a deed, or in a document.

Proximate cause The proximate cause of an event is that which, in a natural and continuous sequence, unbroken by any new cause, produced that event, and without which that event would not have happened.

Proxy One who acts for another.

Prudential Insurance Company Appellant vs. Insurance Commissioner of S. C. South Carolina insurance tax statutes upheld by Supreme Court.

Prudential Insurance Company and Massachusetts Mutual Life Insurance Company vs. Commissioner of Insurance— Michigan Upholds validity of state premium tax.

Prudential Insurance Company vs. State of Indiana Tax on foreign insurance companies premiums involved unconstitutional discrimination.

Public adjuster Individual who for a fee will adjust or represent policyholders in presenting their claims to insurance companies.

Public and institutional property forms A special form and rating system for public property. *See* **Public property.**

Public carrier Individual or company offering to transport people or merchandise for a fee. Such public or common carriers are required by law to accept shipments from all who request and pay for their services.

Public insurance Insurance written by governmental agencies or by private companies but supervised and controlled by the government.

Public Law 15 United States Congressional Act of 1945 exempting insurance from federal antitrust laws to the extent that insurance is regulated by the various states. McCarran Act.

Public liability insurance Provides protection against claims arising out of bodily injury or damaged property of the public. *See* **Liability insurance, bodily injury.**

Public official bond *See* **Federal official bond** and **Bond, public official. Public policy.** The law considers the conservation and promotion of the public welfare to be first and highest duty of government, and it will not countenance any transaction which contravenes a sound public policy.

Public Policy Is the principle under which freedom of contract or private dealings are restricted by law for the good of the community.

Public property   That property which is owned by other than the individual or individuals or private corporations; that is, property whose ownership is vested in the community. This would include such things as public buildings, such as post offices, town halls, county courthouses.

Public report   A subdivision report usually issued by a state agency before the sale of lots in the subdivision. The report is a factual account of the subdivided property, with emphasis on what might be considered its shortcomings. It is not issued until the agency is satisfied that the subdivider has put in place promised improvements and facilities or has made satisfactory financial arrangements to assure their completion and to back any warranties or representations.

Public trustee   A person appointed or required by law to execute and administer a trust.

Punitive damages   Damages awarded separately and in addition to compensatory damages. They are to serve as a punishment for the wrong-doer.

Pup company   A smaller insurance company owned by a larger company.

Purchase agreement   *See* **Agreement for sale.**

Purchase and marketing fee   A fee payable by FNMA sellers upon delivery of loans to FNMA.

Purchase money mortgage   A mortgage executed by the buyer in lieu of the complete payment in cash for the real estate. For example, a $10,000 house purchased by a man who can put up only $4,000, the seller is issued a $6,000 mortgage by the purchaser.

Pure loss cost (Also Burning Cost)   The ratio of reinsurance losses incurred to the ceding company's subject premium.

Pure Endowment   A contract which provides for payment only upon survival of a certain person to a certain date and not in event of that person's prior death. This type of contract is just the opposite of a term contract which provides for payment only in event the insured person dies within the term period specified.

Pure premium   The amount of money required to pay losses covered by insurance without taking into account the cost and expense of operation of the insurance company. *See* **premium, pure.**

Pure risk The uncertainty of a peril that will produce a loss if the event occurs.

Pygenic infection A pus-forming infection. One of the few infections ever covered in accident and sickness insurance. When covered, it is usually specified that it must result from an accident.

Pyramiding An abuse where the insured has been issued and charged for policies of consumer credit insurance without the canceling of current policies. The National Association of Insurance Commissioners in their report of 1954 listed pyramiding as an abuse by certain undesirable elements in credit life insurance.

Q Schedule, New York Code Limitation on the expenses that may be charged to new business. The schedule presents in detail the new business expenses of the insurance company filing that return. Indirectly this schedule has a broad affect on the operations of the company in other states since a limit on the amount establishes a ceiling on commissions, etc.

Qua In the capacity or character of e. g., in an auto accident one might discuss a passenger. Qua (in the capacity of) a passenger in the vehicle or Qua, an employee of the owner of the vehicle.

Quadruple indemnity A provision under which the principal sum (and sometimes other indemnities) will be multiplied by 400 percent in case of death from certain types of accidents. *See* **Multiple indemnity,** and **double indemnity.**

Qualification A portion of a report by an auditor, underwriter, claims investigator accountant, or actuary, that calls attention to the limitations of his report.

Qualified plan *See* **Qualified trust.**

Qualified report A report with exceptions or inadequate facts so that full credence should not be given to the finding. A credit report on an applicant for insurance may qualify some of the findings.

Qualified trust A pension or bonus plan that meets the standards of the Internal Revenue Code, Sec. 165A. Meeting the requirements permits tax minimizing for both the employer and employee.

Quantum Amount or quantity.

Quarantine indemnity A benefit sometimes included in policies making the loss-of-time indemnities apply in case of quarantine of the insured by reason of a contagious disease in his house.

Quartermasters' bonds   Disbursing officers of the military services are required by law to give bond with surety for the faithful performance of their official duties. These bonds or sureties protect the public interest in so far as the office of quartermaster is concerned.

Quasi contract   Situation imposed by law to prevent unjust enrichment or injustice and not dependent on agreement of the parties to the contract.

Quasi-insurance institutions   Those compulsory social insurance activities carried out by various branches of government. Old age and survivors insurance, unemployment insurance, and certain phases of workmen's compensation, industrial accident, are examples of these institutions.

Quasi-judicial bodies   Some federal agencies that are concerned with insurance; such as the Federal Trade Commission, have powers similar to a judicial body. This permits them to enforce their regulations and rules.

Quasi-public corporation   An incorporated organization that is privately operated but in which some general interest of the public is evident. The line of demarcation is not clear when a private company comes into this classification. Charitable and religious companies are clearly quasi-public. Certain insurance activities in health and fire prevention may be considered to be quasi-public.

Quebec Insurance Contract Law   A typical law in Canada, excepting the province from the uniform statutes of the other provinces. Based on French civil law rather than British common law.

Quick assets   Those assets of an insurance company that are rapidly convertible into cash. Items such as till cash, checks deposited and in process of collection, short-term securities such as Treasury bills and notes are examples of quick assets.

Quid pro quo   Something, given in return for another thing of like value.

Quiet enjoyment clause   Provision of lease or deed that gives the new owner or tenant the right of not being disturbed in his possession. *See* **Title insurance.**

Quiet title action   A legal action brought to eliminate any interest on a claim to property by others. The procedure used to perfect title when a quit-claim deed cannot be obtained from others.

Quieting title   Removing a cloud from a title by a proper action in court.

Quit claim   To release or relinquish a claim whether valid or invalid in conveyancing a deed. Quit claim is generally associated with the term quit claim deed and conveys no warrantee.

Quit claim deed   A deed which conveys simply the grantor's right or interest in real estate, without any agreement of covenant as to the nature or extent of that interest, or any other covenants.

Quittance   Discharge from debt or obligation.

Quota share reinsurance   Type of reinsurance contract in which a quota, which is a percentage of every risk falling under terms of the agreement, is ceded.

Quota-share treaty   A reinsurance arrangement under which each insuring company accepts a stated proportion of premiums and losses on the insurance written.

R.E.   Real Estate

REIT   *See* **Real estate investment trust.**

RESPA   Real Estate Settlement Procedures Act.

R.H.I.B.   Rain and Hail Insurance Bureau

R.I.A.   Railroad Insurance Association.

R.L.A.   Retroactive liability insurance.

R.P.   Return premium.

R.R.C.C.   Reduced rate contribution clause.

R.S.   Revised Statutes

R.U.   Railway underwriter.

Radioactive contamination insurance policy   Special coverage for loss due to radioactive material or nuclear reaction. Few insurance policies include this coverage.

Radium insurance   Coverage against loss of and damage to radium elements used by medical institutions or individuals.

Railroad Insurance Rating Bureau   Organization that makes studies of railroad property claims and prepares rates which are filed by members with the respective insurance departments of the various states.

Railroad policy   Accident policies sold in railroad stations by ticket agents or automatic machines.

Railroad subrogation waiver clause   Portion of an insurance contract providing that a release by the insured of a railroad from liability as a condition of obtaining accommodations from the railroad shall not affect the insurance contract or the insured's rights under it. In a fire insurance policy under which the insurance company waives the right to recover from a stated railroad company. In return for the railroad putting in a switch, a factory owner will waive the right of recovery from the railroad company if sparks from a locomotive should set fire to the company's property. Therefore when the company takes out fire insurance the policy should contain a railway subrogation waiver clause in which the insurance company waives the right to recover.

Railway sidetrack agreement   An agreement between a railroad and a company whereby the railroad builds and maintains a switch track on the premises of the company to facilitate shipments, and in which the company often agrees to release the railroad from liability. The company may assume the liability of the railroad.

Railway underwriter   The individual whose duty it is to determine the acceptability of insurance risks involving railroads and their use.

Rain insurance   Insures against loss caused by a measured amount of rainfall within stated period of time. Protects against loss or expense incurred or loss of income expected caused by reduction of patronage of sales or other events by rain, hail, snow, or sleet.

Rain insurance policy   Type of business insurance coverage. Self-explanatory.

Range   In the land laws of the United States, a strip of land six miles wide, running north and south, marked off by government survey.

Rate   The cost of insurance per unit; used as a means or base for the determination of premiums. The price per $100 of insurance for one year is the insurance rate for fire insurance. If a house is to be insured for $5,000 the rate would be multiplied by 50. *See* **Premium rate**.

Rate—Blanket Average   A rate that applies when building and contents or when two or more separate buildings and/or contents are insured under one coverage item of the policy.

Rate cards Cards prepared by rating bureaus stating the premium rate and related information on properties.

Rate-making The process or procedure of developing insurance-pricing structures.

Rate manual Manual containing the rates for various coverages offered by a particular insurer. Other information of importance to the insurers agent may also be included.

Rated-Up Frequently, a person who is considered substandard as an insurance risk is able to secure protection from some company by paying premiums based on a higher mortality table or based on a higher age. Such rating classifies risks according to their departure from normal expectancy.

Rating The evaluation of the moral or other risk of an individual or organization. Dun & Bradstreet, Hooper-Holmes, Retail Credit Bureau, as well as trade rating bureaus may be used by insurance companies to obtain an external source of information on a risk. The investment department of an insurance company may use Standard & Poor's, Moody's, or Fitch's to obtain an idea of the evaluation of specific securities. The making of insurance rates.

Rating bureau Organization which prepares insurance studies and these rates are used by members. It classifies risk and promulgates rates, usually on the basis of statistical data compiled by the bureau or of inspection of risks made by it.

Rating, experience Determination of the premium rate for an individual risk partially or wholly on the basis of that risk's own experience.

Rating, merit Determination of a rate for an individual risk on the basis of its variation in hazard from the average or standard for its class. *See also* **Rating, experience; rating, schedule.**

Rating, retrospective A method of rating that adjusts the final premium of a risk in accordance with the experience of that risk during the term of the policy for which the premium is paid.

Rating, schedule Making or modifying the premium rate for an individual risk on the basis of the physical conditions which affect the probability of loss.

Raw land Land in its natural state with no physical improvements such as grading, sewers, or erected structures. *See* **Improvements on** and **to land.**

Readjustment income The income needed to allow a family time to adjust to a new and usually lower standard of living after the death or disability of the wage-earner.

Real estate   Land and all the rights therein including whatever is made a part of or attached to real estate through the acts of either man or nature.

Real Estate Investment Trust (REIT)   An investment vehicle established for the benefit of a group of real estate investors and managed by one or more trustees who hold title to the assets for the trust and control its acquisitions and investments. A major REIT advantage is that no federal income tax is paid if certain qualifications are met. The REIT is designed to provide an opportunity for large-scale public participation in real estate investment.

Real estate owned (REO)   A term frequently used by lending institutions as applied to ownership of real property acquired for investments or as a result of foreclosure.

Real estate syndicate   A group of investors who pool funds for investment in real property.

Real estate tax   That tax or amount of money levied by taxing authority against the ownership of real estate for purposes of financing the functioning of the government.

Real property   Land and appurtenances, including anything of a permanent nature such as structures, trees, minerals, and the interest, benefits, and inherent rights thereof.

Realty   A collective term sometimes used to designate real estate.

Reassured   *See* **Ceding Company.**

Rebate   A discount or allowance.

Rebating   When a policy is sold at less than the legal rate, or the insured is allowed a remission of the premium, or anything of value whereby payment of full legal premium is defeated, the practice is termed rebating. It is illegal.

Rebuilding or repairing   If the company elects to rebuild or repair the premises damaged or destroyed, under their powers within the Statutory Conditions, it must give notice of its intention so to proceed, within fifteen days after receipt of the Proofs of Loss.

Rebut   To disprove a presumption.

Recapture   An owner's recovery of money invested in real estate, usually referring to a depreciation allowance.

Recapture clause   A clause in an agreement providing for retaking or recovering possession. As used in percentage leases, to take a portion of earnings or profits above a fixed amount of rent.

Receipt   A written acknowledgment of the payment of money.

Receiver   An appointee of a court to collect rents and manage and protect the interest of the lender or creditors during foreclosure or other litigation.

Recession   Repudiation of a contract for a valid reason such as duress, fraud, or misrepresentation.

Reciprocal exchange   An unincorporated association organized to write insurance for its members. Members are both insurers and policyholders. Each member is liable for his proportionate share of total liabilities but may be assessed for additional funds if they are needed.

Reciprocal insurance   Insurance provided by subscribers at a reciprocal exchange. Each subscriber agrees to become liable for his share of the losses and expenses of all subscribers and authorizes the attorney-in-fact to effect his exchange of insurance with the other subscribers. A separate account is often maintained with each subscriber, to which are credited his premiums and his share of other income, and to which are debited his share of losses and other disbursements. *See* **Reciprocal exchange.**

Reciprocal law   A law by which state A provides for granting to insurers or producers of any other state doing business in state A privileges equal to those granted to insurers or prorucers of state A doing business in that other state; or for regulating its domestic insurers or producers in their relations with the other state according to a specified standard if that other state regulates its domestic insurers or producers according to the same standard.

Reciprocity   The system of placing reinsurance on a reciprocal basis, so that a ceding company will only give a share of its reinsurance to a reinsurer who is able to offer reinsurance in return.

Recision   The cancellation or annulment of a transaction or contract by the operation of law or by mutual consent.

Recitals   Statements made in a document leading up to and explaining the nature of the document. They are not the"legally binding "part of the document.

Recommendations   List of suggested changes that are proposed by an inspector. Adoption of the recommended changes can result in lower premiums.

Reconveyance   The transfer of the title of land from one person to the immediate preceding owner. It is used when the performance of debt is satisfied under the terms of a deed of trust.

Recorder The public official in a political subdivision who keeps records of transactions affecting real property in the area. Sometimes known as a registrar of deeds or a county clerk.

Recording The noting in the registrar's office of the details of a properly executed legal document, such as a deed, mortgage, a satisfaction of mortgage, or an extension of mortgage, thereby making it a part of the public record.

Recording agent *See* **Policy writing agent.**

Records destruction insurance policy Type of business insurance coverage. Self-explanatory.

Recourse note A debt instrument under which the lender can take action against the borrower or endorser personally, in addition to foreclosure.

Recovery Money or other valuables that the insurance company obtains from subrogation, salvage, or reinsurance.

Rectification The correction of an error in a register or instrument on the grounds of mutual mistake.

Recurring clause A provision sometimes found in health insurance policies which states the amount of time during which the recurrence of a condition is considered a continuation of a prior period of disability or hospital confinement. Health insurance clause which specifies the period of time that must elapse between disability or claim for the recurrence of that disability or claim to be considered a new benefit period.

Recurring disease A disease characterized by recurrence, such as malaria.

Redemption The right of a mortgagor to redeem the property by paying the debt after the expiration date; the right of an owner to reclaim his property after a sale for taxes. The recovery of property which has been lost through such processes as foreclosure of a mortgage, a tax forfeiture, or some other legal process.

Redemption period The time allowed by law in some states during which a mortgagor may buy back property by paying the amount owed on a foreclosed mortgage, including interest and fees. *See* **Equity of redemption.**

Reduced paid-up insurance A form of insurance available as a nonforfeiture option. It provides for continuation of the original insurance plan, but for a reduced amount. On failure to pay premiums, insurance, in the amount for which the cash value used as a single premium will purchase is optionally available for the remainder of the original policy period.

Reduced rate average clause   *See* **Coinsurance.**

Reduced rate coinsurance clause   *See* **Coinsurance.**

Reduced rate contribution clause   *See* **Average clause.**

Re-examination   One of the three stages in the examination of a witness.

Refer   Request that an adjustor settle a claim.

Referee   One to whom some matter in dispute is referred for a decision.

Reference   *See* **Arbitration.**

Referral risks   Risks beyond the underwriting authority of an office; they must be referred to supervisory office for decision.

Refinancing   The repayment of a debt from the proceeds of a new loan using the same property as security.

Reform of the policy   The correction of an error is termed "reforming the policy". If the agreement for contract, and the terms of the contract are opposed in any part, if in other words a mistake has been made — the Courts can compel a performance of the original contract as evidenced by the terms of the agreement, and correct the mistake. The proofs of such an agreement for contract, however, must be conclusive if such alleged error is to be rectified. Parole evidence may be admitted in support of any claim for error.

Reformation of contract   Proof in a court of equity that the contract does not state the true intentions of both parties will permit reformation of contract to correct the contract.

Refund   An annuity which provides that upon the death of the annuitant the company will continue payments until the total amount paid equals the purchase price.

Refund annuity   *See* **Annuity, cash-refund; Annuity, installment refund.**

Regional agent   Agent below the rank of a general agent but above the rank of a local agent.

Regional office   Similar to branch office in operation, it has, in addition, facilities to handle all lines of business, such as fire, casualty, marine, multi-peril. (*See* **Branch Office**).

Register   A record of all policies charged to an industrial debit.

Registered mail   The United States Post Office Department will insure up to a maximum of $1,000 mail sent registered. If the value is higher than $1,000 it may be insured with insurance companies that provide that service.

Registered mail insurance   Protection against loss of money and securities while in transit via registered mail. Insurance against loss of certain types of intangible property while in charge of the Post Office Department as registered mail. May be through private insurance companies or through U. S. Post Office.

Registered tonnage Cargo capacity of a commercial vessel obtained by computing one ton for each 100 cubic feet of enclosed storage space.

Regular medical expense insurance Insurance coverage for payments toward doctor's fees, for nonsurgical care in the hospital, at home or in a physician's office, and for laboratory tests and X-rays.

Regular medical insurance That type of health insurance covering physicians' services other than surgical procedures.

Rehabilitation The restoration to good use, through repair of structures or improvements of public facilities, of a declining area or neighborhood to arrest and reserve deteriorating influences.

Rehabilitation clause Health insurance clause which is designed to aid a disabled policy holder in vocational rehabilitation.

Reimbursement benefits The actual expense incurred by the insured such as medical, nursing, and hospital treatment. Reimbursement benefits are in contrast to indemnity benefits, which pay a stated amount for whatever disability or injury they cover without regard to the cost to the insured.

Reinstatement Returning a policy to its full protective value after the payment of a claim. This clause may or may not require an additional premium to be paid. Such payment would be known as a reinstatement premium. Restoration of full rights under a contract which has lapsed or had its benefits or terms reduced because of failure to the insured to pay premium as originally agreed. Or, restoration, automatically or on application, of the full amount of a policy contract following a loss; in some cases additional premium is required. The acknowledgment by a mortgagee that an accelerated loan has been brought current by the mortgagor.

Reinstatement premium A premium charged to restore an insurance policy or bond to its original value after payment of a loss. *See* **Reinstatement.**

Reinsurance An agreement between two or more insurance companies by which the risk of loss is proportioned. Thus the risk of loss is spread and a disproportionately large loss under a single policy does not fall on one company. Acceptance by an insurer, called a reinsurer, of all or part of the risk of loss of another insurer. A company issuing an automobile liability policy, with a limit of $100,000 per accident may reinsure its liability in excess of $10,000. A fire insurance company which issues a large policy generally reinsures a portion of the risk with one or several other companies.

Reinsurance, automatic Reinsurance under an automatic reinsurance treaty.

Reinsurance broker An organization that places (brokers) reinsurance through a reinsurance underwriter. This term should not be confused with the insurance "broker" defined earlier in this book.

Reinsurance, excess Reinsurance against loss in an amount in excess of a stipulated primary amount.

Reinsurance, excess or loss *See* **Reinsurance, excess.**

Reinsurance, facultative Reinsurance of individual risks at the option of the reinsurer and the reinsured, whether under a treaty of reinsurance or by negotiation in respect of an individual risk.

Reinsurance, obligatory *See* **Reinsurance, automatic.**

Reinsurance premium The consideration paid by the ceding company to the reinsurer for the reinsurance afforded by the reinsurer.

Reinsurance, quota-share *See* **Reinsurance, share.**

Reinsurance reserve *See* **Unearned premium reserve.**

Reinsurance, share Acceptance by the reinsurer of a share of the risk or risks of the reinsured, the two sharing all losses and expenses as agreed.

Reinsurance, stop-loss Excess reinsurance against all loss incurred after the reinsured's aggregate loss on a line reaches a specified amount, or after the loss ratio reaches a specified figure.

Reinsurance, surplus Reinsurance of amounts over a specified amount of insurance retained by the reinsured carrier, the reinsurer contributing to the payment of losses in proportion to its share of the total amount of the insurance; a form of share reinsurance.

Reinsurance ticket Form attached to the daily report giving facts on reinsurance that has been made.

Reinsurance treaty Agreement between insurance companies sharing insurance. A contract between two insurers under which one, the reinsurer, agrees to reinsure risks written by the other, subject to the conditions of the contract.

Reinsurance treaty, automatic   A reinsurance treaty under which risks written by the reinsured are automatically reinsured by the reinsurer as written, to the extent and subject to the conditions agreed upon in the treaty.

Reinsurance treaty, facultative   A reinsurance treaty under which risks may be submitted to the reinsurer for acceptance or rejection, but if accepted are reinsured in accordance with the terms of the treaty.

Reinsured   An insurer whose risks are reinsured by a reinsurer.

Reinsurer   An insurance company which accepts the obligation of another insurance company by means of some agreement. An insurer reinsuring risks of another insurer under a contract of reinsurance.

Rejoinder   A Defendant's answer to a Plaintiff's reply.

Related company   *See* **Affiliated company.**

Release   To give up, abandon, and discharge a claim of an enforceable right to one as against another. Name of the instrument evidencing such an act. The act or writing by which some claim or interest is surrendered to another.

Release clause   A stipulation in the mortgage or deed of trust that a portion of the security may be released from the lien if certain conditions are met.

Release deed   *See* **Satisfaction of mortgage.**

Release of liability   An agreement by a lender to terminate the personal obligation of a mortgagor in connection with the payment of a debt. FHA and VA require approval by regulatory agencies for a release of liability.

Release of lien   An instrument discharging secured property from a lien.

Release of record   The act of recording a release deed or satisfaction of mortgage to release or eliminate the lien of the mortgage on the public records.

Release price   The amount of compensation, either partial or full, needed for a mortgagee to remove a lien.

Remainder   The estate in property created simultaneously with other estates such as a life estate, by a single grant and consisting of the rights and interests contingent upon and remaining after the termination of the other estate.

Remainder estate   An estate in property created simultaneously with other estates by a single grant and consisting of the rights and interest contingent upon and remaining after the termination of the other estates.

Remise An archaic term found in deeds of release and quit claim meaning to remit or give up.

Remoteness of Damage Unless an act is the immediate or direct cause of the damage, generally speaking the damage is too remote to support a right of recovery. This does not mean that a person starting a chain of events which could reasonably lead to the ultimate damage is not responsible for the ultimate damage. It refers particularly to cases where there has been either some intervening cause or circumstances or the ultimate result could not have been foreseen as a result of the act.

Rendering An artist's or architect's interpretation, in perspective, of a projected development, usually in color.

Renewable term insurance Term insurance providing the right to renew at the end of the term for another term or terms, without evidence of insurability. The rates increase at each renewal as the age of the insured increases.

Renewal The reinstatement in force and effect of something that is about to expire. With an insurance policy it is made either by the issuance of a new policy or renewal receipt or certificate under the same conditions, to take effect upon the expiration of the old policy.

Renewal agreement Provision of some policies in which the insurance company agrees to renew the policy for a stated period.

Renewal certificate A short-form document referring to an original policy which it replaces.

Rent The return in money, labor, chattel provisions which are given by the rentor to the owner of the land in compensation for the use or right of use of the real estate.

Rent and lease policies *Rent policies* are issued to the *owners* of property occupied by tenants, to indemnify the owner against the loss of rentals caused by fire making the property untenable. *Lease policies* secure to the *lessees* of certain specified property any difference in value between the sum paid under the lease and the sum received from the tenants of the leased property. Neither rent nor lease policies have any relation to the value of the building as such.

Rent control Control by a government agency of the amount to be charged as rent.

Rent insurance Contract of insurance for the protection of a building owner's receipts. In the event that a tenant does not pay rent because of such perils as a fire the insurance company will pay such losses.

Rental concession A landlord's agreement to forego part of the advertised rent in an effort to attract tenants.

Rental requirement A condition in the commitment letter stipulating that a specific number of units must be rented at a minimum rental rate before the entire loan amount will be funded.

Rental value The amount of money for which a property should rent in a normal rent market. Thus two comparable properties may have different rents since one is under rent control and the other is not. This in turn affects the value of the property since, in part, the income from a rental unit will determine its value. A term of specifically limited significance and application; the worth for a stated period of the right to use and occupy property; the rent which a prospective tenant is warranted in paying for a stated period of time, i.e., a month, a year, etc., for the right to use and occupy certain described property under certain prescribed or assumed conditions.

Rent/Rental Value Insurance Insurance that provides indemnity (1) for the loss of the rental value of property when the owner or the tenant (if he remains liable for the payment of rent) is deprived of the use of the property because of its damage by a peril insured against, or (2) for loss by the owner-landlord of hte rent that would have been payable by the tenant of the property where the tenant, by the terms of the lease or by statute, is relieved of liability for the payment of rent during the period of untenantability if the property is damaged by a peril covered by the contract.

Rent-up period The time after construction in which a rental property achieves stabilized income and occupancy levels.

Repair and replace insurance policy Type of business insurance coverage. Self-explanatory.

Repairs Ordinary repairs are permitted to a property without notice to the company. Generally speaking, the statutory or other conditions of the policy set a limit of time in which such repairs can be affected. For anything which requires a longer limit the company's consent in writing must be obtained. Also, if the repairs take the form of any reconstruction or remodeling of the building the work is "extra-ordinary" and must from the commencement be assented to by the company. Failure of the insured to observe the conditions relative to repairs may void the policy.

Replacement cost insurance Insurance providing that the insured will be paid the cost of replacing the damaged property without deduction for depreciation. The usual replacement cost form provides that the property must actually be replaced before the insured may collect a claim under it. It is available only for buildings, with some few exceptions.

Replacement insurance Insurance under which the loss payable is the replacement cost of the property new. The excess over the depreciated replacement cost is payable only if the property is actually replaced.

Replacement reserve A cash reserve for the future replacement of fixed assets.

Replevin Re-delivery of goods to the Tenant or Owner.

Reply A Plaintiff's answer to a Defendant's defense.

Reporting contract An insurance contract covering stocks of goods and often types of property in their actual amounts, these amounts being reported periodically by the insured, and the premium being based on them.

Reporting form A policy designed for use when values of the insured property fluctuate during the policy term. Usually an adequate limit of liability is set, and then the insured reports the values actually on hand on a given day of each month. At the end of the year or policy term, these reported values are averaged, and the premium adjusted accordingly.

Reporting policy Covers products, value of which must be reported to the insurance company at stated intervals since their values or volume fluctuates. For example, insurance on the stocks of chain stores which are continually fluctuating between warehouses and stores is provided by a reporting policy, and the insured reports to the company at stated periods the valuation at all points covered in the policy.

Representation Statements made by an applicant on the application that he represents as being substantially true to the best of his knowledge and belief but which are not warranted as exact in every detail. *See* **Declaration, Warranty.**

Reproduction cost Normal cost of the exact duplication of a property as of a certain date.

Repugnancy   Repugnancy is a term used to denote that there is a disagreement or inconsistency between two or more clauses of a written instrument. It is always interpreted against the insurer, and shall rarely if ever avoid a loss.

Rescission of contracts   The abrogating or annulling of contracts.

Reservation   That reservation or right reserved by an owner in selling or leasing a property, a common reservation being in the use of the attic or basement for the storage of personal property of the owner.

Reserve   Funds which are set aside by an insurance company for the purpose of meeting obligations as they fall due. A liability set up by an insurer for a particular purpose.

Reserve for losses   See Loss Reserves.

Reserve, unearned premium   A reserve equal or approximately equal to the total of the unearned premiums on insurance in force with an insurer.

Res gestae   This is one of the exceptions to the hearsay rule against the admissibility of oral evidence. It refers to declarations or exclamations uttered by the parties to an exciting event which were contemporaneous with and accompanying such event and throw light on the motive and intentions of the parties to it. It must not be a mere accounting of the facts afterwards.

Also used with reference to facts surrounding a transaction which is a subject matter for legal proceedings.

Residence   Personal presence in a place with no present intention of removing therefrom.

Residence and outside theft insurance   Contractual protection of the insured's personal property from loss by theft and damage caused by theft or malicious mischief. Insurance against loss by actual or attempted theft, larceny, burglary, or robbery of property on the residence premises of the insured or elsewhere in the Western Hemisphere.

Residence employee   An employee whose duties are incidental to the ownership, maintenance, or use of personal residential premises and to the personal rather than business activities of the insured.

Residence insurance   Insurance pertaining to a personal residence, as distinguished from business premises.

Resident agent   Individual, resident of the state which requires certain policies to be signed by a resident agent of the admitted company.

Residuary   Pertaining to a residue or remainder.

Res ipsa loquitur: Translated means — "The facts speak for themselves." a doctrine or presumption meaning that when an injury occurs to a plaintiff through a situation under the sole and exclusive control of the defendant and where such injury would not normally occur if the one in such control had used due care, then it is presumed the defendant is negligent.

Res judicata Latin "The matter has been decided" — where a court has heard and decided an issue it cannot be brought up again.

Respondeat Superior A legal maxim meaning that in certain cases the master is liable for the wrongful acts of his servant and a principal similarly responsible for the wrongful acts of his agent.

Respondentia Is to cargo what bottomry is to hulls. A combination of money lending and insurance found in early marine insurance policies.

Restoration premium The premium charged to restore a policy or bond to its original value after payment of a loss. *See* **Premium, restoration.**

Restrictions A limitation by private agreement or by public legislative action conditioning the use or occupancy of real estate through such means as covenants and deeds or conditions and leases.

Restrictive covenant A clause in a deed limiting use of the property conveyed for a certain period of time.

Retail Credit Company *See* **Rating.**

Retail store policy A special multi-peril policy designed for small retail stores as distinguished from department stores and supermarkets.

Retainage (retention) The amount withheld out of payment to contractors or subcontractors as per contractual agreement to insure a final and satisfactory completion of the job.

Retainer A contract between Solicitor and Client.

Retaliatory laws State statutes that provide that a company or citizen of a foreign state will be taxed in proportion to what the foreign state taxes a company or citizen of the first state. Laws by which state A provides for imposing requirements on insurers or producers of any other state doing business in state A to the same extent that the other state imposes requirements on insurers or producers of state A.

Retention The amount of liability retained on a given risk; the gross line less reinsurance. That part of the insurance on a risk retained by a reinsured for its own account, the excess or surplus of which, if any, is reinsured.

Retention policy   A contract which the insured agrees to pay all losses up to a specified amount in consideration of a lower premium. This policy is legal only in certain states. Certain states permit a retention glass insurance policy to be sold. Under such a policy the insured pays 50% of the usual premium and all the losses he may suffer from glass breakage up to 50% of the usual premium. When the total loss reaches this figure, the insured then has full coverage for all losses above that figure.

Retirement allowance   Annuity or pension paid to an employee upon retirement.

Retirement annuity   *See* **Annuity, retirement.**

Retirement income   A stipulated amount of income starting at a selected retirement age. This is derived by exercising one of the settlement options available against the policy cash value.

Retirement income insurance   Insurance payable on death before a specified age, with provision of a life annuity certain if the insured attains that age.

Retirement plan   *See* **Pension plan.**

Retiring from a line   Action by an insurance company in canceling or not renewing a line of insurance or risk.

Retroactive extension   Extending retroactively the terms (except amount) of present coverage into the period of prior insurance.

Retroactive liability insurance (RLI)   Insurance written after the insured peril has occurred. The most important instance of this insurance involved writing liability coverage on the MGM Grand Hotel after the fire that resulted in a number of deaths. RLI permits a covered company to show a clearer financial statement since contingent liabilities are now covered.

Retroactive restoration   Reinstatement of a bond or policy to its original face value after a loss has been paid, for the purposes of providing payment should prior losses be discovered at a future date. Automatic restoration of the original amount of an insurance contract or bond, after payment of loss, to cover prior undiscovered as well as future losses not connected with the one previously paid.

Retrocession   The act of reinsuring company that has accepted a risk in again reinsuring the risk with still another company. A cession of reinsurance by a reinsurer to another reinsurer.

Retrocessionaire A reinsurer that accepts a retrocession.

Retrospective rating A technique which permits adjustments of the final premium for a risk based on the loss experience of the insured during the period of protection between maximum and minimum limits. *See* **Rating, retrospective.**

Retrospective rating plan The formula in a reinsurance contract for determining the reinsurance premium for a specified period on the basis of the loss experience for the same period.

Retrospective reserve A particular way of looking at a reserve in which the reserve is thought of as the difference between the accumulation at interest and survivorship of the net premiums received in the past and the accumulation at interest and survivorship of the claims paid.

Return commission That portion of a commission paid by an insurance company to an agent that must be returned in the event a policy is canceled.

Return for no claim Provision in some policies that if no claims have been paid during the term of the policy, the insurance company will refund a portion of the premium.

Return on equity The ratio of cash flow after debt service to the difference between the value of property and the total financing. *See* **Cash-on-cash return.**

Return premium The amount due the insured if a policy is canceled, reduced in amount, or reduced in rate. *See* **Pro rata** and **Short rate.**

Reverse-annuity mortgage A contract designed to supplement the income of retired persons who have paid off their mortgages, but who do not want to move. The lender pays the borrower a fixed monthly annuity, based on a percentage of the current value of the property. Repayment of the loan would not be required until the death of the annuitant, at which time the loan would be discharged through probate.

Reverse leverage Describes a situation that arises when financing is too costly. It results when total yield on cash investment is less than the financing constant on borrowed funds. *See* **Negative cash flow.**

Reversion The right of a lessor to recover possession of leased property upon the termination of the lease, with all the subsequent rights to use and enjoyment of the property.

Reversionary annuity   *See* **Annuity, survivorship.**

Reversionary clause   A clause providing that any violations or restrictions will cause title to the property to revert to the party who imposed the restriction.

Reversionary right   The right to receive possession and use of property upon the termination or defeat of an estate carrying the rights of possession and use and vested in another.

Revocable Beneficiary   A beneficiary whose rights in a policy are subject to the insured's reserved right to revoke or change the beneficiary designation and the right to surrender or make a loan on the policy without the consent of the beneficiary.

Revocation   The act of recalling a power or authority conferred, as the revocation of a power of attorney, a license. etc.

Rider   A document or form containing special provisions that are not contained in the policy contract. Such forms are to be added or attached to the policy. *See* **Endorsement.**

Right of occupancy   A privilege to use and occupy a property for a certain period under some contractual guarantee, such as a lease or other formal agreement.

Right of survivorship   In joint tenancy, the right of survivors to acquire the interst of a deceased joint tenant.

Right of way   The term has two significances: as a privilege to pass or cross, it is an easement over another's land; it is also used to describe that strip of land which railroad companies use for a roadbed, or as dedicated to public use for roadway, walk, or other way. Plural is commonly "right of ways." However, the best thought appears to be toward a fine distinction in usage as follows: (1) a single right or easement for several independent or combined use of pipes, poles, sewers, etc. (2) two or more rights or easements from different parties and over different parcels but for a single use. (3) two or more rights or easements from different parties or for different parties and over different parcels for several independent or combined uses.

Riot   A tumultuous disturbance of the public peace. The exact number needed for a riot is given by individual state law.

Riot and civil commotion insurance   Contractual protection from loss caused by riot, strikes, insurrection, and civil commotions. Insurance against loss due to the violent and tumultuous action of three (in one state, two) or more persons.

Riot insurance policy   Type of business insurance coverage. Self-explanatory.

Riparian Pertaining to or living on the bank of a river, a lake, or of a tidewater; specifically, the use of lands lying between the high water mark and the low water mark. Local legal regulations determine the extent of the riparian right of the upland owner.

Riparian grant The conveyance of riparian rights.

Riparian lease The written instrument setting forth the terms, conditions, and the date of expiration of the rights to use lands lying between the high water mark and the low water mark.

Riparian owners Those who own lands adjoining a watercourse.

Riparian rights All phases of right and title (of the upland owner) in and to the water and land below high water mark. These rights vary and depend upon local legal regulations.

Rising water insurance Type of business insurance coverage. Self-explanatory.

Risk A person or thing insured. CIT
Uncertainty as to the outcome of an event when two or more possibilities exist. CIT

Risk experience program A procedure by which, on large risks, a listing of premiums and losses is referred periodically to the underwriter for review. (*See* **Watch File**).

Risk management The use of appropriate insurance, avoidance of risk, loss control, risk retention, self-insuring, and other techniques that minimize the risks of a business, individual, or organization.

Risk retention Retaining the results of the risk exposure rather than using other techniques, such as insurance or avoidance of the risk.

Robbery The unlawful taking of property by violence, force, or intimidation. By contrast, larceny is theft by stealth.

Robbery insurance policy Type of business insurance coverage protecting against loss from the unlawful taking of property by violence, force, or intimidation.

F. O. Robertson, Appellant vs. the People of the State of California Upheld California statutes on agency licensing.

Rod A measure of length containing 5½ yards or 16½ feet; also, the corresponding square measure.

Route list The itinerary of a fieldman that he sends to his company of the places he plans to call on during the period.

Rule of 78s A method used by a lender (usually on installment loans) for calculating an interest rebate on a loan paid off, or refinanced, prior to its maturity date or for accruing earned discount. The rule involves a factor obtained by adding the value assigned to the consecutive months included in the term of the loan. In a 12-month loan, for example, the first month is given a value of 12, the second month 11, and so on until the last month, which has a value of 1. Thus, the total of the months for a one-year loan is 78. If the loan is repaid at the end of three months, the lender calculates it as having earned 33/78 (12 + 11 + 10) and, therefore, the borrower is entitled to a rebate of 45/78 of the annual interest.

Running down clause That portion of the marine policy that protects against damage by collision with another ship.

Running with the land Affecting the land and the successive owners thereof; usually spoken of a covenant or an easement.

Run-off A termination provision in a reinsurance policy whereby the insurer remains liable for losses occurring after the date of termination on those policies in force on that date.

S.A.   Society of Actuaries.

S/A   Special Agent or State Agent

S.A.A.   Surety Association of America

S.B.L.I.   Savings bank life insurance.

S.E.U.A.   Southeastern Underwriters Association.

S.C.A.   Stock Company Association

S.C.S.E.   Society of Casualty Safety Engineers

S. & F.   Stock and fixtures.

S.L.   Sprinkler leakage.

S. & M.   Stock and machinery.

S.F.P.E.   Society of Fire Protection Engineers

S.M.P.   Special Multi-Peril Policy

S.O.P.   Standard Operating Procedure

S.P.   Sine prole (Died without issue)

S/R   Safety Representative

S.R.   Short rate.

S.R.A.   Senior Residential Appraiser.

S.R.E.A.   Society of Real Estate Appraisers. Senior Real Estate Analyst.

S.R.P.A.   Senior Real Property Appraiser.

Sabotage Malicious destruction of an employer's property by workmen.

Sacrifice *See* **Jettison.**

Safe burglary insurance policy Type of business insurance coverage against loss of or liability for loss of contents of a safe.

Safe deposit box insurance policy Type of business insurance coverage against loss of or liability for loss of contents of a safe deposit box. Also called safe depository insurance.

Safe Driver Plan A system for adjusting standard rates up or down, according to good or bad driving records of insured persons.

Safety Fund Law Legislation permitting insurance company to accumulate from profits a fund which is placed in designated depository to meet emergency claims.

Safety responsibility laws *See* **Financial responsibility laws.**

Salary deduction insurance Life insurance in individual policies, issued to employees whose employer automatically deducts the premium from salary or wages before payment. Not to be confused with "contributory group." *See* **Payroll deduction.**

Salary savings insurance *See* **Payroll deduction insurance.**

Sale-leaseback A technique in which a seller deeds property to a buyer for a consideration and the buyer simultaneously leases the property back to the seller, usually on a long-term basis.

Sales bond *See* **Bond, surety.**

Sales contract A contract embodying the terms of agreement of a sale.

Salesmen's sample floater Insurance coverage on samples carried by salesmen.

Salvage The recovery reducing the amount of loss. As a verb, meaning to save endangered property and to enhance the value of damaged property. In marine insurance it means the cost of saving property exposed to a peril. In suretyship it is that which is recovered from the principal or an indemnitor to offset in whole or in part the loss and expense paid by a surety in satisfying its obligation under a bond.

Salvage corps Organizations maintained by fire insurance companies in big cities that try to prevent damage to insured property during and after a fire.

Salvage value   Scrap value.

Sanborn maps   *See* **Maps.**

Sandwich lease   A leasehold in which the interest of the subles-sor is inserted between the fee owner and the user of the property. The owner A of a fee simple leases to B, who in turn leases to C. The interest of A may be called the leased fee, that of B the sandwich lease, and that of C the leasehold. A lease in which the "sandwich party" is a lessee, paying rent on a leasehold interest to one party, and also is a lessor, collecting rents from another party or parties. Usually the owner of the sandwich lease is neither the fee owner nor the user of the property.

Satisfaction of mortgage   The recordable instrument given by the lender as evidence of payment in full of the mortgage debt. Sometimes known as a **release deed.**

Satisfaction piece   An instrument acknowledging payment of the indebtedness due under a mortgage.

Savings bank life insurance   Insurance written in several states through mutual savings banks. Characterized by having no agents to sell the insurance. It is purchased over the counter and is available in statutory limited amounts in the form of whole life, limited-payment life, endowment, term, and annuities on a participating basis.

Schedule   An enumeration of various properties covered by a policy. A system for computing rates.

Schedule bond   A bond enumerating individuals by name rather than the position. *See* **Bond, schedule.**

Schedule injury   An injury listed in the workmen's compensation law such as loss of a finger or toe, for which specified compensation is payable regardless of whether or not the employee suffers a loss of earning power.

Schedule of insurance   The list of individual items covered under one policy as the various buildings, animals, and other property in farm insurance or the list of the rings, bracelets, etc. insured under a jewelry floater.

Schedule of property   This term is applied to a statement which is attached to a policy, setting forth the various items to be insured, and the amounts applying to each and every one of the items in such schedule. If the schedule is dated, it must be dated before or at the time of the issue of the policy, and not after such date.

Schedule policy A covering under separate insuring agreements, for several hazards which are frequently covered under individual policies. It differs from a comprehensive policy in that hazards not specified in the schedule are not covered. An insurance policy that covers under separate agreements several enumerated causes of loss.

Schedule rating An analysis of the various physical elements of a risk attempting to provide an equitable rate for insurance generally in fire or workmen's compensation. There is a direct relation between the physical conditions and the loss experience. *See* **Rating, schedule.**

Scheduled property The listing of a specific dollar amount against each item covered by one policy.

Scheduled property floater Insurance on specific articles under one policy form.

Scienter "Scienti Non Fit Injuria" most commonly met in insurance with respect to tame animals where the owner must have previous knowledge that the animal presumed to be docile has in fact mischievous or wild disposition at times. Note difference between this and volens — volenti non fit injuria.

Scrap value Value as junk or salvage value.

Scratch daily report A copy of the daily report completed by the underwriter (or rater, or both) to be used by the policy-writer in preparing the policy.

Scratch endorsement A copy of the endorsement completed by the underwriter (or rater, or both) to be used by the policy writer in preparing the endorsement.

Seasonal risk An insured property that is only used for part of the year. A summer cottage at the shore, or a vegetable packing plant are examples of seasonal risks.

Second mortgage A real estate mortgage junior to another mortgage.

Second preliminary notice *See* **Intermediate notice.**

Second surplus reinsurance *See* **Reinsurance surplus.**

Secondary beneficiary The beneficiary next in line to collect should the primary beneficiary be unable to do so.

Secondary financing Financing of real estate with a loan, or loans, that are subordinate to a first mortgage or first trust deed.

Secondary mortgage market An unorganized market where existing mortgages are bought and sold. It contrasts with the primary mortgage market where mortgages are originated.

Section of land One of the portions of one square mile each or 640 acres into which the public lands of the United States are divided; one thirty-sixth part of a township. Much of this public land has been sold to individuals, or homesteaded.

Secured party The party holding a security interest or lien; may be referred to as the mortgagee, the conditional seller, or the pledgee.

Security The collateral given, deposited, or pledged to secure the fulfillment of an obligation or the payment of a debt.

Security agreement An agreement between a secured party and a debtor that creates a security interest.

Security bond *See* **Surety bond.**

Security instrument The mortgage or trust deed evidencing the pledge of real estate security as distinguished from the note or other credit instrument.

Security interest According to the U.C.C., a term designating the interest of the creditor in the property of the debtor in all types of credit transactions. It thus replaces such terms as **chattel mortgage, pledge,** trust receipt, chattel trust, equipment trust, conditional sale, and inventory lien. *See also* **Financing statement.**

Seed money *See* **Front-end money.**

Seisin Frequently spelled siezin. Possession whether of land or chattels; the possession of a freehold estate in land by one having the title thereto. The act of delivery of the land to the new freeholder.

Select mortality tables Mortality tables that reflect the fact that policyholders are selected after a medical or other examination and thus will not reflect the average mortality during the early period of the policy life. This advantage of selection tends to diminish after the passage of a decade.

Selection The choice of risks to prevent adverse selection.

Selection, adverse *See* **Adverse selection.**

Self-administered plan A profit-sharing or pension plan that is funded through a bank or fiduciary or investment company other than an insurance company.

Self-inflicted injury *See* **Intentional injury.**

Self-insurance The systematic provision of a fund to provide for the loss which the individual or firm may have. The endeavor of one who is subject to a risk to lay aside sums periodically which in time will provide a fund to cover any loss which occurs.

Self rating *See* **Prospective rating.**

Self-reinsurance Creation of a fund by an insurer to absorb losses beyond the insurer's normal retention.

Seller-servicer An FNMA term for an approved corporation that sells and services mortgages for FNMA.

Sellers' market The period of an expanding demand; prices are on an upward trend.

Selling price clauses The first clause defines the insurable value of merchandise which has been sold but not delivered as the amount at which it was sold, less any charges not incurred. The second clause applies only to goods made by an insured manufacturer. This sets the value of such goods at the net price at which they could have been sold at the factory instead of the insured's cost to reproduce.

Semicommercial A classification of accident and sickness policies sometimes established to cover forms which are, for all practical purposes, the same as commercial forms but are issued for slightly lower limits and quarterly or monthly premiums.

Semitontine system An insurance provision condemned by the Armstrong Investigating Committee. It provided a surrender value in the event a policy lapsed prior to the period of dividend distribution. *See* **Tontine system.**

Senior interest A participation senior or ahead of another participation.

Separate account A separate fund, held by a life insurance company, that is used to record investment of pension assets.

Separate property Property a husband or wife owns independent of the other; not community property.

Separation Practice, now illegal, for companies that were members of certain associations to refuse to do business with an agent whose companies were not members of the association.

Separation rule A rule that an agent may represent only insurers of a specified class if he is to represent any one insurer of that class.

Septic tank A container in which the solid matter of continuously flowing sewage is deposited and retained until it has been disintegrated by anaerobic bacteria.

Service   Relating to an agreement by the insurer to pay certain providers of health care services, under arrangement with them for rendering such services to covered persons. These arrangements may preclude or limit any additional charges for the defined services.

Service benefit   Insurance in the form of hospital or medical care, for instance, as distinguished from monetary payment for such benefits.

Service of process laws   Legislation similar to that upheld by the Supreme Court in Travelers Health vs. Virginia 339 U.S. 643 in which claimants may obtain service of a process on unlicensed companies in their own state.

Service property   A property devoted to or available for utilization for a special purpose, but which has no independent marketability in the generally recognized acceptance of such a term; such as a clubhouse, a church property, a public school. These properties pose problems of valuation for insurance purposes.

Service station liability insurance   Type of business insurance coverage designed for the particular needs of service stations that handle automobiles and related material.

Servicemen's Insurance *See* **N.S.L.I., U. S. Government Life Insurance,** and **Servicemen's Gratuitous Indemnity.**

Servicing agreement   A written agreement between an investor and mortgage loan correspondent stipulating the rights and obligations of each party.

Setback   The distance that, according to municipal regulations, must separate a structure from the perimeter of its property, usually a curb. Setback lines are defined in building codes, deed restrictions, and zoning requirements.

Settlement option   Provides that the insurance company has the choice of settling the claim in more than one way, such as with money or the same type of property. The option, the insured or beneficiary may have to choose how the money from a policy will be paid.

Settling agents *See* **Claim agents.**

Severability *See* **Divisibility.**

Severance damage   The impairment in value caused by separation. Commonly, the damage resulting from taking of a fraction of the whole property reflected in a lowered utility and value in the land remaining and brought about by reason of the fractional taking.

Sex Male or female designation. Since women on the whole live about five years longer than men, the proper designation for computing mortality is essential. Young females have fewer automobile accidents than young males and this is reflected in automobile insurance rates.

Share reinsurance *See* **Reinsurance, share.**

Sheriff's deed An instrument drawn under order of court to convey title to property sold to satisfy a judgment at law.

Sheriff's sale A sale of real or personal property made by a sheriff or other like ministerial officer, in obedience to an execution or other similar mandate of the court.

Shock loss A claim or loss that is so large as to affect materially the underwriting averages.

Shopping centers The type of shopping center is determined by its major tenant or tenants, not by site area nor building size. A Neighborhood Center provides for the sale of convenience goods and personal service for the day-to-day living needs of the immediate neighborhood. It is built around a supermarket as the principal tenant. A Community Center provides, in addition to convenience goods, a wider range of wearing apparel, hardware, and appliances. It is built around a variety store or junior department store as the major tenant. A Regional Center provides for a full range of general merchandise, including apparel, furniture, and home furnishings in full depth. It is built around one or more department stores.

Short date rates Rates which follow the percentages laid down in the Short Date Tables, and which are in excess of a pro rate proportion of the yearly premium.

Short period insurance This is insurance for periods of less than one year.

Short rate The charge required for insurance or bonds taken for less than one year and, in some cases, the earned premium for insurance or bonds canceled by the insured before the end of the policy period or term of bond.

Short rate cancellation *See* **Cancellation, short rate.**

Short term An insurance contract for less than a year.

Short-term disability income insurance A type of coverage that pays benefits to a disabled individual for a stated period of time not to exceed two years.

Short term trust A reversionary trust under which the income or principal of the trust reverts to the grantor after a specific event or period. Combined with life insurance such short term trusts provide opportunity for tax minimizing under the 1954 Revenue Act.

Sickness insurance   Provides for payment of a substantial part of earned income lost through disability caused by illness and for payment of medical expenses incurred as a result of illness. *See* **Health insurance.**

Sidetrack agreement   An agreement between a railroad and a second party under which the railroad furnishes sidetrack facilities on the latter's premises, the second party releasing the railroad from liability for damages or assuming the railroad's liability for damages to others on account of the maintenance or operation of the sidetrack. *See* **Railway sidetrack agreement** and also **Liability, contractual.**

Signs   Neon signs and painted signs attached to a building are not generally covered in the building policy, nor in the event of them belonging to the tenant, by the tenant's contents policy, unless specifically included. Glass or other fancy signs inside a building also are not covered —unless specifically included. Neither of these things are fixtures or furniture.

Silverware floaters   All-risk inland marine policy covering silverware.

Simple interest   The interest arising from the principal sum only.

Sine die   Adjournment with an unfixed time for the resumption of the hearing.

Sine prole   Died without issue.

Single interest policy   Insurance protecting the interest of only one of the parties having an insurable interest in certain property, as that protecting a mortgagee but not the mortgagor, or protecting the seller but not the buyer of merchandise.

Single premium   *See* **Premium, single.**

Single premium insurance   A life insurance contract that provides that for the consideration of a premium paid only once, the insurance company will assume the liability on the contract. Annuities also may be purchased by a single premium payment.

Site   Lands made suitable for building purposes by dividing into lots, laying out streets, and the like. A location or plot of ground delineated for a specific purpose or function.

Sky lease   *See* **Air rights.**

Slander   Malicious speaking of false and defamatory words concerning another, whereby he is injured. Liability for slander is a risk of newspapers, magazines, radio, television.

Sliding scale commission A system whereby the actual commissions paid by a reinsurer to the ceding company vary inversely with the loss ratio within certain set limits.

Slow burning *See* **Mill construction.**

Slow burning construction *See* **Mill construction.**

Smoke damage insurance Insurance against damage done by smoke from the sudden, unusual, and faulty operation of a heating or cooking unit but only when such unit is connected to a chimney by a smoke pipe and while on the premises described in the policy. Smoke damage from fireplaces and industrial apparatus is excluded. Damage covered by smoke from a hostile fire is covered by a fire insurance policy rather than the smoke damage insurance policy.

Smoke insurance *See* **Smoke damage insurance.**

Smudge insurance *See* **Smoke damage insurance.**

Snap out policy An insurance policy on carbon paper, or carbonless material that permits duplication. The original is given the policy holder; the duplicate is retained by the insurer.

Social Insurance A device for the pooling of risks by their transfer to an organization, usually governmental, that is required by law to provide pecuniary or service benefits to or on behalf of covered persons upon the occurrence of certain pre-designated losses under all of the following conditions: 1. Coverage is compulsory by law in virtually all instances. 2. Except during a transition period following its introduction, eligibility for benefits is derived, in fact or in effect, from contributions having been made to the program by or in respect of the claimant or the person as to whom the claimant is a dependent; there is no requirement that the individual demonstrate inadequate financial resources, although a dependency status may need to be established. 3. The methods for determining the benefits is prescribed by law. 4. The benefits for any individual are not usually directly related to contributions made by or in respect of him but instead usually redistribute income so as to favor certain groups such as those with low former wages or a large number of dependents. 5. There is a definite plan for financing the benefits that is designed to be adequate in terms of long-range considerations. 6. The cost is borne primarily by contributions which are usually made by covered persons, their employers, or both. 7. The plan is administered or at least supervised by the government. 8. The plan is not established by the government solely for its present or former employees. CIT

Social Security Act   Federal legislation providing social insurance on a national scale.

Social security option   Option available to an employee under which he or she may elect to receive higher annuity payments before a certain age, usually the age of retirement, and a lower payment after that age, at which time he will be receiving social security payments from the government.

Society of Real Estate Appraisers   Members of this society are designated as Senior Residential Appraiser (SRA), Senior Real Property Appraiser (SRPA), and Senior Real Estate Analyst (SREA).

Soft costs   Architectural, engineering, and legal fees as, distinguished from land and construction costs, for real estate development.

Sold but not delivered   A stipulation is sometimes included in the policy to the effect that it covers goods "sold but not delivered". his clause takes care of the merchant or manufacturer's liability for goods which have not been legally delivered to the client. (See Delivery of Goods). It is sometimes referred to as the "usual commission clause".

Sole and unconditional ownership clause   As found in fire or property insurance, states that the policy becomes void if the interest of the policyholder is other than sole and unconditional.

Solicitor   As used in insurance terminology, a person authorized by an agent to be his representative. This person may solicit and receive applications for insurance.

Sound value   Usually used after a fire to indicate the value of the insured property immediately before the damage. *See* **Actual cash value.**

Special acceptance   A special agreement by a reinsurer which includes a risk in a reinsurance contract that would not normally be covered by that contract.

Special agent   Individual representing his insurance company in an exclusive territory. He supervises agents of the company and the operations of his insurance company.

Special assessment   A tax levied against certain real estate owners to pay for public improvements that are assumed to specifically benefit their property.

Special damages   Those which are the natural, but not the necessary consequences of the act complained. Actual loss as distinguished from presumed loss.

Special features   *See* **Optional benefits.**

Special hazard   A risk of more than average size, duration, or danger.

Special indemnities   *See* **Optional benefits.**

Special Multi Peril (SMP)   A policy for certain non-personal line risks. Coverage can be afforded for most commonly written property and liability hazards under the single policy.

Special risk or **Specialty risk**   A transfer of risk from one individual to another not based on true insurance principals of reducing the individual risk to the risk of the statistical universe. Underwriters of Lloyd's of London have been known to insure the eyes of artists, the fingers of piano players, and other such special risks.

Special warranty deed   A warranty only against the acts of the grantor himself and all persons claiming by, through, or under him.

Specific insurance   A policy coverage that goes into detail as to the description of the property covered as compared to a blanket coverage, applying separately to specifically named objects or locations. It is inaccurately used in referring to primary insurance, which must be exhausted before excess insurance applies.

Specific performance   A remedy in a court of equity compelling the defendant to carry out the terms of an agreement or contract.

Specific rate   A rate applying to an individual property determined by schedule. *See* **Schedule, class, rates, Minimum rates.**

Specified amount   A dollar amount determined by the VA that must be credited against the veteran's indebtedness at completion of foreclosure. Used as the amount to be bid by the lender at the foreclosure sale and also used in calculation for the lender's claim under the VA guaranty.

Speculative construction   Construction of a building without prior rental, lease, or sale agreements.

Speculative risk   Uncertainty of the probability of an occurrence, of an event that could produce either a gain or loss.

Spendthrift trust or clause   A provision to protect the beneficiary of an insurance settlement from his own indiscretion. The clause provides that benefits shall not be transferable, assignable, or subject to incumbrances, garnishment, or attachment.

Split dollar coverage   Refers to an insurance policy owned jointly by an employer and employee. The annual premium is shared between the two parties involved. It is used chiefly as a means of tieing key executives to a company.

Split funding   A technique wherein a portion of the contributions to a pension plan are paid to an insurance company, with the remainder being invested through a corporate trustee.

Split life insurance   Term insurance and installment annuity are combined in this particular form of insurance.

Spoliation   This is the alteration of a policy by a stranger, i. e. a party other than the insurer or insured, and without their consent and privity. It does not render the policy void, and will not affect the insurance if the original words can be restored with certainty.

Sports liability insurance   Protection against liability for damages resulting in bodily injuries or death occurring as a result of an accident to individuals caused by the assured while engaged in sports.

Spot loans   Single-family loans solicited on an individual basis.

Spread loss   Type of reinsurance agreement. Self-explanatory.

Spread loss reinsurance   A working cover subject to a prospective rating plan.

Sprinkler leakage insurance   Covers damage caused by accidental flow of water from a sprinkler. In some contracts, fire-protection equipment also is included. This protection limits claims to causes other than a hostile fire or certain other specified causes.

Square foot content   The sum expressed in square feet of the area of all rooms on all floors of a building.

Squatter's right   The right at common law created by the occupancy of land for long and undisturbed use but without legal title.

Stabilized operating statement   Detailed projection of all income and disbursements over a selected period of years and averaged for a single year. *See* **Pro forma statement.**

Staff manager   The title of unit manager in an industrial agency, also called superintendent.

Stamping office   A stamping office is a central office or bureau to which agents and companies send certain daily reports and endorsements for auditing before transmittal to the insurance company. If incorrect, notice is sent to the writing office and company, requesting correction.

Standard Insurance written on a basis of the regular mortality and underwriting assumption used by the company.

Standard average clause *See* **Coinsurance clause.**

Standard depth As applied to land (e.g., urban lots), the depth chosen as standard, usually the one which is most common in the neighborhood.

Standard exceptions Commonly found in workmen's compensation insurance. Certain classes or groups of employees are separately classified when rates are established.

Standard form An insurance policy which has been adopted by many insurance companies and approved by respective state insurance departments.

Standard limit See **Limit, basic.**

Standard policy An insurance contract in common use and in many cases complying with state laws as to form and content. *See* **Standard form.**

Standard premium As found in workmen's compensation insurance, is computed on the basis of rates used before the premium is adjusted under premium discount or retrospective rating.

Standard provisions Those clauses that certain state codes prescribe as being inserted in contracts of insurance. Contract provisions in general use by insurers, adopted by a group of insurers, approved by a state insurance department, or required by statute, either literally, in substance, or in a form more favorable to the insured.

Standard Risk (Life) A person who according to a life insurance company's underwriting standards is entitled to insurance protection, without extra rating or special restrictions.

Standby commitment A commitment to purchase a loan or loans with specified terms, with both parties understanding that delivery is unlikely, unless circumstances warrant. The contract is issued for a fee with a commitment to fund in the event that a permanent loan is not obtained within a stated period of time. Such commitments are typically used to enable the borrower to obtain lower-cost construction financing with the understanding that permanent financing of the project will be available on more-favorable terms when the improvements are completed and the project is generating income.

Standby fee   The fee charged by an investor for a standby commitment. The fee is earned upon issuance and acceptance of the commitment.

Standing timber insurance   Highly specialized coverage developed when attempts to borrow on timber were made. Lenders required insurance to prevent loss from catastrophic fire. Since most fires are from April to November, a generally dry season, if policy is in force for any portion of that period, 80 percent of annual premium is considered earned.

Starts   A term commonly used to indicate the number of residential units begun within a stated period of time.

State agent   Agent senior to a special agent and who has an exclusive territory, generally a state. He supervises the agents and the business of his company in the territory.

State fund, competitive   A state fund writing insurance in competition with private insurers.

State fund, monopolistic   A state fund, competition with which is excluded by statute.

State insurance department   A department of a state government whose duty is regulation of the business of insurance and the dissemination of information on insurance.

State unemployment insurance   A form of social insurance that operates by means of a payroll tax which is used to pay calculated benefits to people that qualify as being unemployed within the definitions of the law.

Stated Amount (Auto)   Coverage for a car which for reasons of uniqueness, does not decrease in value with age. (Generally written for antique or special built cars.)

Statement of Claim   A written or printed statement by the plaintiff in an action showing the facts relied upon to support his claim against the defendant and the relief which he claims.

Statement of Defence   A pleading delivered in an action in high court in reply to the Statement of Claim. It answers the allegations in the Statement of Claim by admissions or denials and sets out a fresh set of facts in the form of further allegations may include a counter-claim.

Statement of values   Information required by a rating bureau or underwriter to value each risk separately.

Static impairment   A physical condition in which the body has suffered some loss or injury. Permanent loss of sight or the amputation of a limb are two examples of static impairment.

At times a progressive impairment may by therapy and treatment become static. *See* **Progressive impairment.**

Statistical agent   Association of member companies that prepares statistical studies used in formulation of rates.

Statuary   This and other works of art should always be covered by specific items in the policy and be described minutely. If there are several articles of the kind, they should be scheduled, describing each, and setting an amount of insurance against each.

Status   Legal standing, condition, or relation. Relative position or rank.

Status quo   The state in which things are, or were.

Statute   A law established by the act of the legislature.

Statute of Frauds   In 1677 an English statute that has become an intricate part of our law. Its chief characteristic is that no action can be maintained on certain types of contracts unless a note or memo thereof, signed by the party charged or his agent, can be produced. It is particularly true in matters involving real estate.

Statute of Limitations   A statute placing a time limit on the bringing of actions to within a certain specific period after the accrual of the right to start such an action.

Statutory profit   Premiums earned less losses and expenses.

Statutory warranty deed   A warranty deed form prescribed by state statutes.

Steam boiler insurance policy   Type of business insurance coverage. *See* **Boiler and machinery insurance.** Self-explanatory.

Step-down lease   A lease calling for an initial rent followed by a decrease in rent over stated periods.

Step rate plan   Premium plan that charges a higher rate for older policy holders. The "natural premium" plan.

Step-up lease   A lease which provides for an increase in rent over stated periods, under the assumption that the property will increase in value or that the lessee will be in a better position to pay higher rent as time progresses.

Stipulated Premium Company   See Assessment Insurance.

Stipulated Premium Insurance   A form of assessment insurance. A regular rate is normally charged the policyholder. However the company may under certain conditions require additional payment.

Stirpes   See per-stirpes.

Stock   Insurance company that issues stock as compared to a mutual insurance company. Also merchandise as compared to fixtures, machinery, or furniture.

Stock Company   A company owned by a number of investors or stockholders.

Stock in trade   The term "stock in trade" is always limited to personal property. It varies in technical meaning in consonance with the particular —and peculiar nature of the policyholder's occupation or business. It should never be used without qualifications, such as for instance, "Stock in trade as a grocer and and butcher", and so forth. When the phrase is used in connection with a specified trade or business, it will include the materials essential to the carrying on of that trade or business, and under some circumstances, has been held to extend to cover tools and utensils. However, it is best, if tools and utensils are to be covered, to specifically mention them.

Stock insurance company   A company owned and controlled by stockholders and conducted for profit. It sets a premium charge for insurance, assuming all liabilities on a corporate basis. The owners of the business are paid the profits. *See* **Capital stock company.**

Stock insurer   An insurance firm organized in corporate form that issues stock and is designed to make a profit.

Stock life insurance company   A life insurance company owned and controlled by stockholders who share in the surplus earnings. The company issues, in general, nonparticipating life insurance, but may also issue participating life insurance.

Stocks and shares   Are issued to the owners of the company who then become the shareholders. May be common, ordinary, or preferred. The former share in the profits of the company by way of dividend payments after the preferred holders have received their interest. Participating preferred shareholders also participate in the distribution of net profits with common shareholders, after payment of preferred interest or dividend. No repayment of principal except on liquidation.

Stop loss   Any provision in a policy designed to cut off the company's loss at a given point. A stop loss may be an aggregate payable under the policy, maximum payable for any one disability, or the like. *See* **Excess insurance, reinsurance.**

Stop loss reinsurance   *See* **Excess of loss reinsurance.**

Stoppage in transitu Goods are often sold on credit and delivered to a carrier for transit t othe purchaser at whose risk the goods must, in the absence of special arrangements, remain. The title, however, is subject to the right of the vendor to stop the goods in transit, at any time before they come into the actual possession of the purchaser. If this course is pursued, the vendor reassumes title, and is invested with his original right of ownership of the goods. If they have been covered by the purchaser, and a loss occurs in the hands of the carrier, a question of ownership might arise in case of stoppage in transitu. (See also Delivery of Goods).

Storage The words "storage and keeping" are often applied to articles or substances which are prohibited by the company. Storage means only those articles held for safe keeping, to be delivered in the same condition as when received; keeping generally applies to articles that are kept for sale. Storing or keeping goods which are otherwise prohibited under the conditions of the policy, renders that policy void if loss occurs in consequence, unless the company's permission and consent has been gained and endorsed.

Stored goods insurance policy Type of business insurance coverage. Self-explanatory.

Storekeeper's burglary and robbery policy Insures against losses from robbery or burglary. It is a form of package policy.

Storekeeper's liability policy Insures against bodily injury claims and damage to property due to operation of the business. It is a form of package policy.

Straight life annuity A life annuity policy which does not provide any refund to any beneficiary at the death of the annuitant.

Straight life insurance A plan of insurance for the whole of life with premiums payable until death. *See* **Life insurance, ordinary.**

Stranding The running aground of a ship or vessel.

Strict liability The legal precept covering the degree of care used by manufacturers. The claimant need show only that there was a defect in the product and that loss or injury occurred as a result of the defect. It is not necessary to prove negligence on the part of the manufacturer.

Strike insurance Indemnification designed to protect employers against monetary loss due to strikes.

Strike suit   A legal action brought mostly for nuisance value. *See* **Ex gratia payment.**

Strike-through clause   A reinsurer is liable for his share of a loss even though the ceding company is insolvent. The reinsurer's payment goes directly to the insured.

Subagent   Individual that reports to an insurance company through another agent.

Subcontractor   The person or company under contract to perform work for a developer or general contractor.

Subdivision   A tract of land divided into lots suitable for home building purposes.

Subfloor (diagonal)   Floor which is laid in a diagonal fashion over the floor joists.

Subject premium   The reinsurance rate is added to the ceding company's premium (subject premium) to compute the reinsurance premium.

Subjective risk   The evaluation of a risk by an individual who may not have objective information as to the certainty or uncertainty of the occurrence of a event.

Sublease   The agreement by a tenant which transfers all or part of his rights to another, providing that the original lease permits this new agreement.

Subletting   A leasing by a tenant to another, who holds under the tenant.

Subordinate   Verb meaning to make subject, or junior, to.

Subordination   The act of a party acknowledging, by written recorded instrument, that a debt due is inferior to the interest of another person or company in the same property. Subordination may apply not only to mortgages, but to leases, real estate rights, and any other types of debt instruments.

Subordination clause   A clause in a deed of trust that effects the subordination.

Subpoena   A writ issued in an action or suit, requiring the person to whom it is directed to be present at a specified time and place. It is commonly used to require the presence of all witnesses before a Court, in the Court proceedings.

Subrogation   The right of the insurance company to recover from a third party the amount paid under the policy. For example, if damage is done to your automobile, protected by a collision insurance policy, the insurance company may collect, from the party whose automobile ran into your car, the amount of damages which was paid to you by the process of subrogation.

Subscription policy   A policy which has been subscribed to by two or more insurers. The amount of risk assigned to each subscriber is stated in the policy.

Subsidence   Movement of the land and the damage caused by such a movement. Heavy rains or shifting of land due to mining are examples of subsidence causes.

Substandard   Conditions making a risk less desirable than normal for its class.

Substandard insurance   Insurance of persons who do not meet the standards set for insurance at regular rates. A cestui que vie who is below standard as a mortality risk. A policy issued to such a person, usually calling for an additional amount of premium.

Substandard risk   A risk that is under average or impaired.

Substitution of Liability   The assumption of liability by another individual on a mortgage or trust deed note, with the concurrent release of the original maker by the mortgagee. *See* **Assumption of mortgage.**

Sub-surface right   The right to ownership of everything beneath the physical surface of land, such as oil and minerals.

Subtropical risks   An extra premium on life insurance policies issued to individuals in subtropical countries because of the higher mortality rates in those areas.

Sue and labor clause   Provision of marine policy that requires the insured to attempt salvage. The insurance company pays not only the claim but also the salvage expenses.

Suicide clause   A clause in an insurance policy calling for payment in the event of a suicide if that suicide occurs after a two-year period from the time the policy was written.

Sui puris   A person who can validly contract and bind himself by legal obligation, uncontrolled by another person.

Suit   A legal proceeding brought by one person against another.

Sum of digits   *See* **Rule of 78s.**

Superintendent   In some states, official designation of the commissioner of insurance. Also formerly the title of unit manager in an industrial agency, now usually called staff manager.

Superintendent of insurance   Title used in some states for commissioner of insurance. *See* **Commissioner of insurance.**

Superseded suretyship When a company writes a bond to take the place of another, which is cancelled as of the effective date of the new bond, a rider should be attached (unless the bond itself contains a superseded suretyship provision) agreeing to pay losses that would have been recoverable under the first bond except that the "discovery period" has expired.

Superseded suretyship rider A continuity of coverage clause in the form of a rider attached to a new fidelity bond, taking the place of another bond and agreeing to pay losses that would be recoverable under the first bond except that the discovery period has expired. Losses caused by dishonest employees frequently have been found to have occurred at various times stretching over a period of years. This may involve a chain of several bonds, each one superseding a prior obligation. These losses will be covered if the chain of bonds is unbroken and each has included the superseded suretyship rider.

Supersession A form of economic obsolescence, sometimes called the element of inadequacy, resulting from an inadequate improvement to land.

Supplemental agreement An agreement not a usual part of the policy contract as printed by the company but signed and attached to the contract by the company. It usually concerns a special method of settling the proceeds.

Supplemental Security Income (SSI) The social insurance program of the Social Security Administration. Cash benefits are paid to those covered individuals who are able to demonstrate a need and qualify.

Supplemental Term Insurance A supplemental agreement, available in some life insurance policies, providing for the payment of an additional specified sum in event the insured dies during the given term period. (See Family Income Policy and Family Protection Policy.)

Supplementary contract An agreement by the company to retain the lump sum payable under an insurance policy and to make payments in accordance with the settlement option chosen. *See* **Rider** and **Supplemental agreement.**

Supplementary payments The clause in a liability policy calling for the insurer to pay for defense costs, cost of court bonds, and interest on judgment, as well as judgments handed down by the court of law.

Surety The corporation or individual guaranteeing performance or faithfulness under a bond.

Surety bond   An instrument providing for monetary compensation should there be a failure to perform any specific acts within a stated period.

Suretyship   All forms of obligations to pay the debt or default of another. The function of being a surety.

Suretyship, personal   The giving of a bond by an individual.

Surgeon's liability insurance policy   Type of business insurance coverage. Self-explanatory. *See* **Liability insurance, physician's and surgeon's.**

Surgical Insurance   To cover surgeons fees up to the amounts specified for various types of operations listed in the policy. This coverage is often combined with a hospitalization policy.

Surplus   A company's surplus is the difference between its assets and liabilities. *Net surplus* includes contingency reserves and unassigned funds, while *gross surplus* also includes surplus assigned for distribution as dividends.

Surplus line   *See* **Excess Line Broker.**

Surplus reinsurance   *See* **Reinsurance, surplus.**

Surplus to policyholders   The total of capital, if any, and unassigned (surplus) funds, including voluntary and general reserve funds, and special reserve funds not in the nature of liabilities; the amount beyond liabilities available to meet obligations to policyholders.

Surrender   To voluntarily give up possession. The cancellation of a lease by mutual consent of lessor and lessee.

Surrender charge   The difference between the reserve on a policy and the amount of the cash surrender value. Withheld especially in the earlier years to help repay the drain on surplus arising when the policy was put on the books. Under the standard nonforfeiture valuation laws, now universally used for new poliices in the United States and many Canadian companies, there is no direct surrender charge, the cash values being disassociated from the reserves and calculated directly.

Surrender cost index   The measure of the cost, including interest foregone, of the insurance policy if kept in force for a stated period and then subsequently surrendered for its cash surrender value.

Surrender value   *See* **Cash surrender value.**

Survey   An examination of the insurance requirement of a buyer and the report of such examination. An insurance engineer's study of a risk for underwriting or accident and occupational disease prevention purposes. The process of ascertaining the quantity and or location and boundaries of a piece of land; it may include physical features affecting it, such as grades, contours, structures, etc. A statement of the courses, distances, and quantity of land. A quantitive statement determining and delineating as to form, extent, and position of a tract of land by such means as the taking of linear angular measurements.

Survey agent Individual who is not permitted to write a policy but instead submits an application to his company. The company in turn prepares the policy from the application. *See* **Application agent,** also **Agent, surveying.**

Surveyor Individual adjusting a marine claim.

Surveyor's certificate A formal statement, signed, certified, and dated by a surveyor, giving the pertinent facts about a particular property and any easements or encroachments affecting it.

Survivorship annuity *See* **Annuity, survivorship.**

Suspense file A file in which are kept letters, binders, or applications requiring follow-up.

Swap maternity Immediate maternity coverage is granted in this group health insurance plan. However, any pregnancies in progress upon termination of the plan are not covered.

Sweat equity Equity created in a property by the performance of work or labor by the purchaser or borrower. It directly increases the value of the property.

Switch maternity The husbands of female employees must be in-included in the plan as dependents in order for group health maternity coverage to apply.

Syndicate *See* **Lloyd's Syndicate.**

Syndicate policy Contract of insurance carrying the name and risk of each participating syndicate member company.

T.A.   Trading As
T.B.   Trial Balance
T.D.B.   Temporary disability benefits.
T.I.A.A.   Teachers Insurance and Annuity Association.
T.I.R.B.   Transportation Insurance Rating Bureau
T.N.E.C.   Temporary National Economic Committee.
Tabular mortality Mortality as shown on the mortality table in use, that is, expected mortality.

Takedown The act of a borrower drawing needed funds against a previously made loan commitment. The advance of money by a lender to a borrower under a loan agreement, loan commitment, or line of credit.

Takeout commitment A promise to make a loan at a future specified time. It is most commonly used to designate a higher-cost, shorter-term, back-up commitment as a support for construction financing until a suitable permanent loan can be secured.

Takeout investor An investor who agrees to make a long-term (permanent) loan that will be used to pay off a short-term loan, usually a construction loan.

Takeout loan A first mortgage loan that is committed and expected to be made upon completion of a specific real estate project. *See* **Permanent loan.**

Tandem plan A mortgage assistance program whereby GNMA agrees to purchase qualified, below-market interest rate mortgages at prices favorable to sellers. The mortgages purchased by GNMA are accumulated and periodically sold at auction as either GNMA securities or whole mortgages.

Tangible property Property that, by its nature, is susceptible to the senses. Generally land, fixed improvements, furnishings, merchandise, cash, and other items of capital used in carrying on an enterprise.

Target risks Policyholders or prospects for insurance, whose business develops large premiums, are considered targets for competing insurance agents and brokers. Also used to describe risks of large value or limits and severe hazards that are difficult to insure or for companies to reinsure.

Tariff rate The insurance rate established by the rating organization having jurisdiction over the class and territory.

Tax To assess or determine judicially the amount of levy for the support of certain government functions for public purposes. A charge or burden, usually pecuniary, laid upon persons or property for public purposes; a forced contribution of wealth to meet the public needs of a government.

Tax abatement Amount abated; deduction; decrease rebate, especially of a tax or burden improperly laid. The act of abating such tax or burden.

Tax and board Percentages of the paid premium for state and local taxes and for the support of the various rating offices, bureaus, and rating boards.

Tax deed A deed issued by a public authority as a result of a tax sale of the property.

Tax foreclosure Seizure of property, because of unpaid taxes, by the duly authorized officials of the public authority impowered to tax.

Tax lien A claim against property for the amount of its due and unpaid taxes.

Tax penalty That extra charge or forfeiture of an amount because of delinquent payment of taxes.

Tax rate The rate of tax per $100 of assessed value of real property.

Tax receivership The function of a receiver appointed by a court or under a statute upon default of taxes.

Tax redemption The recovery of property by settlement through the payment of the delinquent taxes and any penalties that have accrued as a result of such delinquency.

Tax sale Sale of property because of the nonpayment of taxes. This will usually be by auction. It may be by means of sealed or open bids.

Tax sale certificate A certificate given to one who purchases land at a tax sale.

Tax title The title by which one holds lands purchased at a tax sale.

Taxable value The value set upon the property by which the tax levy is computed. In some cases the tax value may have but small relationship to the market value since the market value will fluctuate more rapidly and is not set in a fairly arbitrary manner.

Taxing authority A statutory authority invested in a governmental body to levy and collect taxes for public purposes.

Taxpayer One who pays taxes. A building erected for the primary purpose of producing revenues to meet the taxes on the land. When the land has ripened, the taxpayer is demolished and a more substantial structure put up in its place. Thus the building and property with the "taxpayer" is producing some return, generally enough to pay the taxes.

Team's liability insurance policy Type of business insurance protecting owners of athletic teams from liability.

TEFRA Tax Equity and Fiscal Responsibility Act of 1982: Complex legislation to plug tax loopholes and stimulate economy by lower rate of taxation.

Temporary disability benefits Weekly benefits payable to employees for nonoccupational accidents and sickness. This term or the abbreviated form T.D.B. is commonly used when referring specifically to coverage under temporary disability benefit laws. *See* **Disability insurance, Disability benefit law.**

Temporary disability laws State laws that provide disability income for individuals who are disabled either on or off the job for a stated period of time.

Temporary Life Annuity A contract providing for the payment of an annuity for a limited period only, or until the annuitant's death within the specified period.

Temporary National Economic Committee investigation Study by a Congressional committee with particular reference to monopoly power in the United States. One phase of the study was of the insurance industry.

Tenancy A holding or mode of holding, in a state of tenure, temporary possession of that which belongs to another. The period of a tenant's occupancy; an estate less than freehold, a holding of real estate under a lease, either written or oral.

Tenancy at sufferance That tenancy which results when a tenant holds over after the expiration of his lease.

Tenancy at will That estate which may be terminated by either the lessor or the lessee at any time.

Tenancy by entirety The joint ownership of a structure.

Tenancy in common Form of estate held by two or more persons, each of whom is considered as being possessed of the whole of an undivided part.

Tenant One who holds or possesses real estate by any kind of title, either in fee, for life, for years, or at will. In a more limited and popular sense, a tenant is one who has the temporary use of real estate which belongs to another.

Tenant contributions All costs that are a pro rata responsibility of the tenant over and above the contract rent specified in the lease, such as area maintenance.

Tenant's Policy A form of homeowners policy sold to people who rent rather than own their own homes.

Tender This may be (a) a written offer to supply certain commodities, or (b) an offer of money in payment of a debt or obligation.

Tender of unearned premium The portion of the premium unearned must always be tendered in case of the termination of a contract before its full term has expired. The tender of such unearned premium should be made at the time of cancellation, and if the tender be refused, the exact amount should be offered and counted in the presence of the policy-holder. If the tender is still refused, such tender will be sufficient to maintain the cancellation. The agent must, however, hold the money ready, at all reasonable times and proper places, to pay over to the policy-holder if he demands it. The agent must avoid any act that would indicate that the policy was in force after such tender has been made.

Tenure   A mode of holding land.

Term   The period of time for which a lease or an insurance policy is issued.

Term Insurance   *A convertible term* policy can be replaced at expiration with a new policy without taking a physical.

Term life   Life insurance protection during a certain number of years, but expiring without policy cash value if the insured survives the stated period.

Term loan   A loan by insurance companies or banks for a period generally in excess of five years. The loan is made to business firms and typically has an agreement on the part of the debtor to restrict his performance to an area circumscribed by various ratios.

Term mortgage   A loan having a specified term during which interest is paid but the principal is not reduced. The entire principal plus any unpaid accrued interest is due and payable at the end of its term.

Term noncancellable   A designation sometimes applied to policies which omit the cancellation provision but are not guaranteed renewable. They are noncancellable for the term of the policy. However, it is considered better not to use this designation since it tends to be confusing to the layman. All reference to noncancellability should be avoided unless the policy is not only noncancellable but also guaranteed renewable.

Term of policy   The period for which the policy runs. This is usually the period for which a premium has been paid in advance. In some instances it may be for a year, or longer even though the premium is paid on a semiannual or other basis.

Term policy   Usually, a fire or casualty policy written for more than one year. The name has a different meaning when used in reference to life insurance.

Term rate The price per $100 of insurance for insurance lasting a year or longer. Short-term rates refer to the price per $100 of insurance for periods lasting less than a year.

Term rules The various formulas for computing the application of a rate where the period of the policy is for over one year. A three-year-rate would not be three times the yearly rate because of reduced overhead costs.

Termination Default in premium payment rendering the death or endowment benefits of the policy void and resulting in the application of one of the nonforfeiture values. *See* **Lapse.**

Termite Any of numerous pale-colored, soft-bodied, social insects of the order Isoptera, which feed primarily on wood.

Termite shield A metal protective shield applied on top of the foundation wall to prevent subterranean termites from attacking the structural wood members supporting the building. Termite insurance is concerned with the exposure that the building presents to infestation.

Territorial limits *See* **Geographical limits.**

Tertiary beneficiary The third beneficiary. The person who collects the settlement or the remains of a settlement if the primary and secondary are unable to do so.

Testamentary trust A trust established by will.

Testate To dispose of one's property by a valid will.

Testator The person making a will.

Testimony Evidence of a witness given in Court.

Theater public liability insurance A form of public liability insurance for theaters. *See* **Liability insurance.**

Theatrical floater Inland marine coverage for theatrical properties, costumes, and scenery against loss or damage other than wear and tear.

Theft The taking or removing of property with intent to deprive the rightful owner. It includes such crimes as robbery, burglary, and larceny.

Theory probability *See* **Law of large numbers.**

Thiasoi Ancient Greek benevolent society that was influential in developing the idea of life insurance.

Third party action An action brought by a defendant in one action against another party, e. g. an injured workman, a sub-contractor. The sub-contractor may institute "third party proceedings" against the principal contractor if he feels such a principal contractor is basically liable for the loss.

Third-party insurance   Protection for the insured against liability arising out of bodily injury to others or damage to their property. Insurance other than life against loss due to liability to third parties, or for the benefit of third parties.

Three-D Policy (dishonesty, destruction, and disappearance)   A fidelity policy covering losses of such things as money and security, depositors' forgery and/or counterfeiting.

Three-fourths value clause   A clause in a policy contract providing that the insurer will not pay on any loss more than three-fourths of the actual cash value of the property covered by the contract at the time of loss.

Ticket stub insurance   *See* **Travel ticket policies.**

Tickler   A file designed to call attention to certain factors at the proper time. The policy-expiration and premiums-due ticklers are examples of this device.

Time element insurance   Type of insurance contract that pays when the policyholder has lost the use of the insured property for a period of time. The claim payment is based on the period of time to correct the situation.

Time is of the essence   A phrase which, if included in a contract, means that performance within a specified time is a material element of the transaction.

Time limits   The period of time within which notice of claim or proof of loss must be filed.

Title   The means whereby the owner of lands has the legal possession of his property. It also refers to the instrument which is evidence of the right.

Title binder   *See* **Binder, insurance.**

Title deeds   The successive deeds upon which title rests. The owner of the land is properly entitled to these instruments which go with the land.

Title defect   Any legal right held by others to claim property or to make demands upon an owner.

Title exception   An exception appearing in a title policy against which the company does not insure.

Title guarantee policy   The title insurance provided as an alternative to an abstract of title. The insurance is written by a title insurance company; payment is made by the owner.

Under the policy an agreement binds the insurer to indemnify the insured for such losses as specifically delineated by reason of defects in the title of the real estate providing there are no exceptions listed in the title insurance policy. Since the title insurance company investigates the property prior to issuing a policy it serves as an indication of their mature evaluation of the risk involved. Also called Torrens certificate of title.

Title insurance policy A contract by which the insurer, usually a title insurance company, agrees to pay the insured a specific amount for any loss caused by defects of title to real estate, wherein the insured has an interest as purchaser, mortgagee, or otherwise.

Title I The section of the FHA insurance program for home improvements and mobile homes.

Title search An examination of public records, laws, and court decisions to disclose the past and current facts regarding ownership of real estate. A normal part of a real estate sale and required by law in most municipalities. *See* **Clear title.**

Tontine A reverse form of life insurance that did not pay on any deaths of the insured until they had lived through the tontine period. The few that were then alive thus shared the very high benefit. In Europe it had various applications as a gambling device. In the United States the tontine insurance was a modification of the original and the insurance company put a stated amount of gross receipts of premiums into a special tontine fund to be paid only to those living at the end of the stated period. This type of insurance is not available now and was disapproved by the Armstrong Investigation.

Tornado A violent wind associated with a funnel-shaped cloud that moves along a fairly narrow path.

Tornado insurance Contractual coverage against loss caused to property by unusually high winds.

Torrens certificate A document, issued by the proper public authority called a registrar acting under the provisions of the Torrens Law. The certificate indicates the party or parties in whom title resides.

Torrens system of land registration A form and system of state insurance for land titles.

Tort A wrongful act, injury, or damage, but one that does not involve a breach of contract for which a civil action be brought.

Total disability Disability which prevents the insured from performing any duty of his usual occupation or from performing any occupation for remuneration. The actual definition depends on the wording of the policy.

Total loss The complete destroying or ruining of the property insured. The claim of sufficient size to require settlement of the maximum amount of insurance on the covered property.

Total loss, actual *See* **Total loss.**

Total loss, constructive *See* **Constructive total loss.**

Tort A legal wrong committed on a person or property apart from a responsibility in a contract.

Tort-feasor A wrongdoer or trespasser.

Tourists' baggage floater Type of all risk personal insurance on personal effects. Also called tourist's floater. *See* **Personal effects floater.**

Towing charges The expense of towing a disabled or damaged automobile from the place of accident to a garage.

Townhouse A residential unit on a small lot which has coincidental exterior limits with other similar units. Title to the unit and its lot is vested in the individual buyer along with a fractional interest in common areas, if any.

Tract An area of land.

Tract book This is a synonym for plat book, which is a record showing the name of the owner of each plot, its size, location in the land area designated to be covered by the book. Useful in title insurance.

Tract loan A loan to a developer secured by land being subdivided for proposed construction of single-family homes.

Tractor trailer A motor truck which is used to tow or pull a trailer.

Trade fixtures Property affixed to the realty by a tenant, which he has a right to remove at the end of his lease.

Trade report *See* **Credit report.**

Traditional net cost A measure of the surrender cost of a life insurance policy that does not consider the cost of the interest that has been foregone.

Transfer books Ledgers required to be kept by the county auditor, showing all transfers of real estate within the county.

Transfer fees Fees collected from the buyer or seller of a property to defray county or city charges for changing the records.

Transit policy Contractual coverage for loss or damage to merchandise while it is being moved.

Transportation insurance Insurance against loss to personal property while in the course of transportation. Also called transportation floater insurance.

Traumatic injury Damage of a physical nature caused by accidental means. Not caused by disease or illness.

Travel accident policy A policy limited to indemnities for accidents while traveling, usually by common carrier.

Travel ticket policies Accident insurance issued for the duration of a specified trip by a common carrier. Originally such coverage was issued by an extra stub attached to a ticket and is still sometimes referred to as ticket stub insurance. It is now usually a separate policy, ordinarily issued at a ticket window or station, frequently through automatic vending machines.

Travelers Health Association and R. E. Pratt as Treasurer Thereof and in his Personal Capacity vs. Commonwealth Of Virginia Upheld states authority under "blue sky laws" to require those selling certificates of insurance to obtain permits.

Treaty A contract of reinsurance between various insurance companies. *See* **Reinsurance treaty.**

Trespasser One who goes on another's premises without right or permission, even though it may be by mistake. The owner must abstain from doing him any wilful or wanton injury but otherwise a trespasser must accept the property as he finds it.

Trip transit insurance Transportation insurance against loss to personal property on a single trip between two specified points.

Triple indemnity *See* **Multiple indemnity.**

Triple protection Whole life and term life insurance are combined in this particular form of insurance. The term insurance, which terminates at a certain age, is generally twice as large in dollar amounts as the whole life.

Truckman's liability insurance Contractual coverage which indemnifies the operator or owner of a truck or trucks that used them to carry for hire goods of others. It protects against liability the truckman may have resulting from damage or loss that has occurred to the transported property and is required by the Interstate Commerce Commission for common carriers under their supervision.

True group A form of group insurance whereby individuals are covered by one master policy. Individual contracts are not issued.

Trust An equitable right or interest in property distinct from the legal ownership thereof. A property interest held by one person for the benefit of another, usually under temporary or conditional terms such as that ownership is transferred to a trustee until an heir becomes of legal age.

Trust agreement A supplemental settlement agreement which distributes the proceeds in a special way, much as a regular fiduciary trust does.

Trust deed That deed which establishes a trust, conveying legal title of property to a trustee, states his authority and conditions which bind him in dealing with the property held in the fiduciary capacity as a means sometimes to secure the lenders against loss; thus it may serve a similar function to a mortgage. The term is usually and peculiarly applied to such a deed when made to secure a debt.

Trust indenture An agreement under which a third party holds the instrument in trust as security for the payment of the debt.

Trust or commission clause A clause extending the coverage of the insurance contract to the insured's interest in a legal liability for property belonging to others and held by the insured in trust, on commission, on storage, for repairs or otherwise held.

Trustee One who holds the title to the property for the benefit of another. This may be either an individual or a company such as a bank and trust company. Since the trust company has a more permanent existence than the life of an individual, it will frequently be combined with an individual trustee in a trust procedure.

Trustee in bankruptcy An agent of the court authorized to liquidate the assets of the bankrupt, protect them, and bring them to court for final distribution for the benefit of the bankrupt and all his creditors.

Tuition fees insurance Coverage of losses of schools due to interruption that might hinder student enrollment.

Turnkey leasing The leasing of completed housing constructed by private sponsors to a housing authority for use by low-income tenants.

Turnkey project A project in which a builder-contractor-developer contracts with a government or approved private agency to construct and deliver a completed facility that includes all items necessary for occupancy.

Twilight zone   That section of an area in which a definite downward economic transition is in progress or has taken place. Such zone may involve moral hazard and adverse selection.

Twisting   Practice of inducing any policyholder to lapse or cancel a policy for the purpose of replacing such policy with another to the detriment of the policyholder. The practice is considered to be unethical as well as illegal.

U.A.B.   Underwriters Adjustment Bureau

U.A.C.   Underwriters Adjusting Company

U.C.C.   Uniform Commercial Code.

U.J.F.   Unsatisfied Judgment Fund

U.L.   Underwriters' Laboratories

U.L.C.   Underwriters Laboratory of Canada

U. & O.   Use and occupancy.

U.O.A.   Use of other automobiles.

U.P.   Unearned premium.

U.S.A.   Underwriters Service Association

U.S.A.I.G.   United States Aircraft Insurance Group.

U.S.A.S.I.   United States of America Standards Institute

U.S.Co.   Underwriters Salvage Company

U.S.G.L.I.   United States Government Life Insurance.

Uberrimae fidei   Of utmost good faith — Certain transactions require the utmost of good faith on both sides, and both parties must disclose relevant facts. It is a fundamental principle of all insurance contracts.

Ultimate mortality table   A mortality table that eliminates the more favorable mortality of the select period. The C.S.O. Table is an ultimate mortality table. *See* **Select table** for comparison.

Ultra vires   An act beyond the powers legally granted a corporation.

Umbrella liability policy   A combination of comprehensive general and comprehensive personal liability insurance.

Umpire   A third person appointed to decide an arbitration.

Umpire clause   Part of some insurance contracts that provides that, in the event that the individual or company filing a claim and the insuring company cannot agree on the settlement of a loss, each party may select an arbitrator and then the two arbitrators select an umpire. The insured and the insurance company agree to abide by the decision of the majority vote of the arbitrators and umpire.

Unallocated benefit A reimbursement provision, usually for miscellaneous hospital and medical expenses, which does not specify how much will be paid for each type of treatment, examination, dressing, or the like, but only sets a maximum which will be paid for all such treatments.

Unauthorized company An insurer unlicensed in the state in which it is referred to as unauthorized. No agent may solicit for it in that state under legal penalties for both the agent and the company.

Unauthorized insurance A policy of insurance written by a company not licensed by the state or country in which the policy has been sold. Insurance with a nonadmitted insurance carrier.

Unbalanced improvement An improvement which is not the highest or best use for the site on which it is placed. The moral hazard and adverse selection may result from insurance of unbalanced risks.

Uncancellable *See* **Noncancellable.**

Unconditional Vesting That form of vesting in a contributory plan under which entitlement to a vested benefit is not conditional upon the nonwithdrawal of the participant's contributions. CIT

Underimprovement An improvement which is not the highest or best use for the site on which it is placed by reason of being smaller in size or lesser in cost than a building which would bring the site to its highest and best use. *See* **Unbalanced improvement.**

Underinsurance A condition in which not enough insurance is carried to cover the insurable value, and especially to satisfy a coinsurance clause. Insurance less in amount than the possible loss to which it applies.

Underinsured motorist provision A type of coverage for a situation in which the motorist does meet the state law requirements for liability insurance but a judgment is rendered in excess of these limits.

Underlying The amount of insurance or reinsurance on a risk which attaches before the next higher excess layer of insurance or reinsurance attaches.

Underlying policy *See* **Master policy.**

Underwriter The individual whose duty it is to determine the acceptability of insurance risks. A person whose duty it is to select risks for insurance and to determine in what amounts and on what terms the insurance company will accept the risks. Also, an insurer.

Underwriting gain Amount equal to 100 less the total of the loss and expense ratios.

Underwriting profit That portion of the earnings of an insurance company that comes from the function of underwriting. It excludes the earnings from investments either in the form of income from securities or sale of securities at a profit. The remainder is found by deducting incurred losses and expenses from earned premiums.

Undue exertion Voluntary overexertion.

Unearned increment An increase in the value of property caused by such phenomena as population increase, community expansion, increased desirability of the situs, the fortuitous location of some large project nearly. The increase in value is not due to any effort on the part of the owner.

Unearned premium That part of the original premium not yet earned by the insurance company and therefore due the policyholder if the policy should be canceled. *See* **Premium, unearned.**

Unearned premium insurance Insurance against loss by the insured of unearned premium due to payment of a claim made prior to the end of the term for which the premium was paid. Contractual reimbursement to the insured; if, as a result of a loss, he has paid insurance premiums for future periods that as a result of the loss he would not have needed future insurance protection. A loss on the second day of a policy written for a year would have the effect of being an expense for over an eleven-month period, during which time the insurance company would not be insuring the risks since the risk did not exist any longer and thus it would be unearned.

Unearned premium reserve The fund set aside by an insurance company to provide for the payment of unearned premiums on cancelled policies. *See* **Reserve, unearned premium.**

Unearned reinsurance premium That part of the reinsurance premium applicable to the unexpired portion of the policies reinsured.

Unemployment insurance A type of social insurance for unemployed covered individuals that is paid through state organizations after a waiting or qualifying period.

Unencumbered property A property that is free and clear.

Unfair Competition and Practice A number of states have set out specifically those deeds and acts of a life insurance agent which are deemed unfair competition and practice. They include Twisting, Rebating, Defamation of persons or companies, and committing any act tending towards monopoly of the business.

Unfunded Trust See Life Insurance Trust.

Uniform Commercial Code (UCC) A commercial comprehensive law regulating commercial transactions. It has been adopted, with modification, by most states.

Uniform forms Standardized policies used by more than one insurance company.

Uniform provision A set of provisions, the wording of which is specified by law, which must be included in certain policies issued in a jurisdiction requiring the use of the uniform provisions. In general, they set the operating conditions of the policy. The uniform provisions have been adopted and recommended for passage in all states by the National Association of Insurance Commissioners, to replace the older standard provisions.

Unilateral contract One in which a promise is given in exchange for an act or forbearance. It is a promise by one party to do certain things in the event the other party performs a certain act.

Unimproved Real estate which is vacant or lacks any material improvements required to make the property useful.

Uninsured motorist coverage *See* **Family protection automobile coverage.**

Unit benefit plan An arrangement for purchasing periodically an amount of annuity such as a percentage of wages as part of a retirement pension.

U. S. A., Appellant vs. South-Eastern Underwriters Association, et. al. Held insurance business is commerce.

United States Government Life Insurance *See* **Veterans' Administration Insurance Division** and **N.S.L.I.**

Universal mercantile schedule Technique for computing fire insurance rates which has been adopted by other types of insurance rate makers.

Unlicensed reinsurance Reinsurance placed with companies not licensed to do business in that state or province.

Unoccupied Furnished but not lived in. The standard fire insurance policy prohibits vacancy and unoccupancy beyond a specified period. Permission for unlimited vacancy and unoccupancy is usually given in the forms for use in protected territory without charge. In unprotected territory the permission is given as necessary and a charge is made.

Unoccupied buildings insurance policy Type of business insurance described in **Unoccupied**.

Unprotected *See* **Protected.**

Unsafe A term used in schedule rating to describe a condition for which a penalty is applied, and which can usually be corrected. With the removal of the charge and condition there is a reduction of the insurance rate. Some schedules use the term "fault of management"; some use "after charge."

Unsatisfied judgment funds A fund created by state law in several states. Reimbursement is made to persons having claims arising out of automobile accidents who have been unable to collect from the party responsible for the accident because the party is not insured or is financially not in a position to pay.

Urban Land Institute (ULI) An independent, non-profit research and educational organization incorporated in 1936 to improve the quality and standards of land use and development. It conducts practical research in the various fields of real estate knowledge, identifies and interprets land use trends in relation to changing needs, and disseminates information to promote orderly and efficient land use.

Urban property City property or closely settled property.

Urban renewal The redevelopment or rehabilitation of a slum in an uban area.

Use The purpose for which a property or an automobile will be used.

Use and occupancy *See* **Business interruption.**

Use and occupancy insurance Insurance contract that indemnifies against certain expenses such as payroll, and reduced income as a result of the insured peril such as fire. *See* **Business interruption insurance.**

Use value That value determined on the basis of the amount paid for the actual use of the property as compared with the holding of the property out of use.

Usury The excess over the legal rate charged to a borrower for use of money. Each state has its own definition of the exact rate and conditions that result in usury.

Utility An economic concept of subjective value of the power to satisfy the needs or wants of individuals.

Utmost good faith A phrase in a legal document calling for the highest standards of integrity on the part of the insured and the insurer.

VA *See* **Veterans Administration.**

V.F.D. Volunteer Fire Department

V. & M.M. Vandalism and malicious mischief.

Vacancy and rent loss Vacancy refers to any type of rental property or unit that is unrented. In the estimate of gross income of a property an allowance or discount is usually made for vacancy. Rent loss can result from a number of reasons, such as a loss in income during periods of remodelling or rehabilitation, low occupancy rates, and the tenant's inability to pay.

Vacancy factor A percentage rate expressing the loss from gross rental income due to vacancy and collection losses.

Vacant Not lived in and void of furnishing. *See* **Unoccupied**.

VA Certificate of Reasonable Value The VA issues a Certificate of Reasonable Value at a specific figure, agreeing to guarantee a mortgage loan to an eligible, qualified veteran buyer upon completion and purchase of the house. The veteran must be aware of the VA's appraised value of the property.

Valuation An estimate or act of processing of value. This will frequently be done through the process of an appraisal.

Valuation clause A clause in a marine policy in which the insured and insurer agree on the value of the covered property.

Value Ability to serve useful purposes or to command goods, including money, in exchange; utility; desirability; the quantity of goods, including money, which should be commanded or received in exchange for the thing valued; the present worth of all the rights to future benefits arising from ownership of the thing valued. *See* **Actual cash value.**

Value of all consideration See Consideration.

Valued policy A policy which provides that a special amount shall be paid in event of a total loss of the property. Most fine arts and some other inland marine policies have this provision. In fire insurance any such provisions are illegal in most states. However, in some states there are valued policy laws which require that fire insurance on buildings be treated as valued policies.

Valued policy law State law requiring an insurance company to pay the total face amount of a policy in the event that the insured has a total loss.

Vandalism and malicious mischief The willful injury or destruction of property; e.g., throwing stones through the window of a home and damaging home furnishings would be vandalism and can be insured against by extending coverage of a fire insurance policy.

Vandalism insurance policy Type of insurance coverage protecting against loss caused by the willful injury or destruction of property.

Variable annuity An annuity agreement whereby the insurance company agrees to pay an amount of money to the beneficiary of the annuity. The amount will vary with the value of equities purchased as investments by the insurance companies. Most annuities are fixed as to the annual amount of payment but the variable annuity is not. Proponents of variable annuities believe that they provide a better hedge against inflation than the fixed annuities; however, variable annuities are not permitted to be sold in many states. *See* **Equity annuity.**

Variable life insurance Insurance in which the amount may fluctuate during the term of the policy. The variable may be some index such as the Consumer Price Index or an index of securities.

Variable Rate Mortgage A mortgage agreement that allows for adjustment of the interest rate in keeping with a fluctuating market and terms agreed upon in the note.

Variance An approved special charge in construction codes, zoning requirements, or other property-use restrictions.

Vendee One who purchases any kind of property, especially real estate.

Vendor One who sells any kind of property, especially real estate.

Vendor's lien An equitable lien which the vendor of land has thereon for the unpaid purchase money.

Venture A single undertaking or voyage.

Venue The place where an action is tried as distinguished from jurisdiction.

Verbal   When used with reference to a contract, or to evidence, means spoken, not written.

Versus   (Latin "Against") used in the title of a case that means the plaintiff "against" the defendant.

Vested Benefit   A benefit the payment of which is not contingent upon a participant's continuation in specified employment.   CIT

Vesting   The attainment by a participant of a benefit right, attributable to employer contributions, this is not contingent upon a participant's continuation in specified employment.   CIT

Veterans Administration (VA)   An independent agency of the federal government created by the Servicemen's Readjustment Act of 1944 to administer a variety of benefit programs designed to facilitate the adjustment of returning veterans to civilian life. The VA home loan guaranty program is designed to encourage lenders to offer long-term, low-downpayment mortgages to eligible veterans by guaranteeing the lender against loss.

Veterans' insurance   *See* **N.S.L.I., Servicemen's Gratuitous Indemnity, U. S. Government Insurance.**

Vicarious   Liability imposed upon a person even though he is not a party to the particular occurrence, e. g. the owner of a motor vehicle is vicariously responsible for injuries even though he is not driving the car at the time of the ocurrence.

Vice propre   An inherent characteristic that may cause loss of value. *See* **Inherent vice.**

Violation   *See* **Rating Bureau.**

Vis major   An act of God. An accident for which no one is responsible.

Void   An insurance contract that is prohibited by law and thus cannot be held to be a valid contract. A tontine contract is void.

Voidable contract   A valid contract that may be rescinded by one of the parties due to such grounds as fraud, duress, insanity, incompetency, or minority.

Volens   "Volenti non fit injuria" means that to one consenting no wrong is done. Where a person voluntarily assumes a risk and directly or indirectly consents or assents to it then if he suffers injury he cannot later deny his position and claim damages. Note the difference between this and Scienti Non Fit Injuria.

Voluntary compensation insurance   A type of insurance found in some states by which the company agrees to pay injured employees who are not subject to the compensation law benefits which they would have received if they were covered. In some states the compensation law applies only to employees engaged in certain hazardous occupations. Under a voluntary compensation policy an employee engaged in a nonhazardous occupation could receive the same benefits as are provided by the compensation law.

Voluntary conveyance A mortgagor's act of conveying title on a mortgaged property to the holder of the mortgage to avoid foreclosure.

Voluntary overexertion Undue exertion.

Voluntary reserve The term reserve is misleading since there are not liabilities. They really represent the designation of surplus for particular purposes. They are not held to meet specific policy obligations.

Volunteer One who gives his services without reward or promise of reward.

Voyage clause Marine insurance clause stating the period of time or number of trips the aggregate of which form one voyage.

W Workmen's compensation.
W.A.B. Western Actuarial Bureau
W.C. Workmen's Compensation
W.D. Water Damage
W.I.C. War Insurance Corporation.
W.O.H. Work on Hand
W.P.A. With Particular Average
W.U.A. Western Underwriters Association.
W.W.A. With will annexed.

Waiting period The time which must elapse before an indemnity is paid. At the inception of disability, a period in respect of which benefits are not payable.

Waiver The surrender of a right or privilege which is known to exist. Excuse from future premiums during, usually, the total and permanent disability of the payor, as that disability is defined in the policy and commonly if occurring after a waiting period.

Waiver of coinsurance Fire contract clause which states that coinsurance does not apply unless the amount of loss exceeds a certain amount.

Waiver of lien The written evidence from the contractor (or supplier of material) surrendering the right of lien to enforce collection of debt against property.

Waiver of premium A provision that under certain conditions an insurance policy will be kept in full force by the insurance company without the payment of premiums. It is used most often as a total and permanent disability benefit and may be available in certain other cases.

Waiver of restoration premium A provision in certain contracts, especially in bonds, wherein the company agrees not to charge any additional premium for reinstating the contract after loss has occurred.

War clause A clause in an insurance contract relieving the insurer of liability, or reducing its liability, for loss caused by war.

War risk clause Part of an insurance contract that limits coverage. In the event of loss due to war, the insurance company does not accept liability for loss claims.

War risk insurance Coverage against damage or loss caused by enemies while at war. Commercially it is written by marine companies on vessels. Damage to buildings on land was insured in the United States during the Second World War by an instrumentality of the federal government with participation by and handling by insurance companies. *See* **Free of capture and seizure clause** and **War Insurance Corporation.**

Ware vs. Travelers Insurance Company Interpretation of resident agents' laws.

Warehouse bond, customs Bonds furnished only on forms prescribed by the United States Treasury Department that are required by federal laws and regulations in connection with the importation of dutiable merchandise.

Warehouse to warehouse clause Marine cargo clause which provides coverage from the originating warehouse to the terminating warehouse.

Warehouseman's liability insurance policy Type of business insurance protecting warehousemen from liability.

Warehousing The borrowing of funds by a mortgage banker on a short-term basis at a commercial bank using permanent mortgage loans as collateral. This form of interim financing is used until the mortgages are sold to the permanent investor.

Warrant   To assure the title to property through the means of an express covenant to that effect in the deed of conveyance stating that the title of a grantee shall be good and his possession undisturbed.

Warranted value   A term erroneously used in place of warranted price.   Value is always warranted in as much as it is dependent on services or benefits which will or could actually be received by the owner.   Price paid or asked; however, may or may not be warranted.

Warranties and Representations   Legally, all statements made by the applicant in connection with application for insurance are considered, in the absence of fraud to be representations.

Warranty   The statement by the insured, the truth of which becomes a condition of the validity of the policy.   Statement or stipulation in a policy as to the existence of a fact or a condition of the subject of the insurance, which, if untrue, will void the policy. *See* **Representation.**

Warranty deed   The deed by which a freehold is guaranteed in writing by the grantor and his successors.   Instrument, in writing, by which a real estate is created or alienated and whereby the freehold is guaranteed by the grantor, his heirs, or successors.

Warranty, implied   A warranty assumed to be a part of the insurance contract even though not expressly included.   In connection with products liability insurance, the warranty assumed to be made by one who sells a product that it is fit for the purpose for which it is sold.

Warsaw Convention Agreement   Concurrence of signing members of a pact to establish international agreement on limits of liability of air lines operating international flights for baggage loss or damage or for bodily injury or death of passengers.

Watch file   A procedure by which losses on small risks are referred to the underwriter for his attention.

Watchman clause   Phrase of insurance contract that provides for lower insurance rates and premiums on properties protected by a watchman than those not so protected.

Water damage insurance policy   Type of business insurance coverage protecting against loss due to specified damage caused by water.   Contractual protection against damage or loss that results from accidental presence of water where water is not supposed to be. It is not flood insurance.

Water power rights A property consisting of the right to the use of water as power, developed or undeveloped.

Water rights A property consisting of the rights to a water supply.

Water table The distance from the ground surface to the depth at which natural groundwater is found.

Wave damage insurance Contractual protection against loss or damage caused by waves and the action of waves.

Wave wash Damage caused by severe wave action. A loss attributed to wave wash is not covered under policy terms.

Weather insurance *See* **Rain insurance.**

Webb-Pomerene Act Law which permits combinations for purposes of foreign trade that would not be permitted in domestic trade. Marine insurance companies handling foreign risks have greater freedom of cooperation and underwriting under this act.

Wedding present floater Contractual insurance protection of almost all risks for wedding presents for a stated period before and after a wedding.

Weekly premium insurance *See* **Debit systems.**

Weight and height table A table of statistics giving such information as average weight and height for men and women by age. Such tables may be prepared by the Actuarial Society of America and the Association of Life Insurance Medical

Whole coverage Any form of insurance which provides for payment of all losses without any deductions. This is the opposite from a deductible policy.

Whole Dollar Premium The premium for each exposure is rounded to the nearest dollar for each coverage or each endorsement. For purposes of this rule an amount of $.51 (in some states $.50) is considered as a dollar.

Whole life insurance A plan of insurance for the whole of life, payable at death. It includes straight life on which premiums are payable until death, or limited payment life on which premiums are payable for a specified number of years.

Wholesale insurance A modification of group policy to a number of employees as defined in state statutes (between 25 and 50 employees). Instead of a master policy, individual policies are issued.

Will An instrument, almost always in writing, prepared by an individual in contemplation of his death in which instructions for the disposition of his estate are contained. The disposition of one's property to take effect after death.

Willful injury *See* **Intentional injury.**

Windstorm insurance policy Type of business insurance coverage against loss due to windstorm. Contractual protection against loss or damage caused by cyclones, hurricanes, and high winds.

Wire off Telegraphic instructions to an agent to cancel a specific policy on receipt of the telegram.

Without prejudice Part of a nonwaiver agreement that holds that the insured who signs the agreement cannot legally construe certain actions, such as the determination of the value of a claim by the insurance company to be an admission of liability on their part.

Without recourse Words used in endorsing a note or bill to denote that the future holder is not to look to the endorser in case of nonpayment.

Witness One who gives evidence in any case or matter.

Work and materials clause Provision of a fire insurance policy that permits the insured to store, process, and use material and handle them in the manner customary for his line of business.

Working capital Liquid assets available for the conduct of daily business.

Working capital ratio The ratio of current assets to current liabilities. It is one of the most commonly used ratios to indicate a company's financial position.

Working cover An excess reinsurance contract providing coverage in certain areas in which the number of losses has been anticipated.

Workmen's Compensation catastrophy coverage Primary insurer's purchase excess of loss reinsurance to cover their unlimited compensation and medical liability as a result of the workmen's compensation laws in many states.

Workmen's compensation insurance Social insurance that provides that employees may collect from their employer for injuries sustained in the course of his employment.

Workmen's compensation insurance policy Type of business insurance coverage protecting an employer against liability imposed by a workmen's compensation law.

Workmen's Compensation Law A statute imposing liability on employers to pay benefits and furnish care to employees injured, and to pay benefits to dependents of employees killed, in the course of and because of their employment. The employer is generally relieved of liability for common law damages.

World-wide coverage A clause in some policies that provides coverage in any place in the world. Jewelry, fur, personal effects, and personal property floaters may have this clause.

Wrap-around A mortgage that secures a debt which includes the balance due on an existing senior mortgage and an additional amount advanced by the wrap-around mortgagee. The wrap-around mortgagee thereafter makes the amortizing payments on the senior mortgage. An example: a landowner has a mortgage securing a debt with an outstanding balance of $3,000,000. A lender now advances the same mortgagor a new $1,500,000 and undertakes to make the remaining payments due on the $3,000,000 debt, and takes a $4,500,000 wrap-around junior mortgage on the real estate to secure the total indebtedness.

Wrap up *See* **Umbrella liability policy.**

Writ A writ is a form of document commanding the Defendant to enter an Appearance within so many days, if he wishes to dispute the Claimant's claim.

Write To insure, or to sell insurance.

Write a policy To fill in the appropriate spaces on an insurance policy.

Written business Those applications that have been signed by the applicant, but on which no premiums have been paid. See distinction between delivered, examined, paid, placed, issued, and written business.

Written premiums *See* **Premiums, written.**

Wrongful Abstraction This term refers to all forms of stealing and, for all practical purposes, is synonymous with theft.

It is under these two definitions (theft and wrongful abstraction that the insured is protected from the wrongdoer who gains admission to the locked premises by use of a key or opens the safe by discovering the combination.

X.C.L. Excess current liabilities.

X.P. Fire resistive protected (classification).

X.U.   Fire resistive unprotected (classification).

X-Bracing   Cross bracing in a partition to provide rigidity.

X 17 Table   New mortality table.

Y.R.T.   Yearly Renewable Term

Yachts fire coverage   A fire coverage rather than marine risk that is written on a standard fire insurance policy but issued through the marine department of the insurer, which has an endorsement covering the ship ashore or afloat.

Yachts, protection and indemnity   Protection of the yacht owner from liability for loss of life and personal injury and property damage. This protection is in two forms and excludes workmen's compensation claims, which may be covered by obtaining a special endorsement.

Yearly renewable term insurance   Term policies for one-year periods. Group insurance and reinsurance are frequently written on a yearly renewable term basis.

Yield   The annual percent of return on an investment. Insurance companies must know the yield that they have on their investments, and the yield must be adequate when combined with capital gains or losses and underwriting gains or losses to meet their charges.

Yield, current   That rate of return expressed in percentage that is calculated by dividing the annual dividend, coupon, or payment, such as rent, by the price paid for the investment.

Yield test   Measurement applied to bond investments in the portfolios of insurance companies. It is the relationship of the yield of bonds the insurance company has in its portfolio individually to the yield of fully taxable United States Government bonds of the same maturity. Yields of such corporate bonds of over 1½ percent higher than the United States Government bonds require that they be valued at market price rather than amortized value.

Yield to maturity   That rate of return expressed in a percentage that will be obtained on an investment if the investment is held to maturity. It takes into consideration that few investments are bought exactly at par and thus have a capital gain or loss in addition to the rate of return stated on the face of the instrument. For example, a bond with a face interest of 4% bought at 95 (that is $950) and maturing in one year will actually yield to maturity 9.41% as follows: 4% of $1,000 (the face value of the bond) equals $40, appreciation on the bond between purchase price of $950 and redemption value of $1,000 equals $50. The $40 interest and the $50 capital gain equals $90. Thus a return of $90 on the original investment of $950 or a yield to maturity of 90 divided by 950 or 9.4+%. Most insurance companies have tables of yields based on various interest tables.

Young person Any person who is under 18 years of age but no longer a child.

York Antwerp Rules Body of regulations used by major maritime countries providing the procedure for settling a loss which involves a number of different interests; such as the owners of a ship, the owners of a cargo, the owners of related freight interests. A set of rules for the adjustment of general average loss.

Youthful Insured An insured (male or female) under age 25 years of age.

Z Table A mortality table giving recent ultimate experience on insured lives, computed from experience on contracts of insurance issued during 1925 through 1934 by major companies. This table was important in the processing of the Commissioners Standard Ordinary Table (CSO).

Zone system Technique developed by the National Association of Insurance Commissioners for the triennial examination of insurance companies. Teams of examiners are formed from the staff of various states and have major direction from the insurance department of the insurance companies' home state insurance departments.

Zoning The employment of the police power by a public body regulating the character and the intensity of the use of property in the public interest. The effectiveness of zoning is important in the establishment of rates and maps.

Zoning ordinance Exercise of police power of a municipality in regulating and controlling the character and use of property.

DIRECTORY
OF
STATE COMMISIONERS
OF INSURANCE

DIRECTORY OF
STATE COMMISIONERS OF INSURANCE

State Insurance Department officials have the responsibility for enforcing state insurance laws. They also serve as intermediaries to settle disputes between policyholders (or beneficiaries) and insurance companies.

Alabama Commissioner of Insurance
Administrative Bldg., 64 N. Union St.
Montgomery, AL 36130

Alaska Director of Insurance
State Office Bldg., Pouch D, Mail Stop 0800
Juneau, AK 99811

Arizona Director of Insurance
Commerce Bldg., 1601 W. Jefferson St.
Phoenix, AZ 85007

Arkansas Commissioner of Insurance
400 University Tower Bldg., 12th and University Ave.
P.O. Box 4499, Little Rock, AR 72204

California Commissioner of Insurance
600 S. Commonwealth Ave., Los Angeles, CA 90005

Colorado Commissioner of Insurance
106 State Office Bldg., 201 E. Colfax Ave.
Denver, CO 80203

Connecticut Commissioner of Insurance
425 State Office Bldg., 165 Capitol Ave.
Hartford, CT 06106

Delaware Commissioner of Insurance
Robert Short Memorial Bldg., 21 The Green
Dover, DE 19901

District of Columbia Superintendent of Insurance
512 North Potomac Bldg., 614 H Street, NW
Washington, D.C. 20001

Florida Commissioner of Insurance
The Capitol, Tallahassee, FL 32301

Georgia Commissioner of Insurance
238 State Capital, Atlanta, GA 30334

Hawaii Commissioner of Insurance
1010 Richards St., P.O. Box 3614
Honolulu, Hawaii 96811

Idaho Director of Insurance
State Office Bldg., 700 W. State St.
Boise, ID 83720

Illinois Director of Insurance
Bicentennial Bldg., 320 W. Washington St.
Springfield, IL 62767

Indiana Commissioner of Insurance
509 State Office Bldg., 100 N. Senate Ave.
Indianapolis, IN 46204

Iowa Commissioner of Insurance
Lucas State Office Bldg., E. 12th and Walnut St.
Des Moines, IA 50319

Kansas Commissioner of Insurance
State Office Bldg., Topeka, KS 66612

Kentucky Commissioner of Insurance
151 Elkhorn Ct., P.O. Box 517
Frankfort, KY 40602

Louisiana Commissioner of Insurance
950 N. 5th St., P.O. Box 44214, Capitol Sta.
Baton Rouge, LA 70804

Maine Superintendent of Insurance
State House, Station 34, August, ME 04333

Maryland Commissioner of Insurance
Stanbalt Bldg., 501 St. Paul Pl.
Baltimore, MD 21202

Massachusetts Commissioner of Insurance
Leverett Saltonstall State Office Bldg.
100 Cambridge St., Boston, MA 02202

Michigan Commissioner of Insurance
1048 Pierpont St., P.O. Box 30220
Lansing, MI 48909

Minnesota Commissioner of Insurance
500 Metro Square Bldg., 7th and Robert Sts.
St. Paul, MN 55101

Mississippi Commissioner of Insurance
1804 Walter Sillers Bldg., 550 High St.
P.O. Box 79, Jackson, MS 39205

Missouri Director of Insurance
515 E. High St., P.O. Box 690
Jefferson City, MO 65102

Montana Commissioner of Insurance
Sam W. Mitchell Bldg., 205 Roberts St.
P.O. Box 4009, Helena, MT 59620

Nebraska Director of Insurance
State Office Bldg., 301 Centennial Mall, S.
P.O. Box 94699, Lincoln, NE 68509

Nevada Commissioner of Insurance
Nye Building, 201 S. Fall St.
Capitol Complex, Carson City, NV 89710

New Hampshire Commissioner of Insurance
169 Manchester St., Concord, NH 03301

New Jersey Commissioner of Insurance
201 E. State St., C.N. 325
Trenton, NJ 08625

New Mexico Superintendent of Insurance
428 PERA Bldg., P.O. Drawer 1269
Santa Fe, NM 87501

New York Superintendent of Insurance
Two World Trade Center, New York, NY 10047

North Carolina Commissioner of Insurance
Dobbs Bldg., 430 N. Salisbury St.
P.O. Box 26387, Raleigh, NC 27611

North Dakota Commissioner of Insurance
State Capital, 5th Floor, Bismarck, ND 58505

Ohio Director of Insurance
2100 Stella Ct., Columbus, OH 43215

Oklahoma Commissioner of Insurance
408 Will Rogers Memorial Office Bldg.
2401 N. Lincoln Blvd., Oklahoma City, OK 73105

Oregon Commissioner of Insurance
Commerce Building, 158 12th Street, N.E.
Salem, OR 97310

Pennsylvania Commissioner of Insurance
1326 Strawberry Sq., 4th and Walnut Sts.
Harrisburg, PA 17120

Rhode Island Commissioner of Insurance
100 N. Main St., Providence, RI 02903

South Carolina Commissioner of Insurance
Kettrell Center, 2711 Middleburg Dr.
P.O. Box 4067, Columbia, SC 29240

South Dakota Director of Insurance
Insurance Bldg., Broadway and Nicollet St.
Pierre, SD 57501

Tennessee Commissioner of Insurance
114 State Office Bldg., 5th and Charlotte Ave.
Nashville, TN 37219

Texas Commissioner of Insurance
State Insurance Bldg., 1110 San Jacinto Blvd.
Austin, TX 78786

Utah Commissioner of Insurance
326 S. 5th East St., Salt Lake City, UT 84102

Vermont Commissioner of Insurance
120 State St., Montpelier, VT 05602

Virginia Commissioner of Insurance
Jefferson Bldg., 1220 Bank St.
P.O. Box 1157, Richmond, VA 23209

Washington Commissioner of Insurance
Insurance Bldg., 1306 Capitol Way
Mail Stop AQ-21, Olympia, WA 98504

West Virginia Insurance Commissioner
2100 Washington St., E., Charleston, WV 25305

Wisconsin Commissioner of Insurance
Loraine Bldg., 123 W. Washington Ave.
P.O. Box 7873, Madison, WI 53707

Wyoming Commissioner of Insurance
1 Pioneer Ctr., 2424 Pioneer Ave.
Cheyenne, WY 82002

American Samoa Insurance Commissioner
Pago Pago, AS 96797

Puerto Rico Commissioner of Insurance
Intendente Alejandro Ramirez Bldg.,
Covadonga Dr., Stop 1
P.O. Box 3508, San Juan, PR 00904

Virgin Islands Commissioner of Insurance
Lieutenant Governor's Office Bldg., 18 Kongens Gade
P.O. Box 450, Charlotte Amalie, St. Thomas VI 00801

DIRECTORY
OF
ORGANIZATIONS RELATED TO
THE INSURANCE INDUSTRY

DIRECTORY OF ORGANIZATIONS RELATED TO THE INSURANCE INDUSTRY

Including Agencies, Associations, Bureaus, Conferences, Councils, Forums, Foundations, Institutes, Schools, Services, and Societies

Alliance of American Insurers
20 N. Wacker Dr., Chicago, IL 60606

American Academy of Actuaries
Suite 515, 1835 K St. NW, Washington, D.C. 20006

American Association of Insurance Services
1035 S. York Rd., Bensenville, IL 60106

American Association of Managing General Agents
1001 Connecticut Ave. NW, Washington, D.C. 20036

American Association of University Teachers of Insurance
(see American Risk and Insurance Association)

American Bureau of Shipping
69 Broadway, New York, NY 10006

American Cargo War Risk Reinsurance Exchange
14 Wall St., Rm. #2120, New York, NY 10005

American College, The
Bryn Mawr, PA 19010

American Council of Life Insurance
1850 K Street NW., Washington, D.C. 20006

American Hull Insurance Syndicate
14 Wall St., New York, NY 10005

American Institute for Property and Liability Underwriters, Inc.
Box 314, Malvern, PA 19355

American Institute of Marine Underwriters
14 Wall St., New York, NY 10005

American Insurance Association
85 John St., New York, NY 10038

American Insurers Highway Safety Alliance
20 N. Wacker Dr., Chicago, IL 60606

American Life Convention
(merged with American Council of Life Insurance)

American Life Insurance Association
(merged with American Council of Life Insurance)

American Management Association
135 W. 50th St., New York, NY 10020

American Marine Insurance Clearing House
14 Wall St., Rm. #2120, New York, NY 10005

American Museum of Safety
85 John St., New York, NY 10038

American Risk and Insurance Association
College of Business, Univ. of Georgia, Athens, GA 30602

American Service Bureau, Inc.
211 E. Chicago Ave., Chicago, IL 60611

American Society of Chartered Life Underwriters
270 Bryn Mawr Ave., Bryn Mawr, PA 19010

Associated Aviation Underwriters
90 John St., New York, NY 10038

Associated Factory Mutual Fire Insurance Companies
(merged with Factory Mutual System)

Association for Advance Life Underwriting
1922 F St. NW, Washington, D.C. 20006

Association of Average Adjusters of the United States
123 William St., New York, NY 10038

Association of Casualty Accountants and Statisticians
(see Society of Insurance Accountants)

Association of Casualty and Surety Companies
(see American Insurance Association)

Association of Insurance Attorneys
110 S. Central Ave., St. Louis, MO 63105

Association of Life Insurance Counsel, The
51 Madison Ave., New York, NY 10010

Association of Life Insurance Medical Directors
4601 Market St., Philadelphia, PA 19101

Association of Mutual Fire Insurance Engineers
(merged with Insurance Loss Control Association)

Association of Superintendents of Insurance of the Provinces of Canada
c/o L. P. Wood, 6th Floor, 555 Yonge St.
Toronto, Ontario, M4Y 1Y7 Canada

Canadian Life and Health Insurance Association, Inc.
Suite 2500, 20 Queen St., West
Tornoto, Ontario M5H 3S2 Canada

Casualty Actuarial Society
One Penn Plaza, New York, NY 10001

Chamber of Commerce of the United States—Insurance Department
1615 H St. NW, Washington, D.C. 20062

Chartered Insurance Institute, The
20 Aldermanbury, London, E.D. 2, England

Coal Mine Rating Bureau
1015 Locust St., St. Louis, MO 63101

College of Insurance
123 William St., New York, NY 10038

Conference of Actuaries in Public Practice
208 S. LaSalle St., Chicago, IL 60604

Conference of Casualty Insurance Companies
Box 68695, 3707 Woodview Trace, Indianapolis, IN 46268

Crop Hail Insurance Actuarial Association
Room 700, 209 W. Jackson Blvd., Chicago, IL 60606

Defense Research Institute, Inc.
733 N. Van Buren St., Milwaukee, WI 53202

Disability Insurance Training Council
145 North Ave. Hartland, WI 53029

Eastern Underwriters Association
(merged with Insurance Services Office)

Factory Mutual System
1151 Boston-Providence Tpk., Norwood, MA 02062

Federation of Insurance Counsel
　1205 Red Rambler Rd., Jenkintown, PA 19046

Fire Insurance Research and Actuarial Association
　(now part of Insurance Services Office)

Fire Marshals' Association of North America
　Suite 220, 600 Maryland Ave. SW,
　Washington, D.C. 20024

Foreign Credit Insurance Association
　One World Trade Center, New York, NY 10048

Fraternal Field Manager's Association
　123 W. Washington St. Belleville, IL 62220

General Agents and Managers Conference of NALU
　1922 F St. NW, Washington, D.C. 20006

General Cover Underwriters Association
　127 John St., New York, NY 10038

Government Life Insurance for Veterans
　Veterans Administration, Washington, D.C. 20420

Charles W. Griffith Memorial Foundation for Insurance
　1775 College Rd., Columbus, OH 43210

Health Insurance Association of America
　1701 K St. NW, Washington, D.C. 20006

Health Insurance Institute
　1850 K St. NW, Washington, D.C. 20006

Home Office Life Underwriters Association
　c/o Mutual Life Ins. Co., 1740 Broadway, New York, NY

S. S. Huebner Foundation for Insurance Education
　3641 Locust Walk, Philadelphia, PA 19104

Industrial Risk Insurance
　85 Woodland, Hartford, CT 06102

Inland Marine Insurance Bureau
　(see Insurance Services Office)

Inland Marine Underwriters Association
　14 Wall St., Rm. #2100, New York, NY 10005

Institute of Home Office Underwriters
　Box 82448, Lincoln, NE 68501

Institute of Life Insurance
(merged with American Council of Life Ins.)

Insurance Accountants Association (Society of Insurance Accountants)
1750 Elm St., Manchester, NH 03107

Insurance Accounting and Statistical Association
Mutual Plaza, Durham, NC 27701

Insurance Advertising Conference
175 W. Jackson Blvd., Chicago, IL 60604

Insurance Company and Bank Purchasing Agents Association
85 Woodland, Hartford, CT 06102

Insurance Company Education Directors Society
518 E. Broad St., Columbus, OH 43216

Insurance Crime Prevention Institute
15 Franklin St., Westport, CT 06880

Insurance Economics Society of America
Suite 590, 1700 Pennsylvania Ave. NW,
Washington, D.C. 20006

Insurance Executives Association
(see American Insurance Association)

Insurance Hall of Fame, Inc.
c/o Griffith Foundation, 1775 College Rd.,
Columbus, OH 43210

Insurance Information Institute
110 William St., New York, NY 10038

Insurance Institute for Highway Safety
Suite 600, Watergate Office Bldg.
2600 Virginia Ave. NW, Washington, D.C. 20037

Insurance Institute of America
Providence Rd., Malvern, PA 19355

Insurance Institute of Canada
12 St. Patrick, Toronto, Ontario M5T 2X8 Canada

Insurance Loss Control Association
2425 E. Grand River Ave., Lansing, MI 48912

Insurance Rating Board
(see Insurance Services Office)

Insurance Services Office
    160 Water St., New York, NY 10038

International Association of Fire Chiefs
    1329 18th St. NW, Washingotn, D.C. 20036

International Association of Industrial Accident Boards and Commissions
    Suite 201, Ashley Bldg.
    1321 Executive Center Dr., Tallahassee, FL 32301

International Association of Insurance Counsel
    Suite 3705, 20 N. Wacker Dr., Chicago, IL 60606

International Aviation Theft Bureau
    7315 Wisconsin, Bethesda, MD 20814

International Claim Association
    400 Broadway, Cincinnati, OH 45202

International Insurance Adivsory Council of the Chamber of Commerce of the U.S.
    1615 H St. NW, Washington, D.C. 20062

James. S. Kemper Foundation
    120 S. LaSalle St., Chicago, IL 60603

Life Insurance Advertisers Association
    Suite 200, 900 Des Moines St., Des Moines, IA 50316

Life Insurance Association of America
    (see American Council of Life Insurance)

Life Insurance Marketing and Research Association
    8 Farm Springs, Farmington, CT 06032

Life Insurers Conference
    1004 N. Thompson St., Richmond, VA 23230

Life Office Management Association
    100 Colony Sq., Atlanta, GA 30361

Life Underwriters Association of Canada
    41 Lestmill Rd., Don Mills, Ontario M3B 2T3 Canada

Life Underwriter Training Council
    1922 F St. NW, Washington, D.C. 20006

Loss Executives Association
    c/o John Coleman, Secy., American Foreign Ins. Co.,
    Wayne, NJ 07470

Million Dollar Round Table of the National Association of Life Underwriters
    2340 River Rd., Des Plaines, IL 60018

Mill Mutual Fire Prevention Bureau
    2 N. Riverside Pl., Chicago, IL 60606

Multi-line Insurance Rating Bureau
    (see Insurance Services Office)

Multi-peril Insurance Conference
    (see Insurance Services Office)

Mutual Atomic Energy Liability Underwriters
    One E. Wacker Dr., Chicago, IL 60601

Mutual Reinsurance Bureau
    1780 S. Bell School Rd., Cherry Valley, IL 61016

National Association of Casualty and Surety Agents
    Suite 1625, 5454 Wisconsin Ave.,
    Chevy Chase, MD 20815

National Association of Credit Management
    475 Park Ave. S, New York, NY 10016

National Association of Fire Investigators
    53 W. Jackson Blvd., Chicago, IL 60604

National Association of Health Underwriters
    145 North Ave., Hartland, WI 53029

National Association of Independent Insurance Adjusters
    175 W. Jackson Blvd., Chicago, IL 60604

National Association of Independent Insurers
    2600 River Rd., Des Plaines, IL 60018

National Association of Auditors and Engineers
    P.O. Box 776, Manhasset, NY 11030

National Association of Insurance Brokers, Inc.
    Suite 700, 311 First St. NW, Washington, D.C. 20001

National Association of Insurance Commissioners
    350 Bishops Way, Brookfield, WI 53005

National Association of Insurance Women
    1847 E. 15th St., Tulsa, OK 74104

National Association of Life Companies, Inc.
    Suite 1060, 3340 Peachtree Rd. NE, Atlanta, GA 30026

National Association of Life Underwriters
1922 F St. NW, Washington, D.C. 20006

National Association of Mutual Insurance Companies
Box 68700, 3707 Woodview Trace, Indianapolis, IN 46268

National Association of Professional Insurance Agents
400 N. Washington St., Alexandria, VA 22314

National Association of Public Insurance Adjusters
Suite 210, 131 E. Redwood St., Baltimore, MD 21202

National Association of Surety Bond Producers
Suite 1625, 5454 Wisconsin Ave.,
Chevy Chase, MD 20815

National Automobile Theft Bureau
10330 S. Roberts Rd., Palos Hills, IL 60482

National Automobile Underwriters Association
(see Insurance Services Office)

National Board of Fire Underwriters
(see American Insurance Association)

National Bureau of Casualty Underwriters
(see Insurance Services Office)

National Cargo Bureau, Inc.
Suite 2757, 1 World Trade Center, New York, NY 10048

National Council of Self-Insurers
Rm. 2910, 420 Lexington Ave., New York, NY 10017

National Council on Compensation Insurance
One Penn Plaza, 250 W. 34th St., New York, NY 10119

National Crop Insurance Association
Suite 322, 2860 S. Circle Dr., South Bldg.,
Colorado Springs, CO 80906

National Fire Protection Association
Batterymarch Park, Quincy, MA 02269

National Foundation of Health, Welfare, and Pension
18700 Blue Mound Rd., Brookfield, WI 53005

National Fraternal Congress of America
Rm. 720, 250 W. Monroe St., Chicago, IL 60606

National Insurance Actuarial and Statistical Association
(see Insurance Services Office)

National Insurance Association
2400 S. Michigan Ave., Chicago, IL 60616

National Insurance Buyers Association
(merged with Risk and Insurance Management Society)

National Safety Council
444 N. Michigan Ave., Chicago, IL 60611

Nuclear Insurance Rating Bureau
160 Water St., New York, NY 10038

Property Loss Research Bureau
20 N. Wacker Dr., Chicago, IL 60606

Reinsurance Association of America
Suite 512, 1025 Connecticut Ave. NW,
Washington, D.C. 20036

Reporting Form Service Office
55 John St., New York, NY 10038

Risk and Insurance Management Society
National Office and New York Chapter
Suite 1504, 205 E. 42nd St., New York, NY 10017

Self-Insurance Institute of America
Suite 165, 1700 East Dyer Rd., Santa Anna, CA 92705

Society of Actuaries
208 S. LaSalle St., Chicago, IL 60604

Society of Chartered Property and Casualty Underwriters
Kahler Hall, Providence Road (CB#9),
Malvern, PA 19355

Society of Fire Protection Engineers
60 Batterymarch St., Boston, MA 02110

Society of Insurance Accountants
14 Ardsley Rd., Glen Ridge, NJ 07028

Society of Insurance Brokers
c/o Reed Stenhouse, Inc., Suite 2400,
Three Embarcadero Center, San Francisco, CA 94111

Society of Insurance Research
Box 933, Appleton, WI 54912

Southeastern Claim Executives Association
c/o Southern Trust Ins. Co., P.O. Box 250,
Macon, GA 30329

Surety Association of America
100 Wood Ave. S., Iselin, NJ 08830

Teachers Insurance and Annuity Association
730 Third Ave., New York, NY 10017

Underwriters Adjusting Company
80 Maiden Lane, New York, NY 10038

Underwriters' Laboratory, Inc.
333 Pfingsten Rd., Northbrook, IL 60062

Underwriters Salvage Company of Chicago
1400 Busse Rd., Elk Grove Village, IL 60007

United States Salvage Association, Inc.
14 Wall St., New York, NY 10005

Western Actuarial Bureau
(see Insurance Services Office)

Western Loss Association
c/o Hanover Insurance, 222 S. Riverside Pl.,
Chicago, IL 60604

Western Underwriters Association
(see Insurance Services Office)

Workmen's Compensation Reinsurance Bureau
59 John St., New York, NY 10038